Merchant-Ivory: Interviews

Conversations with Filmmakers Series
Gerald Peary, General Editor

Merchant-Ivory
INTERVIEWS

Edited by Laurence Raw

University Press of Mississippi / Jackson

www.upress.state.ms.us

The University Press of Mississippi is a member of the Association
of American University Presses.

First printing 2012

∞

Library of Congress Cataloging-in-Publication Data

Merchant, Ismail.
  Merchant-Ivory : interviews / edited by Laurence Raw.
      p. cm. — (Conversations with filmmakers series)
  Includes bibliographical references and index.
  Includes filmography.
  ISBN 978-1-61703-237-0 (cloth : alk. paper) — ISBN 978-1-61703-238-7 (ebook)
  978-1-4968-5370-7 (paperback)
1. Merchant, Ismail—Interviews. 2. Ivory, James—Interviews. 3. Jhabvala, Ruth Prawer,
1927—Interviews. 4. Motion pictures producers and directors—India—Interviews.
5. Motion pictures producers and directors—United States—Interviews. 6. Screenwriters—India—Interviews. I. Raw, Laurence. II. Title.
  PN1998.3.M466A3 2012
  792.702'80922—dc23   2011041457

British Library Cataloging-in-Publication Data available

Contents

Introduction

Mention the phrase "Merchant-Ivory" to most filmgoers of a certain generation and they automatically bring a specific aesthetic to mind: period dramas with languid camerawork, long takes, and deep staging, long and medium shots rather than close-ups or rapid cross-cutting. The camerawork seems dictated less by a desire to follow the characters, but to offer the aesthetic pleasure of admiring period settings and costumes. High-angle shots, slow pans, and tracking shots deliberately foreground the lovingly recreated *mise-en-scène* (Higson 2005, 38). In 1997 the *Guardian* newspaper published an article "Modern Recipes no. 21: Costume Drama" in which they parodied what they perceived as the typical Merchant-Ivory style: "Carefully landscape the garden and fill with pathways. Fill the britches and frocks with ham and perambulate through the garden, turning every few minutes. [. . .] For a slightly novel flavor, place the garden in South America or Africa, but don't stint on the britches and frocks" ("Modern Recipes" 2007, 21). Even Janet Maslin, in the foreword to Robert Emmet Long's excellent *James Ivory in Conversation* (2005), describes Merchant-Ivory's films as "broodingly elegant" in characterization, "literate in their own right," with "a virtually automatic prestige, [. . .] refinement and—yes—[. . .] a stately decorous manner" (Maslin 2005, ix–xi).

What this collection of interviews spanning a period of forty years demonstrates is that Merchant-Ivory address a far broader range of issues than their critics would have us believe. As independent filmmakers, they have developed an idiosyncratic approach that resists facile classification. Merchant-Ivory have insisted on maintaining their independence. Although flirting from time to time with the major Hollywood studios, they have largely concentrated on raising their own finance. In "Hollywood versus Hollywood" (1976), Ivory ruefully recounts his experiences of working with AIP (American International Pictures) on *The Wild Party*, as the studio re-cut the film without his knowledge and refused him permission to screen the director's cut at festivals. Ivory quarreled with the film's British distributors, who accused him of making derogatory comments in public that had a "devastating effect" on the box-office. While other experiences have not been so fraught—even in the 1960s the Hollywood studios had shown interest in Merchant-Ivory's Indian films—the company has chosen to go it alone, even if the business of raising finance can prove torturous. In "Dialogue on Film" (1987) Merchant suggests that "fund-raising is never easy, particularly if you want to do something of your own. [. . .] But if you want to do something good, you really have to knock on doors and convince people about what you are going to do." In "A Truly Flourishing Plant" (1992) Merchant suggests that this independence gives the company the chance to "make films painstakingly, with the emphasis on a good script, and on characters, relationships, atmosphere. These films say something about our life and we can't make mindless movies." James Ivory agrees: in "James Ivory on his 'Final Destination'" (2010) he claims that the company's oeuvre constitutes a "three-part autobiography. [. . .] They [the films] are full of our interests and the stuff that was meaningful to us in different kinds of ways, and in some cases deeply psychological."[1]

Such comments would seem to undermine Higson's assumption that their work is in some way impersonal, dominated by preoccupations of style rather than content. In "Merchant-Ivory" (1973), Ivory freely admits that he traveled to India after graduating from the University of Oregon because he wanted to go there, and that he tried to make "particular films," analyzing the kind of cross-cultural issues that he had experienced himself as a foreigner in India. Screenwriter Ruth Prawer Jhabvala suggests in "Interview with Ruth Prawer Jhabvala" (1987) that whereas her efforts were not necessarily inspired by events in her life, she liked to render the situations "personally authentic, as though it could have happened to me, if my responses had been those of the character in the story." This comment explains why many of Merchant-Ivory's films have focused on cross-cultural issues, many of which have been inspired by Jhabvala's own experiences of growing up in Nazi Germany, studying at the University of London, and subsequently residing in India and New York. Merchant emphasizes in "James Ivory and Ismail Merchant: An Interview" (1968) that the company cultivated an atmosphere wherein Ivory and Jhabvala could explore their personal conflicts cinematically: "The basic thing [about us] is the respect for feelings, for work which we have in our organization. I think our strength is that everyone wants to do for the betterment of the film."

While many of Merchant-Ivory's most successful films (both artistically and financially) have been costume dramas, they have been conceived in a particular way, with sets and costumes existing to serve the plot, rather than vice versa. In "Dialogue on Film" (1987), Ivory claims that the visual look of Forster's *A Room with a View* was "suggested by the writing itself." In "Conversation with Ruth Prawer Jhabvala" (2000), the screenwriter expresses a liking for Henry James's "grand material, wonderful scenes, great characters, [and] such wonderful relationships between characters," but simultaneously emphasized the importance of avoiding fidelity concerns in writing her screenplays: "You can take up the theme [. . .] and the feel of the characters, the ambience and their relationships, that is what you try and—but never, never literally." James Ivory tells us more about Jhabvala's technique in an interview with Mike Goodridge (2002): "She often picks up on things which feel repetitive and rewrites scenes we haven't shot accordingly, or [. . .] she will simplify speeches or vice versa, if someone turns out to be brilliant, she will pump up their part." The emphasis on plot and characterization persists throughout Merchant-Ivory's extensive oeuvre, including contemporary films based on original stories as well as adaptations and costume dramas. Merchant stresses to the Indian interviewers in 1968 that any of their films have to have "a definite story; it may not have a plot as such because I do not believe in plots—there has to be [a] relationship between characters, a particular atmosphere, a particular environment, something of human interest."

One of the triumvirate's principal mentors was Satyajit Ray, who not only provided the music for two of their early Indian films, but provided invaluable guidance about how to tell an intensely personal, character-driven tale. In 1968 Merchant calls Ray "a pillar of strength to us," while Ivory acknowledges his debt of gratitude in the Goodridge interview: "I have never really found a better way to set my scenes than the way Ray taught me, or a way I *like* better, to put it another way. [. . .] I realize that I wouldn't have done it that way if it had not been for Ray's lingering influence."

In the same interview, Ivory admits that Ray taught him to treat actors with respect: "if you hire good actors, then they are artists through and through, and what they give you is the gift of their talent." Most Merchant-Ivory films are actor-centered, giving filmgoers the opportunity to appreciate what Howard Mancing describes as the "superior vividness" of performance (Mancing 2006, 197). The experience is not straightforward—in spite of the claims made by the *Guardian* article quoted earlier on, we do not simply witness classically trained actors (mostly British) in crinolines and britches giving decorous performances. Rather Merchant-Ivory encourages actors to create a series of image-streams and thereby create "a vital sense of unfolding embodiment" (Blair 2006, 182). An example of how this works on screen can be seen in Anthony Hopkins's performance as Stevens in *The Remains of the Day* (1993). According to Merchant in 1993, Hopkins is a performer "who doesn't have to explain or shout, a man who can twitch an eye and an audience will see and feel what is happening so far as his emotions are concerned." Ivory's approach to directing, with its roots in cognitive neuroscience, treats a character not as an entity with a series of motivations but rather conceived it as "a set of choices and behaviors—a process rather than a discrete entity," supported by what the actor brings to the role in terms of "imagination, voice/speech, body, and intellect" (Blair 2006, 183). Attention focuses on what the actor is doing at any and every moment throughout the film. With this idea in mind, Ivory described his rehearsal process in "Dialogue on Film": "the whole thing is blocked out on location. [. . .] If you're working with real locations— say, just a room—and the actors have to move around in that room in a convincing way, they may have bits of business that take them here and there. They've got to feel comfortable." This process of letting the actors find their own way into a role often proves stunningly effective. Merchant recalls a particular moment involving Anthony Hopkins and Peter Vaughan in *The Remains of the Day*: "And when you see their hands together when Hopkins is trying to remove Peter Vaughan's hand from the trolley where he has fallen, their hands have such a resemblance! This man's entire attention and concentration is on little things—gestures are what they will do for the character." Treating actors in this way also renders the stories more credible to filmgoers, as we witness characterizations in which each note, gesture, or word feels fully inhabited and fully connected to the overall flow of the piece. Perhaps this helps to explain why box-office names such as Christopher Reeve agreed to work on *The Bostonians*, as Ivory claims in a 1984 interview with Pat Anderson: "It made him happy to be working with the other people—not in a star-like situation where he was the dominant person and everything revolved around him, but rather as part of the ensemble. [. . . .] He's master of the spoken phrase. People don't know that."

With so much emphasis placed on characterization, it is perhaps not surprising that Merchant-Ivory's films appear slow-moving. Ivory insists to Goodridge that he does not want filmgoers to admire the sets and costumes, but rather provide the time and space for actors to develop their performances: "it's all rehearsed before we start. [. . .] The scene is broken down into shots so we know what we're going to do, and we follow that plan. But sometimes the scene is covered in one long master-shot, which we then break into with closer shots for emphasis." This would appear to contradict Higson's claim that Merchant-Ivory's narratives are predominantly comprised of long and medium shots.

The emphasis on character also helps to implement one of Merchant-Ivory's principal thematic concerns, running throughout their work—the impact of the "clash of cultures" on individuals. Partly this has been inspired by their collective experiences of living and working in different cultures: Merchant was born in Bombay and educated mainly in America; and according to Judith Trojan, writing in 1973, this gives him an "outsider's view of some of the byways of an India trying to come to terms with Western styles." Ivory himself claims in "The Elegance of James Ivory" (1995) that they remain outside the mainstream of filmmaking—even though some of their films have been financed by the major studios, they have had a turbulent relationship with them: "There's not a script we didn't send to the studios. Usually they turned them down—in the seventies, anyway. Then, with *A Room with a View*, we became very popular." This sense of being an outsider certainly irked the Indian interviewers talking to James Ivory in 1968; one of them asked the director whether he could perhaps "contribute something more difficult" to the topic of Anglo-Indian relations—i.e., produce something about the effect of postcolonialism on contemporary (1968) Indian society. Ivory replied: "We don't have the Indian mentality. [. . .] Our point of view is really that of foreigners." Neither he nor Merchant wanted to become insiders; they preferred to remain on the outside offering an alternative perspective on Indian society. Their film *The Householder* (1963) was made in two languages—English and Hindi—but Ivory in particular told the Indian interviewers that he did not want to make another Hindi film unless he could speak good Hindi.

In a 1972 interview with Stephan Varble, Ivory emphasizes the strengths and weaknesses of an outsider's perspective on society. On the one hand this point of view offers new insights on familiar issues such as race, gender, and class (as Merchant also claims); on the other hand outsiders might find it impossible to establish any kind of meaningful dialogue with cultural insiders. Both *Shakespeare Wallah* and *The Guru* (1968) show that "things cannot work out for these people [expatriates] [. . .]. They don't belong in India. They shouldn't be. India wants to get them out." Talking to Judith Trojan two years later, Ivory speculates on whether he, as an American filmmaker, might have experienced the same cultural exclusion. For all his efforts in *The Guru* to show how artists "have a side to their character, which doesn't always bear close inspection," his film received an adverse reaction from Indian audiences, who objected to the way a foreigner had represented local mystical traditions. As someone who has lived in Europe, India, and now New York, Jhabvala believes to a large extent that people should learn to value their cultural experiences. She tells John Gillett in 1979 that she has to live in a place and try to understand it before she can write about it. On the other hand outsiders should not expect too much from their encounters with a foreign culture; nor should they profess to know too much about it. The fundamental issue running throughout Merchant-Ivory's oeuvre is one of effective cross-cultural communication: while insiders and outsiders will seldom see eye to eye, at least they can make efforts to empathize with one another. Ivory implies this in a 1999 interview with Geoffrey Macnab when he describes the English people thus: "I think they're nakedly emotional [. . .] often far more than they themselves may realize" (100).[2]

However none of the triumvirate offers any easy solutions to this issue. Rather they believe that their task lies in raising awareness; to make filmgoers aware of the importance of cultural sensitivities (encompassing more specific issues such as class difference) that assume paramount significance in any exchange, whether verbal or nonverbal. Merchant claims in a 2003 interview with Chris Neumer that their core audiences appreciate "a clash of culture" in their films, which operates on different levels, "from India, to East and to the West." *Mr. and Mrs. Bridge* (1990) and *The Remains of the Day* show what happens to people who consciously repress such conflicts; Ivory tells Graham Fuller in 1990 that the two central characters in *Mr. and Mrs. Bridge* (played by Paul Newman and Joanne Woodward) are forced to play "the game of silence" that renders them oblivious to the world and the feelings of those closest to them. Merchant describes the process of repression thus in 1993: "We never allow side winds to enter our lives. It's a kind of blindness." Perhaps the only solution is to accept the idea of contradiction—rather like the Bengali writer Nirad C. Chaudhuri, profiled in the Merchant-Ivory documentary *Adventures of a Brown Man in Search of Civilization* (1972). Ivory describes Chaudhuri in 1972 as "a product of the British Raj and immersed in dreams of England," who thought that the idea of westerners going to India for spiritual nourishment was ludicrous: "he has discovered the best and worst of both cultures and is very willing to offer us his conclusions," however tentative they might be.

Merchant-Ivory has been well aware of the labels pinned on them by critics: Brian Case quotes two examples in 1993: "David Thom[p]son wrote of 'a rather unobtrusively tasteful diffidence' about James Ivory's work. Pauline Kael, reviewing *A Room with a View*, found him 'essentially a director who assembles the actors, arranges the *bric-à-brac*, and calls for the camera.'" Ivory tells Carolyn Hill in 1994 a year that the so-called "elegance" of his films is "found in the script—and not only as just an objective. [. . .] You can have people in all sorts of fancy clothes and have the most elegant big cars, but if it's a lousy script, you're nowhere." On another occasion Ivory speculates to Geoffrey Macnab that it is the English, above all, who tend to voice such comments.[3] Perhaps they don't really like authors such as James, or Forster in particular: "They see him [Forster] as a hectoring old auntie who should shut up." By criticizing Ivory's adaptations of Forster, they were implicitly asking Ivory to shut up as well. Merchant seems apparently unconcerned about the whole issue; in 2003 he tells Chris Neumer that the triumvirate make films for civilized audiences drawn from no particular socio-economic background, who are united by their desire for "something interesting, exciting, entertaining, and they are satisfied with that."

Throughout their long careers, Merchant, Ivory, and Jhabvala have become associated with the cinematic equivalent of the well-made play, with the emphasis placed on character rather than incident. Apart from a few exceptions—*A Room with a View, The Remains of the Day*—their work has never attracted substantial box-office returns, but nonetheless commands a loyal following. In a recent review of W. Somerset Maugham's short story "A Round Dozen," I suggested that Maugham, like Terence Rattigan, was particularly proficient in creating plays of "narrowly reclaimed opportunity," in which characters—many of whom live in genteel yet oppressive circumstances—achieve some form of self-discovery. They might not be able to change their worlds, but at least they know more about them (Raw 2009). Merchant-Ivory's oeuvre ploughs the same thematic territory; nothing much happens in many of their films, but we learn a lot about the characters and how they cope (or fail to cope) with cross-cultural encounters, including class-conflicts. By allowing his actors to develop a series of image-streams, whether visual, kinetic, or verbal, Ivory shows how such struggles determine the characters' reactions to the situations they face throughout the films.

As for the criticism that Merchant-Ivory offer us little more than lifeless costume-parades: perhaps Ivory is right in claiming (albeit implicitly) that this view is predominantly expressed by English writers objecting to the fact that the films—especially those with an English setting, or involving English characters—have been written, directed, and produced by outsiders. Maybe they need to pay closer attention to the kind of material included in this collection, which provides an invaluable guide to what Merchant-Ivory have been trying to say about their films and their contribution to cross-cultural understanding over the past five decades.

All the interviews are reprinted as originally published, apart from a few silent corrections in terms of punctuation, spelling, and grammar.

I'd like to offer my thanks to Leila Salisbury, the director of the University Press of Mississippi, for commissioning this book. She has been a great source of support, particularly in the months following the death of my father in early 2010.

Obtaining permissions to reproduce any copyright material can be a long drawn-out affair. In the case of this anthology, the task was made much easier with the help of many people from different organizations: Kendra Armwood of AOL Permissions; Alex Batho, business manager, *Time Out*; Michael Charles of Amco Agency Ltd; Robert Dacopoulos of the AFI Mayer Library, Los Angeles; Roy Frumkes, managing editor of *Films in Review*; Mike Goodridge, editor, *Screen International*; Patricia A. Hart, associate general counsel of Washington University in St. Louis; Darrell Hope, editor, *DGA News*; Philip Horne; Urmila Joshi of the National Film Archive of India; Valerie Jones, Rob Winter, and Ian O'Sullivan of the British Film Institute; Geoffrey Macnab; Chris Neumer, editor of *Stumped* magazine; Ron Nowicki; Gerald Peary; Laura Pritchard, senior rights assistant, Elsevier Press; Natasha Schmidt, assistant editor, *Index on Censorship*; Lucy Silberman, associate managing editor of *Interview*; Judith Trojan[4]; Roger Thornton, head of publicity, Quartet; and Romney Whitehead, digital asset manager, BBC Worldwide.

I would like to thank the staffs of the AFI Mayer Library, Bilkent University Library (Ankara, Turkey), the British Film Institute, British Library, and the National Film Archive of India for their assistance in finding these articles.

I would like to thank the following individuals and institutions for granting permission to reproduce the articles in this book: the National Film Archive of India for "James Ivory and Ismail Merchant: An Interview" (1968); *Interview* magazine for "Interview with James Ivory"

(1972); the British Film Institute for "Merchant-Ivory" (1973), "Where Could I Meet Other Screenwriters?" (1978), and "The Trouble with Olive" (1985); Judith Trojan for "The Merchant-Ivory Synthesizers" (1974); *Index on Censorship* for "Hollywood versus Hollywood" (1976) and "Ismail Merchant: The Maker of Dreams" (1995); Roy Frumkes of *Films in Review* for "James Ivory: An Interview" (1984); the family of Charles Newman for "Ismail Merchant: From Snowballs to Eskimos" (1984); Ron Nowicki, former publisher of the *San Francisco Review of Books*, for "Interview with Ruth Prawer Jhabvala" (1987); BBC/*The Listener* for "A Film of Two Halves" (1990); Amco Agency for "A Truly Flourishing Plant" (1992); *Time Out* for "Buttling Under" (1993); permission to reprint the article "The Elegance of James Ivory—1994 D. W. Griffith Award Winner," from *DGA News* 20, no. 2, courtesy of the Director's Guild of America, Inc.; Quartet and Geoffrey Macnab for "James Ivory" (1999); Philip Horne for "Conversation with Ruth Prawer Jhabvala" (2000); *Stumped* magazine for the transcript of "Ismail Merchant" (2003); Elsevier Publishing for "James Ivory Interview" (2002) and "Interview with Ruth Prawer Jhabvala" (2003); Mike Goodridge for "James Ivory Interview" (2002); and AOL Permissions for "James Ivory on his 'Final Destination'" (2010).

LR

Notes

1. Since Merchant's death in 2005, Merchant-Ivory has reconstituted itself as a two-person company comprising Merchant and Jhabvala.

2. Higson claims that this is characteristic of most of Merchant-Ivory's work, even costume dramas such as *Howards End* (1992) (192).

3. Pauline Kael is an American, David Thomson is English, so perhaps Ivory's comments are rather generalized.

4. Award-winning journalist Judith Trojan has written and edited more than a thousand film and TV reviews and celebrity profiles, magazines, newsletters, and several books. Her interviews have run the gamut from best-selling authors Mary Higgins Clark, Ann Rule, and Frank McCourt and Academy Award–winning costume designer Ann Roth and screenwriter Eric Roth to seminal documentary filmmakers Ken Burns, Al Maysles, and Perry Miller Adato, and broadcast TV's legendary Carroll O'Connor (Archie Bunker), folk icon Judy Collins, and Sesame Street's Big Bird and Oscar the Grouch (Caroll Spinney), among many others. Ms. Trojan most recently helmed the Christopher Awards, a program that for the past sixty-one years has honored feature films, TV/cable programs, and books for adults and children that "affirm the highest values of the human spirit."

Chronology

1927   Ruth Prawer born on May 7, in Cologne, Germany, to Marcus and Eleanor Prawer.

1928   James Ivory born on June 7, in Berkeley, California, to Hallie Millicent and Edward Patrick Ivory.

1936   Ismail Noormohamed Abdul Rehman born on December 25, to Hazra and Noormohamed Haji Abdul Rehman, a Mumbai textile dealer.

1939   Ruth Prawer's family flees the Nazis in Germany, emigrating to Britain.

1947   Ismail Rehman caught up in the partitioning of India. His father, the president of the Muslim League—which later helped to form the state of Pakistan—refuses to move from India.

1948   Prawer becomes a British citizen.

1951   Prawer receives an M.A. in English literature from Queen Mary College, University of London, and marries Cyrus H. Jhabvala, an Indian Parsi architect. She moves to India.

1953   Ivory directs a documentary *Four in the Morning*, while a student at University of California School of Cinematic Arts.

1955   Jhabvala publishes her first novel, *To Whom She Will*.

1957   Ivory graduates from University of Southern California with a graduation thesis film that he writes and directs: *Venice: Themes and Variations*. Jhabvala publishes her second novel, *Esmond in India*.

1958   Ismail Rehman (now known as Ismail Merchant) studies at New York University.

1959   Ivory writes and directs *The Sword and the Flute*, another short film.

1960   Jhabvala publishes her third novel, *The Householder* (filmed 1963).

1961   *The Creation of Woman*, produced by Merchant, nominated for an Oscar and shown at Cannes Film Festival. Ivory creates Merchant-Ivory Productions with Jhabvala and Ismail Merchant.

1963   Jhabvala publishes *Get Ready for the Battle*. *The Householder*, directed by Ivory from Jhabvala's book, produced by Merchant and screenplay by Jhabvala.

1964   *The Delhi Way*, documentary written and directed by Ivory narrated by Leo Genn.

1965   *Shakespeare Wallah*, screenplay by Jhabvala and Ivory, directed by Ivory, produced by Merchant.

1969   *The Guru*, written for the screen by Jhabvala, directed by Ivory, produced by Merchant.

1970   *Bombay Talkie*, screenplay by Ivory and Jhabvala, produced by Merchant, directed by Ivory with Jennifer Kendal, Shashi Kapoor.

1972   *Adventures of a Brown Man in Search of Civilization*, written and directed by Ivory for BBC TV (documentary).

1973   *Savages*, directed by Ivory, produced by Merchant. *ABC Afterschool Specials: William—The Life and Times of William Shakespeare* written by Jhabvala and Ivory (TV). *Helen, Queen of the Nautch Girls*, short, screenplay by Ivory, produced by Merchant.

1974   *Mahatma and the Mad Boy*, produced and directed by Merchant.

1975   *Autobiography of a Princess*, directed by Ivory, screenplay by Jhabvala, produced by Merchant. *The Wild Party*, directed by Ivory, produced by Merchant. Jhabvala wins the Booker Prize for her novel *Heat and Dust* (filmed 1981). Jhabvala moves to New York. *The Place of Peace*, written by Jhabvala.

1976   *Sweet Sounds*, documentary short produced by Merchant.

1977   *Roseland*, story and screenplay by Jhabvala, directed by Ivory, produced by Merchant.

1978   *Hullabaloo Over Georgie and Bonnie's Pictures*, written by Jhabvala, directed by Ivory, produced by Merchant. *Mata Hari*, portmanteau film coproduced by Merchant.

1979   *The Europeans*, screenplay by Jhabvala, produced by Merchant, and directed by Ivory. *3 by Cheever: The Five Forty-Eight*, directed by Ivory.

1980   *Jane Austen in Manhattan*, directed by Ivory, written by Jhabvala, produced by Merchant.

1981   *Quartet*, screenplay by Jhabvala, produced by Merchant, and directed by Ivory.

1983   *Heat and Dust*, screenplay by Jhabvala, produced by Merchant, and directed by Ivory. *The Courtesans of Bombay*, documentary written by Ivory and Jhabvala and directed by Merchant.

1984   *The Bostonians*, screenplay by Jhabvala, produced by Merchant, and directed by Ivory. Jhabvala wins BAFTA Award for Best Adapted Screenplay (*Heat and Dust*).

1985   *Noon Wine*, TV film with Merchant and Ivory as executive producers.

1986   *A Room with a View*, screenplay by Jhabvala, produced by Merchant, and directed by Ivory. Film wins three Oscars for Best Art Direction, Best Costume Design, and Best Screenplay for Jhabvala. *My Little Girl*, Merchant as executive producer. Jhabvala becomes naturalized American citizen.

1987   Merchant and Ivory win BAFTA Award and *Evening Standard* Award for Best Film (*A Room with a View*). *Maurice*, screenplay by Ivory, produced by Merchant, directed by Ivory (wins Silver Lion at Venice Film Festival).

1988   *The Perfect Murder*, Merchant as executive producer. *The Deceivers*, Merchant as producer. *Madame Sousatzka*, screenplay by Jhabvala.

1989   *Slaves of New York*, produced by Merchant, directed by Ivory.

1990   *Mr. and Mrs. Bridge*, screenplay by Jhabvala, produced by Merchant, directed by Ivory (wins Venice Film Festival Award for Best Film).

1991   *The Ballad of the Sad Café*, Merchant as producer.

1992   *Howards End*, screenplay by Jhabvala, produced by Merchant, and directed by Ivory. Film wins three Oscars for Best Supporting Actress (Emma Thompson), Best Art Direction, and Best Screenplay for Jhabvala. Merchant and Ivory win BAFTA Award and *Evening Standard* Film Award for Best Film (*Howards End*). Ivory wins 45th Anniversary Prize at Cannes for *Howards End*.

1993   *The Remains of the Day*, written by Jhabvala, produced by Merchant, and directed by Ivory.

1994   Ivory wins London Critics Circle Award for Director of the Year for *The Remains of the Day*. *Street Musicians of Bombay* (documentary), Merchant as executive producer. *In Custody*, directed by Merchant.

1995   *Jefferson in Paris*, screenplay by Jhabvala, produced by Merchant, and directed by Ivory. *Lumiere and Company*, portmanteau film co-directed by Ivory. *Feast of July*, Merchant as executive produc-

er. Ivory receives Lifetime Achievement Award from Director's
Guild of America.

1996   *Surviving Picasso*, screenplay by Jhabvala, produced by Merchant,
and directed by Ivory. *The Proprietor*, directed by Merchant.

1998   Merchant wins Lifetime Achievement Award at the Asian American Film Festival. *A Soldier's Daughter Never Cries*, screenplay by
Ivory and Jhabvala, produced by Merchant, and directed by Ivory. *Side Streets*, Merchant as executive producer. *The Tree* (documentary), Merchant as executive producer.

1999   *Cotton Mary*, co-directed by Merchant.

2000   *The Golden Bowl*, screenplay by Jhabvala, produced by Merchant
and directed by Ivory.

2001   *The Mystic Masseur*, directed by Merchant. Merchant wins Joseph L. Mankiewicz Excellence in Filmmaking Award from the
Director's View Film Festival.

2002   *Refuge*, Merchant as executive producer. *Merci Docteur Rey*, Merchant as executive producer.

2003   *Le Divorce*, screenplay by Ivory and Jhabvala, produced by Merchant and directed by Ivory (wins the Wella Prize at the Venice
Film Festival in same year).

2005   *The White Countess*, directed by Ivory. *Heights*, Merchant as co-
producer. Ivory and Merchant win Costume Designers Guild
Award for Distinguished Director-Producer. May 25, Merchant
dies in London following surgery for abdominal ulcers.

2009   *The City of Your Final Destination*, screenplay by Jhabvala, directed by Ivory.

Filmography

1957
VENICE: THEMES AND VARIATIONS
Writer/Director: **James Ivory**
Cinematographer: **James Ivory**
Editing: Stellos Roccos
Cast: Alexander Scourby (narrator)
US 28 minutes, black and white, documentary

1959
THE SWORD AND THE FLUTE
Writer/Director/Producer: **James Ivory**
Cinematographer: Mindaugis Bagdon (Mindaugus Bagdon)
Editing: **James Ivory**
Music: Ali Akbar Khan, Chatur Lal, D. R. Parvatikar, Ravi Shankar, T. Visvanathan
Cast: Saeed Jaffrey (narrator)
India 24 minutes, black and white, documentary

1960
THE CREATION OF WOMAN
Production Company: Trident Films
Writer/Director: Charles F. Schwep
Producers: Charles F. Schwep, **Ismail Merchant**
Cinematography: Wheaton Galentine
Set Design: James McIntyre
Editing: Jan Wing Lum
Music: Frank Moore (musical director)
Cast: Bhaskar Roy Chowdhury, Dinu, Anjali Devi (dancers), Saeed Jaffray (narrator)
US 14 minutes, black and white

1963
THE HOUSEHOLDER
Production Company: Merchant-Ivory Productions
Director: **James Ivory**
Screenplay: **Ruth Prawer Jhabvala**
Producer: **Ismail Merchant**
Cinematography: Subrata Mitra
Set Design: Bettina Gill
Editing: Raja Ram Khetle
Music: Ustad Ali Akbar Khan
Cast: Shashi Kapoor (Prem Sagar), Leela Naidu (Indu), Durga Khote (The Mother), Achala Sachdev (Mrs. Saigal), Harindranath Chattopadhyay (Mr. Chadda)
India 100 minutes, black and white

1964
THE DELHI WAY
Production Company: Merchant-Ivory Productions and the Asia Society of New York
Writer/Director/Producer/Cinematography/Editing: **James Ivory**
Music: Ustad Vilayat Khan, Ustad Shantaprasad
Cast: Leo Genn (Narrator)
India 50 minutes, black and white, documentary

1965
SHAKESPEARE WALLAH
Production Company: Merchant-Ivory Productions
Director: **James Ivory**
Screenplay: **James Ivory**, **Ruth Prawer Jhabvala**
Producer: **Ismail Merchant**
Cinematography: Subrata Mitra
Costume Design: Jennifer Kapoor (Jennifer Kendal)
Editing: Amit Bose
Music: Satyajit Ray
Cast: Shashi Kapoor (Sanju), Felicity Kendal (Lizzie Buckingham), Geoffrey Kendal (Mr. Tony Buckingham), Laura Liddell (Mrs. Carla Buckingham), Madhur Jaffrey (Manjula), Utpal Dutt (Maharaja), Praveen Paul (Didi), Pinchoo Kapoor (Guptaji)
India 120 minutes, black and white

1969
THE GURU
Production Company: Merchant-Ivory Productions in association with
Twentieth Century-Fox and Arcadia Films
Director: **James Ivory**
Screenplay: **James Ivory**, **Ruth Prawer Jhabvala**
Producer: **Ismail Merchant**
Cinematography: Subrata Mitra
Costume Design: Bansi Chandragupta
Editing: Prabhakar Supare
Music: Ustad Vilayat Khan
Cast: Rita Tushingham (Jenny), Michael York (Tom Pickle), Utpal Dutt
(Ustal Zafar Khan), Madhur Jaffrey (Begum Sahiba), Barry Foster (Chris),
Aparna Sen (Ghazala), Saeed Jaffrey (Murad)
India 112 minutes, color

1970
BOMBAY TALKIE
Production Company: Merchant-Ivory Productions
Director: **James Ivory**
Screenplay: **James Ivory**, **Ruth Prawer Jhabvala**
Producer: **Ismail Merchant**
Cinematography: Subrata Mitra
Costume Design: A. Ranga Raj (A. Rangaraj)
Editing: David Gladwell
Music: Jakishan Dayabhai Pankal, Shankarsingh Raghuwanshi
Cast: Shashi Kapoor (Vikram), Jennifer Kendal (Lucia Lane), Zia Mo-
hyeddin (Hari), Aparna Sen (Mala), Utpal Dutt (Bose), Nadira (Anjana
Devi), Pinchoo Kapoor (Swamiji)
India 112 minutes (UK 105 minutes), color

1972
ADVENTURES OF A BROWN MAN IN SEARCH OF CIVILIZATION
Production Company: Merchant-Ivory Productions in association with
the BBC
Director: **James Ivory**
Writer: **James Ivory**
Producer: **Ismail Merchant**
Cinematography: Walter Lassally
Editing: Kent McKinney

Cast: Nirad C. Chaudhuri (Himself), Barry Foster (Narrator)
UK 54 minutes, color, documentary

1973
SAVAGES
Production Company: Merchant-Ivory Productions in association with
Angelika Films
Director: **James Ivory**
Screenplay: George Swift Trow, Michael O'Donoghue, based on an idea
by **James Ivory**
Producer: **Ismail Merchant**
Cinematography: Walter Lassally
Costume Design: Jack Wright
Editing: Kent McKinney
Music: Joe Raposo
Cast: Lewis J. Stadlen (Julian Branch), Anne Francine (Carlotta), Thayer
David (Otto Nurder), Susan Blakely (Cicely), Russ Thacker (Andrew),
Sam Waterston (James)
US 106 minutes, color

1973
WILLIAM—THE LIFE AND TIMES OF WILLIAM SHAKESPEARE
Production Company: American Broadcasting Company
Director: Ian MacNaughton
Teleplay: **James Ivory**, **Ruth Prawer Jhabvala**
Producer: Alexander H. Cohen
Cinematography: Terry Maher
Editing: Howard Lanning
Cast: John Gielgud, Ralph Richardson, Lynn Redgrave, Simon Ward,
Paul Jones (various roles)
US 52 minutes, color, television film

1973
HELEN, QUEEN OF THE NAUTCH GIRLS
Production Company: Merchant-Ivory Productions
Director: Anthony Korner
Writer: **James Ivory**
Producer: **Ismail Merchant**
Editing: Andrew Page

Cast: Helen (Herself), Anthony Korner (Narrator)
India/UK 31 minutes, black and white, documentary

1974
MAHATMA AND THE MAD BOY
Production Company: Merchant-Ivory Productions
Director: **Ismail Merchant**
Writer: Tanveer Farooqi
Producer: **Ismail Merchant**
Cinematography: Subrata Mitra
Costume Design: Bansi Chandragupta
Editing: Andrew Page
Music: Ram Narajan
Cast: Sajid Khan (The Mad Boy), Ruby Mayer (The Woman Feeding a Dog), Shastri Maharaj (The Gandhi-ite Speaker)
India 27 minutes, color

1975
AUTOBIOGRAPHY OF A PRINCESS
Production Company: Merchant-Ivory Productions
Director: **James Ivory**
Screenplay: **Ruth Prawer Jhabvala**
Producer: **Ismail Merchant**
Cinematography: Walter Lassally
Costume Design: Jacqueline Charriot-Lodwidge
Editing: Humphrey Dixon
Music: Vic Flick
Cast: James Mason (Cyril Sahib), Madhur Jaffrey (The Princess), Keith Varnier (Delivery Man), Timothy Bateson (Blackmailer), Diane Fletcher (Blackmailer)
UK 60 minutes, color

1975
THE WILD PARTY
Production Company: Merchant-Ivory Productions in association with American International Pictures and The Wild Party Production Company
Director: **James Ivory**
Screenplay: Walter Marks, based on the narrative poem by Joseph Moncure March

Producer: **Ismail Merchant**
Cinematography: Walter Lassally
Costume Design: Ron Talsky
Editing: Kent McKinney
Music: Walter Marks
Cast: Raquel Welch (Queenie), James Coco (Jolly Grimm), Perry King (Dale Sword), Tiffany Bolling (Kate), David Dukes (James Morrison)
US 95 minutes (France 100 minutes, Germany 88 minutes, 108 minutes DVD version), color

1975
THE PLACE OF PEACE
Production Company: Granada Television
Director: Robert Knights
Screenplay: **Ruth Prawer Jhabvala**
Producer: Jonathan Powell
Cast: Jane Lapotaire, Beatrix Lehmann, Roger Rees (Willie)
UK 50 minutes, color, television film

1976
SWEET SOUNDS
Production Company: Merchant-Ivory Productions
Director: Richard Robbins
Writer: Richard Robbins
Producer: **Ismail Merchant**
Cinematography: Fred Murphy, Richard Inman Pearce
Editing: Humphrey Dixon
Cast: Jean Whitelock, Laura Wilson (Teachers of Mannes College of Music), John Desser (solo cello), Hai-Kyung Suh (solo piano)
US 29 minutes, color, documentary

1977
ROSELAND
Production Company: Merchant-Ivory Productions in association with Oregon Four
Director: **James Ivory**
Screenplay: **Ruth Prawer Jhabvala**
Producer: **Ismail Merchant**
Cinematography: Ernest Vincze
Costume Design: Diane Finn Chapman

Editing: Humphrey Dixon, Richard Schmiechen
Music: Michael Gibson
Cast: Teresa Wright (May), Lou Jacobi (Stan), Geraldine Chaplin (Marilyn), Christopher Walken (Russel), Conrad Janis (George), Denny Shearer (Young Eddie), Lilia Skala (Rosa)
US 104 minutes, color

1978
HULLABALOO OVER GEORGIE'S AND BONNIE'S PICTURES
Production Company: Merchant-Ivory Productions in association with London Weekend Television
Director: **James Ivory**
Writer: **Ruth Prawer Jhabvala**
Producer: **Ismail Merchant**
Cinematography: Walter Lassally
Costume Design: Purnima Agarwal, Jenny Beavan
Editing: Melvyn Bragg, Humphrey Dixon
Music: Vic Flick
Cast: Peggy Ashcroft (Lady Gee), Larry Pine (Clark Haven), Saeed Jaffray (Sri Narain), Victor Banerjee (Georgie), Aparna Sen (Bonnie), Jane Booker (Lynn)
UK/India 85 minutes, color, television film

1978
MATA HARI
Director: David Carradine
Producers: Paul Hunt, **Ismail Merchant**
Cinematography: Paul Hunt
Costume Design: Gert Brinkers
Cast: Calista Carradine (Mata Hari), David Carradine (Adam Zelle), Paul Hunt (English Soldier)
US 63 minutes, color

1979
THE EUROPEANS
Production Company: Merchant-Ivory Productions
Director: **James Ivory**
Screenplay: **Ruth Prawer Jhabvala**, from the novel by Henry James
Producer: **Ismail Merchant**
Cinematography: Larry Pizer

Costume Design: Judy Moorcroft
Editing: Humphrey Dixon
Music: Richard Robbins
Cast: Lee Remick (Eugenia Young), Robin Ellis (Robert Acton), Wesley Addy (Mr. Wentworth), Tim Choate (Clifford), Lisa Eichhorn (Gertrude), Nancy New (Charlotte)
UK 90 minutes, color

1979
3 BY CHEEVER: THE FIVE FORTY-EIGHT
Production Company: Thirteen/WNET
Director: **James Ivory**
Screenplay: Terrence McNally, from the story by John Cheever
Producer: Peter Weinberg
Cinematography: Andrzej Bartkowiak
Costume Design: Julie Weiss
Editing: David E. McKenna
Music: Jonathan Tunick
Cast: Laurence Luckinbill (John Blake), Mary Beth Hurt (Jane Dent), Laurinda Barrett (Louise Blake)
US 58 minutes, television film

1980
JANE AUSTEN IN MANHATTAN
Production Company: Merchant-Ivory Productions in association with Polytel International
Director: **James Ivory**
Screenplay: **Ruth Prawer Jhabvala**
Producer: **Ismail Merchant**
Cinematography: Larry Pizer
Costume Design: Jenny Beavan
Editing: David E. McKenna
Music: Richard Robbins
Cast: Anne Baxter (Lilliana Zorska), Robert Powell (Pierre), Michael Wager (George Midash), Tim Choate (Jamie), Nancy New (Jenny), Sean Young (Ariadne Charlton)
US/UK 111 minutes, color

1981
QUARTET
Production Company: Merchant-Ivory Productions in association with
Lyric International
Director: **James Ivory**
Screenplay: **Ruth Prawer Jhabvala**, from the novel by Jean Rhys
Producer: **Ismail Merchant**
Cinematography: Pierre Lhomme
Costume Design: Judy Moorcroft
Editing: Humphrey Dixon
Music: Richard Robbins
Cast: Alan Bates (H. J. Heidler), Maggie Smith (Lois Heidler), Isabelle Adjani (Marya 'Mado' Zelli), Anthony Higgins (Stephan Zelli), Sheila Gish (Anna)
UK/France 101 minutes, color

1983
HEAT AND DUST
Production Company: Merchant-Ivory Productions
Director: **James Ivory**
Screenplay: **Ruth Prawer Jhabvala**, from her novel
Producer: **Ismail Merchant**
Cinematography: Walter Lassally
Costume Design: Barbara Lane
Editing: Humphrey Dixon
Music: Richard Robbins
Cast: Christopher Cazenove (Douglas Rivers), Greta Scacchi (Olivia), Julian Glover (Crawford), Susan Fleetwood (Mrs. Crawford), Jennifer Kendal (Mrs. Saunders), Julie Christie (Anne), Shashi Kapoor (The Nawab), Madhur Jaffrey (Begum Mussarat Jahan)
UK 133 minutes, color

1983
THE COURTESANS OF BOMBAY
Production Company: Merchant-Ivory Productions
Director: **Ismail Merchant**
Writers: **James Ivory**, **Ruth Prawer Jhabvala**
Cinematography: Vishnu Mathur
Editing: Amit Bose, Rita Stern

Cast: Saeed Jaffrey (Narrator), Zohra Segal (Herself)
UK 74 minutes, television documentary

1984
THE BOSTONIANS
Production Company: Merchant-Ivory Productions in association with
WGBH, Rediffusion, and Almi Entertainment Finance Corporation
Director: **James Ivory**
Screenplay: **Ruth Prawer Jhabvala**, from the novel by Henry James
Producer: **Ismail Merchant**
Cinematography: Walter Lassally
Costume Design: Jenny Beavan, John Wright
Editing: Mark Potter Jr., Katherine Wenning
Music: Richard Robbins
Cast: Vanessa Redgrave (Olive Chancellor), Christopher Reeve (Basil
Ransom), Jessica Tandy (Miss Birdseye), Madeleine Potter (Verena Tar-
rant), Wesley Addy (Dr. Tarrant), Linda Hunt (Dr. Prance)
UK/US 122 minutes, color

1985
NOON WINE
Production Company: Merchant-Ivory Productions in association with
PBS
Director: Michael Fields
Writer: Michael Fields, from a story by Katherine Anne Porter
Executive Producers: **James Ivory, Ismail Merchant**
Cinematography: Juan Ruiz Anchia
Costume Design: Hilary Rosenfeld
Editing: Jeanne Jordan
Music: Paul Chihara
Cast: Fred Ward (Royal Earle Thompson), Stellan Skarsgård (Olaf Hel-
ton), Pat Hingle (Homer T. Hatch), Jon Cryer (Teenage Herbert)
US 81 minutes, color, television film

1986
A ROOM WITH A VIEW
Production Company: Merchant-Ivory Productions in association with
National Film Finance Corporation, Curzon Film Distributors, Film Four
International, and Goldcrest
Director: **James Ivory**

Screenplay: **Ruth Prawer Jhabvala**, from the novel by E. M. Forster
Producer: **Ismail Merchant**
Cinematography: Tony Pierce-Roberts
Costume Design: Jenny Beavan, John Wright
Editing: Humphrey Dixon
Music: Richard Robbins
Cast: Maggie Smith (Charlotte Bartlett), Helena Bonham Carter (Lucy Honeychurch), Denholm Elliott (Mr. Emerson), Julian Sands (George Emerson), Simon Callow (The Rev. Arthur Beebe), Daniel Day-Lewis (Cecil Vyse)
UK 117 minutes, color

1986
MY LITTLE GIRL
Production Company: Black Swan Productions in association with Merchant-Ivory Productions
Director: Connie Kaiserman
Screenplay: Connie Kaiserman, Nan Mason
Producer: **Ismail Merchant**
Cinematography: Pierre Lhomme
Costume Design: Susan Gammie
Editing: Katherine Wenning
Music: Richard Robbins
Cast: James Earl Jones (Ike Bailey), Geraldine Page (Molly), Mary Stuart Masterson (Franny Bettinger), Peter Gallagher (Kai), Jennifer Lopez (Myra)
US 118 minutes, color

1987
MAURICE
Production Company: Merchant-Ivory Productions in association with Cinecom Pictures and Film Four International
Director: **James Ivory**
Screenplay: **Ruth Prawer Jhabvala**, from the novel by E. M. Forster
Producer: **Ismail Merchant**
Cinematography: Pierre Lhomme
Costume Design: Jenny Beavan, John Wright, William Pierce
Editing: Katherine Wenning
Music: Richard Robbins

Cast: James Wilby (Maurice Hall), Hugh Grant (Clive Durham), Rupert Graves (Alec Scudder), Denholm Elliott (Dr. Barry), Simon Callow (Mr. Ducie), Barry Foster (Dean Cornwallis), Ben Kingsley (Lasker-Jones)
UK 140 minutes, color

1988
THE PERFECT MURDER
Production Company: Merchant-Ivory Productions in association with Perfect Movie Productions
Director: Zafar Hai
Screenplay: Zafar Hai, H. R. F. Keating
Producer: Wahid Chowhan
Executive Producer: **Ismail Merchant**
Cinematography: Walter Lassally
Costume Design: Sally Turner
Editing: Charles Rees
Music: Richard Robbins
Cast: Naseeruddin Shah (Inspector Ghote), Stellan Skarsgård (Axel Svensson), Amjad Khan (Lala Heera Lal), Madhur Jaffrey (Mrs. Lal)
UK/India 93 minutes, color

1988
THE DECEIVERS
Production Companies: Merchant-Ivory Productions and Michael White Productions in association with Cinecom Pictures, Film Four International, and Masters Film Productions
Director: Nicholas Meyer
Screenplay: Michael Hirst, from the novel by John Masters
Producers: **Ismail Merchant**, Tim van Rellim
Cinematography: Walter Lassally
Costume Design: Jenny Beavan, John Bright
Editing: Richard Trevor
Music: John Scott
Cast: Pierce Brosnan (William Savage), Saeed Jaffrey (Hussein), Shashi Kapoor (Chandra Singh), Keith Michell (Colonel Wilson), Gary Cady (Lt. Maunsell)
India/UK 102 minutes, color

1988
MADAME SOUSATZKA
Production Companies: Cineplex-Odeon Films
Director: John Schlesinger
Screenplay: John Schlesinger, **Ruth Prawer Jhabvala**, from the novel
by Bernice Rubens
Producer: Robin Dalton
Cinematography: Nat Crosby
Costume Design: Amy Roberts
Editing: Peter Honess
Music: Gerald Gouriet
Cast: Shirley MacLaine (Madame Sousatzka), Peggy Ashcroft (Lady Em-
ily), Twiggy (Jenny), Shabana Azmi (Sushila Sen), Leigh Lawson (Ronnie
Blum)
UK 122 minutes, color

1989
SLAVES OF NEW YORK
Production Companies: Merchant-Ivory Productions and Tri-Star Pic-
tures in association with Gary Hendler
Director: **James Ivory**
Screenplay: Tama Janowitz, from her own stories
Producer: **Ismail Merchant**
Cinematography: Tony Pierce-Roberts
Costume Design: Carol Ramsey
Editing: Katherine Wenning
Music: Richard Robbins
Cast: Bernadette Peters (Eleanor), Chris Sarandon (Victor Okrent), Mary
Beth Hurt (Ginger Booth), Madeleine Potter (Daria), Mercedes Ruehl (Sa-
mantha), Steve Buscemi (Wilfredo)
US 124 minutes, color

1990
MR. AND MRS. BRIDGE
Production Companies: Merchant-Ivory Productions, Miramax, and
RHI Entertainment in association with Cineplex-Odeon Films
Director: **James Ivory**
Screenplay: **Ruth Prawer Jhabvala**, from the novels by Evan S. Con-
nell

Producer: **Ismail Merchant**
Cinematography: Tony Pierce-Roberts
Costume Design: Carol Ramsey
Editing: Humphrey Dixon, Andrew Marcus
Music: Richard Robbins
Cast: Paul Newman (Walter Bridge), Joanne Woodward (India Bridge), Saundra McClain (Harriet), Margaret Welsh (Carolyn Bridge), Simon Callow (Dr. Alex Sauer), Blythe Danner (Grace Barron), Austin Pendleton (Mr. Gadbury)
UK/US 126 minutes, color

1991
THE BALLAD OF THE SAD CAFÉ
Production Companies: Merchant-Ivory Productions and Channel Four Films
Director: Simon Callow
Screenplay: Michael Hirst, from the novel by Carson McCullers and the play by Edward Albee
Producer: **Ismail Merchant**
Cinematography: Walter Lassally
Costume Design: Marianna Elliott
Editing: Andrew Marcus
Music: Richard Robbins
Cast: Vanessa Redgrave (Miss Amelia), Keith Carradine (Marvin Macy), Rod Steiger (Rev. Willin), Austin Pendleton (Lawyer Taylor), Cork Hubbert (Cousin Lymon)
UK/US 100 minutes, color

1992
HOWARDS END
Production Company: Merchant-Ivory Productions in association with Sumitomo Corporation, Imagica Corporation, Cinema Ten Corporation, Japan Satellite Broadcasting, Ide Productions, and Film Four Productions
Director: **James Ivory**
Screenplay: **Ruth Prawer Jhabvala**, from the novel by E. M. Forster
Producers: **Ismail Merchant**, Ann Wingate
Cinematography: Tony Pierce-Roberts
Costume Design: Jenny Beavan, John Bright
Editing: Andrew Marcus

Music: Richard Robbins
Cast: Vanessa Redgrave (Ruth Wilcox), Helena Bonham Carter (Helen Schlegel), Emma Thompson (Margaret Schlegel), Prunella Scales (Aunt Juley), Anthony Hopkins (Henry J. Wilcox), James Wilby (Charles Wilcox)
UK/Japan 140 minutes, color

1993
THE REMAINS OF THE DAY
Production Companies: Merchant-Ivory Productions and Columbia Pictures
Director: **James Ivory**
Screenplay: **Ruth Prawer Jhabvala**, from the novel by Kazuo Ishiguro
Producers: **Ismail Merchant**, John Calley, Mike Nichols
Cinematography: Tony Pierce-Roberts
Costume Design: Jenny Beavan, John Bright
Editing: Andrew Marcus
Music: Richard Robbins
Cast: Anthony Hopkins (James Stevens), Emma Thompson (Miss Kenton), Christopher Reeve (Jack Lewis), James Fox (Lord Darlington), Peter Vaughan (William Stevens), Hugh Grant (Reginald Cardinal)
UK/US 134 minutes, color

1994
STREET MUSICIANS OF BOMBAY (aka COURTESANS OF BOMBAY)
Production Company: Merchant-Ivory Productions in association with Film Four
Director: Richard Robbins
Producer: Wahid Chowhan
Executive Producer: **Ismail Merchant**
Cinematography: Jehangir Choudhury
Editing: Amit Bose
Music: Ustad Sultan Khan, Richard Robbins
Cast: Trevor Nichols, Rosemary Martin (Narrators)
UK 59 minutes, color, television documentary

1994
IN CUSTODY
Production Companies: Merchant-Ivory Productions and Channel Four Films

Director: **Ismail Merchant**
Screenplay: Shahrukh Husain, Anita Desai, from the novel by Desai
Producer: Wahid Chowhan
Cinematography: Larry Pizer
Costume Design: Lovleen Bains
Editing: Roberto Silvi
Music: Zakir Hussain, Ustad Sultan Khan
Cast: Shashi Kapoor (Nur), Shabana Azmi (Imtiaz Begum), Om Puri (Deven)
UK/India 126 minutes, color

1995
JEFFERSON IN PARIS
Production Companies: Merchant-Ivory Productions and Touchstone Pictures
Director: **James Ivory**
Screenplay: **Ruth Prawer Jhabvala**
Producer: Ismail Merchant
Cinematography: Pierre Lhomme
Editing: Isabelle Lorente, Andrew Marcus
Music: Richard Robbins
Cast: Nick Nolte (Thomas Jefferson), Gwyneth Paltrow (Patsy Jefferson), Thandie Newton (Sally Hemmings), Greta Scacchi (Maria Cosway), Simon Callow (Richard Cosway)
US/France 139 minutes, color

1995
LUMIERE AND COMPANY (original title LUMIÈRE ET COMPAGNIE)
Production Companies: Cinétévé, La Sept-Arte, Igeldo Komunikazioa, Søren St?mose AB
Directors: John Boorman, Costa-Gavras, Hugh Hudson, **James Ivory**, et al.
Screenplay: Philippe Poulet
Cinematography: Didier Ferry
Costume Design: Françoise Nicolet
Editing: Roger Ikhlef, Timothy Miller
Cast: Neil Jordan, Alan Rickman, et al.
France/Denmark/Spain/Sweden 88 minutes, color

1995
FEAST OF JULY
Production Companies: Merchant-Ivory Productions and Touchstone Pictures in association with Peregrine Productions
Director: Christopher Menaul
Screenplay: Christopher Neame, from the novel by H. E. Bates
Producer: Christopher Neame
Executive Producer: **Ismail Merchant**
Cinematography: Peter Sova
Costume Design: Phoebe de Gaye
Editing: Chris Wimble
Music: Zbigniew Preisner
Cast: Ben Chaplin (Con Wainwright), James Purefoy (Jedd Wainwright), Greg Wise (Arch Wilson), Gemma Jones (Mrs. Wainwright), Tom Bell (Ben Wainwright), Embeth Davitz (Bella Ford)
US/UK 116 minutes, color

1996
SURVIVING PICASSO
Production Companies: Merchant-Ivory Productions and David L. Wolper Productions
Director: **James Ivory**
Screenplay: **Ruth Prawer Jhabvala**, from the book by Arianna Stassinopoulos Huffington
Producers: **Ismail Merchant**, David L. Wolper
Cinematography: Tony Pierce-Roberts
Costume Design: Carol Ramsey
Editing: Andrew Marcus
Music: Richard Robbins
Cast: Anthony Hopkins (Pablo Picasso), Natascha McElhone (Françoise Gilot), Julianne Moore (Dora Maar), Joss Ackland (Henri Matisse), Jane Lapotaire (Olga Picasso)
US 125 minutes, color

1996
THE PROPRIETOR
Production Companies: Merchant-Ivory Productions, Ognon Pictures, Fex Production Filmcilik in association with Largo Entertainment, Canal +, Channel Four Films, and Eurimages
Director: **Ismail Merchant**

Screenplay: Jean-Marie Besset, George W. S. Trow
Producers: Humbert Balsan, Donald Rosenfeld
Cinematography: Larry Pizer
Costume Design: Patrick Colpaert
Editing: William Webb
Music: Richard Robbins
Cast: Jeanne Moreau (Adrienne Mark), Sean Young (Virginia Kelly/ Sally), Sam Waterston (Harry Bancroft), Christopher Cazenove (Elliott Spencer), Austin Pendleton (Willy Kunst)
France/UK/USA 113 minutes, color

1998
A SOLDIER'S DAUGHTER NEVER CRIES
Production Companies: Merchant-Ivory Productions and Capitol Films in association with British Screen
Director: **James Ivory**
Screenplay: **James Ivory**, **Ruth Prawer Jhabvala**, from the novel by Kaylie Jones
Producer: **Ismail Merchant**
Cinematography: Jean-Marc Fabre
Costume Design: Carol Ramsey
Editing: Noelle Blossom
Music: Richard Robbins
Cast: Kris Kristofferson (Bill Wills), Barbara Hershey (Marcella Wills), Leelee Sobieski (Charlotte Anne 'Channe' Wills), Jane Birkin (Mrs. Fortescue), Dominique Blanc (Candida)
France/UK/USA 127 minutes, color

1998
THE TREE (original title GAACH)
Production Company: Merchant-Ivory Productions
Director: Catherine Berge
Producer: Nayeem Hafizka
Executive Producer: **Ismail Merchant**
Cinematography: Ivan Kozelka
Editing: Georges-Henri Mauchant, Catherine Poitevin
Music: Zakir Hussain
Cast: Soumitra Chatterjee (Himself)
US 66 minutes, documentary

1999
COTTON MARY
Production Company: Merchant-Ivory Productions
Directors: **Ismail Merchant**, Madhur Jaffrey
Screenplay: Alexandra Viets
Producers: Nayeem Hafizka, Richard Hawley
Cinematography: Pierre Lhomme
Costume Design: Sheena Napier
Editing: John David Allen
Music: Richard Robbins
Cast: Greta Scacchi (Lily MacIntosh), Madhur Jaffrey (Cotton Mary), James Wilby (John MacIntosh), Gemma Jones (Mrs. Freda Davids)
France/UK/USA 124 minutes, color

2000
THE GOLDEN BOWL
Production Companies: Merchant-Ivory Productions and TFI International
Director: **James Ivory**
Screenplay: **Ruth Prawer Jhabvala**, from the novel by Henry James
Producer: **Ismail Merchant**
Cinematography: Tony Pierce-Roberts
Costume Design: John Bright
Editing: John David Allen
Music: Richard Robbins
Cast: Kate Beckinsale (Maggie Verver), Nick Nolte (Adam Verver), Anjelica Huston (Fanny Assingham), James Fox (Bob Assingham), Jeremy Northam (Prince Amerigo), Madeleine Potter (Lady Castledean), Uma Thurman (Charlotte Stant)
US/France/UK 130 minutes, color

2001
THE MYSTIC MASSEUR
Production Company: Merchant-Ivory Productions in association with Pritish Nandy Communications and Video Associates Ltd.
Director: **Ismail Merchant**
Screenplay: Caryl Phillips, from the novel by V. S. Naipaul
Producers: Nayeem Hafizka, Richard Hawley, Pritish Nandy
Cinematography: Ernest Vincze
Costume Design: Michael O'Connor

Editing: Roberto Silvi
Music: Zakir Hussain, Richard Robbins
Cast: Om Puri (Ramlogan), Aasif Mandvi (Ganesh Ramseyor), Ayesha Dharker (Leela G. Ramseyor), Jimi Mistry (Pratap Cooper), James Fox (Mr. Stewart)
UK/India/USA 117 minutes, color

2002
REFUGE
Production Company: Park & 60 Second Productions
Director: Narain Jashanmal
Screenplay: Narain Jashanmal
Producers: Narain Jashamal, Pravesh Sippy
Executive Producer: **Ismail Merchant**
Cinematography: Tom Grubbs
Costume Design: Eveline Jashanmal
Editing: Narain Jashanmal, Peter Sabat
Music: Paul Rose
Cast: Santa Choudhury (Girl), Madeleine Potter (Sylvia Oakes), Philip Tabor (Oliver Oakes)
UK 70 minutes, color

2002
MERCI DOCTEUR REY
Production Company: Merchant-Ivory Productions in association with Eat Your Soup Productions
Director: Andrew Litvack
Screenplay: Andrew Litvack
Producers: Rahila Bootwala, Nathalie Gastaldo
Executive Producer: **Ismail Merchant**
Cinematography: Laurent Machuel
Costume Design: Pierre-Yves Gayraud
Editing: Giles Gardner
Music: Geoffrey Alexander
Cast: Dianne West (Elizabeth Beaumont), Jane Birkin (Pénélope), Stanislas Merhar (Thomas Beaumont), Vanessa Redgrave (Herself), Simon Callow (Bob)
France/USA 91 minutes, color

2003
LE DIVORCE
Production Companies: Merchant-Ivory Productions and Radar Pictures
Director: **James Ivory**
Screenplay: **James Ivory**, **Ruth Prawer Jhabvala**, from the novel by
Diane Johnson
Producer: **Ismail Merchant**
Cinematography: Pierre Lhomme
Costume Design: Carol Ramsey
Editing: John David Allen
Music: Richard Robbins
Cast: Kate Hudson (Isabel Walker), Naomi Watts (Roxeanne de Persand),
Leslie Caron (Suzanne de Persand), Glenn Close (Olivia Pace), Sam Wa-
terston (Chester Walker)
US 117 minutes, color

2005
THE WHITE COUNTESS
Production Companies: Merchant-Ivory Productions, Sony Pictures
Classics, Shanghai Film Group in association with Global Cinema
Group, Rising Star, and China Film Co-Production Corporation
Director: **James Ivory**
Screenplay: Kazuo Ishiguro
Producer: **Ismail Merchant**
Cinematography: Christopher Doyle
Costume Design: John Bright
Editing: John David Allen
Music: Richard Robbins
Cast: Ralph Fiennes (Todd Jackson), Natasha Richardson (Countess Sofia
Belinskya), Lynn Redgrave (Olga Belinskya), Vanessa Redgrave (Princess
Vera Belinskya), Madeleine Potter (Grushenka)
UK/USA/Germany/China 135 minutes, color

2005
HEIGHTS
Production Company: Merchant-Ivory Productions
Director: Chris Temio
Screenplay: Amy Fox, from her play
Producers: **Ismail Merchant**, Richard Hawley
Cinematography: Jim Denault

Costume Design: Marina Draghici
Editing: Sloane Klevin
Music: Ben Butler, Martin Erskine
Cast: Chandler Williams (Juilliard Macbeth), Bess Wohl (Juilliard Lady Macbeth), Glenn Close (Diana), Isabella Rossellini (Liz), Philip Tabor (Paul)
US 93 minutes, color

2009
THE CITY OF YOUR FINAL DESTINATION
Production Company: Merchant-Ivory Productions and Hyde Park International
Director: **James Ivory**
Screenplay: **Ruth Prawer Jhabvala**, from the novel by Peter Cameron
Producers: Paul Bradley, Pierre Proner
Cinematography: Javier Aguirreesarobe
Costume Design: Carol Ramsey
Editing: John David Allen
Music: Jorge Drexler
Cast: Anthony Hopkins (Adam), Laura Linney (Caroline), Charlotte Gainsbourg (Arden Langdon)
US 117 minutes, color

Merchant-Ivory: Interviews

James Ivory and Ismail Merchant: An Interview

Jag Mohan, Basu Chatterji, and Arun Kaul/1968

From *Close-Up* no. 2 (October/ December 1968): 5–19, 46. Reprinted by permission of the National Film Archive of India.

At the time of the final editing of the film *Guru*, both Ismail Merchant and James Ivory were in Bombay for a long stretch. *Close-Up* took advantage of their presence and interviewed them. The team of *Close-Up* interviews was Jag Mohan, Basu Chatterji, and Arun Kaul, headed of course by Jag Mohan. The interview started at the temporary office of Ismail Merchant at about 4:00 pm, and ended at 10:00 pm. Yagya Sharma, a young documentary filmmaker, tape-recorded the interview.

Q: How did Merchant and Ivory become Merchant and Ivory Productions—that is, joined together as a team?
Ismail Merchant: Well. I was studying in the US, and I had just finished a year in Los Angeles where I had been observing all the different aspects of filmmaking. I had then made a film called *The Creation of Woman* which had won the Academy Award nomination and was invited to the Cannes Film Festival. That was in 1961. On the way to Cannes I stopped at New York for ten to fifteen days and was invited to see the film *The Sword and the Flute*. Of course, I had heard about this film when I was still a student in 1958 and always wanted to see it and this was the perfect opportunity. So I went and there I met James Ivory who had just returned from India after making *The Delhi Way*. We decided that we would go to India and make films together, he as the director and I as the producer. At that time Ray's *Apur Sansar* was running up town in New York and we wanted to see it. I had not seen a Ray film before. And once

I had seen one, I saw each film five or six times and was quite convinced that our work should follow and try to do something of the same pattern, but make it in the English language which is much more international and has a bigger market.

James Ivory: Now you are going too fast [*to Merchant*]. You are not filling in all the detail. You have not told everything. First of all Ismail wanted to make a feature film in India and I had at that time no idea of making a feature film in India or anywhere, except vaguely as something to aim for when I could afford it and I could not, at that time. Anyway, Ismail said he wanted to make a feature film in India and that he had already begun to make plans by striking up a kind of partnership with some American who wanted to make a film here. I introduced him to an American anthropologist, Gitel Steed, who had written a script for a kind of semi-documentary, semi-feature film. She wanted to set it in a village in Gujarat where she had been working for almost a year as an anthropologist. She had also interested the American director Sydney Myers in directing the film. I don't know if you know Sydney Myers's works. He is a marvelous director; he has not done anything much lately but has made a wonderful film called *The Silent One*. He was to direct this film and I rather foolhardily said that I would photograph it. I did not realize then what a tremendous chore it is really to photograph a film. I had photographed three documentaries including one film in India and it had been quite easy, so I said I would do this. So we came to India. In my case I had to do some more work on a documentary film that the Asia Society had commissioned us to make, *The Delhi Way*. This film is not much known here in India, which is a pity because I like this film very much. Well, Gitel Steed was in New York and Ismail wanted to produce it, so he went back and I started casting. She was to come back with Sydney Myers, but that film finally fell through as films do and we were left wondering what to do. Ismail had read *The Householder* as a novel when he was in California and suggested filming it. By this time we had already met Shashi Kapoor and Leela Naidu and Durga Khote and all people who were in *Householder* because they were also to be in this film of Gitel Steed's. So we decided to make *Householder*, just like that—again in a rather foolhardy way and grandiose way too, because it was to be made in Hindi and in English. Here was my opportunity to direct a feature film, but of course it was a very, very difficult thing for me because then I did not know Hindi at all. That is how Merchant-Ivory really got started.

Q: Which part of the States do you come from and how did you become interested in things Indian?

Ivory: Well, it is quite a history. The first glimpse I had of India or any sort of contact with India was through Jean Renoir's *The River* when I was still at the University of Southern California taking cinema courses, and I loved that film and saw it many times and it made a tremendous impression on me. Then for about four or five years, I did not think about India. In the meantime I had been through the Army and then had been to Venice, where I made a film about Venetian paintings called *The Venice Theme and Variations*. I had a friend in San Francisco who was a dealer in original drawings and etching and other European works of arts, Japanese prints, and Indian miniatures. One day I went to see him, he had just sold some Indian miniatures or shown them to a client and they were all spread out on the table, forty to fifty miniatures. It was the first time I had seen them, and got interested right away. And as I had just made this film about Venetian paintings, I said, well, why not make a film on Indian miniatures? Again, rather a foolhardy quick decision, because I had to learn a tremendous amount about Indian paintings before I could really make the film. I did not even know the difference between a Rajput and a Moghul. After I had worked on it for maybe three or four months, I saw *Pather Panchali* in San Francisco and it made a profound impression on me and I saw it many, many times. And really, to this day I can remember going to that film, and everything about that afternoon. After that I finished my film on Indian paintings which is called *The Sword and the Flute*. It has been shown here so many times that it must have worn away ten feet of film by now. That is how I really got interested in India.

Q: You shot the entire film in the States?

Ivory: Yes. The paintings were all in American collections.

Q: And then you got the commission to do *The Delhi Way*, which enabled you to come to India.

Ivory: Correct. The Asia Society saw those two earlier films and in those days they had quite a lot of exchange programs with India. They wanted to make a documentary on India and asked whether I would go and make a film there? I said, naturally I would. I was absolutely free to make any kind of film that I wanted provided that it was shot in Delhi; it had to be a film about Delhi.

Q: Now Mr. Merchant. Here is a case of an American coming all the way to India and you had gone to the States. We of course know you were a St. Xavier's student but what made you migrate to the US?

Merchant: Right from the beginning I had had a fascination for the American way of life that I gathered from books, stories, and films, and after my graduation from St. Xavier's, I got admission to New York University. New York fascinated me. Most people say, well, you should go to a small campus where you would really get an idea of average American life, but actually what interested me was the people and the activity, and somehow the activity of New York connected with my ideas, and I decided that I would go into films or television and be involved in show business, as you call it. I had evening classes at the University and during the day I worked in an advertising agency. While I was working I also did some television programs, directed, produced, or acted in them. Then someone said I should make a film. So I got together some friends, they put up money, got Bhaskar Roy Choudhuri to be in this film, and we did *The Creation of Woman* in our spare time.

Q: Now we know the background of both of you. So when you landed in Delhi and met Prawer Jhabvala and got the story of *The Householder* done, how did you get about financing the film?

Merchant: You know there is one more thing about this story which I think would interest you. When I was in Los Angeles, I decided to make the film, you know there is always a sort of pattern. In Hollywood, you go to a writer, screen writer, and give him the idea. If he is interested, he writes a screenplay and you go and make a film. At that time I visited Metro Studios and I was introduced to Isobel Lennart. She is a prominent screenwriter in America. She wrote *Sundowners* and various other pictures and she said, "I don't think I would be interested in doing anything in India at the moment but there is a very interesting book come out called *The Householder* which I have just read which I think is one of the best books I have read in a long time and it would make a very good film." So I immediately bought the book, read it, and I sort of noted it in my little diary to make it into a film. So my first feature film was suggested by a very big Hollywood writer and this is how I came to know about *The Householder* and started working on it. Then it was soon forgotten and when Gitel Steed's film fell through, I suggested *The Householder* to Jim. So Jim read it and had a very positive response to it and since he had known Delhi we set the whole story in Delhi. We telephoned Ruth Jhabvala and met her.

Q: Ruth Prawer Jhabvala, she is of Polish extraction?
Ivory: Polish German.

Q: And you met her here for the first time?
Merchant: That's right. Both Jim and I went together.
Ivory: I had met her before.

Q: Shashi Kapoor was by then married to Jennifer [Kendal]. Was that the starting point for *Shakespeare Wallah*?
Merchant: No. *Shakespeare Wallah*, as a matter of fact, was Jim's own idea and he thought of it much before he made *The Householder*. Madhur and Sayeed Jaffrey, both husband and wife, lived in New York and Jim had known them for a long time. He heard of a group of actors performing plays all over India from them (The Jaffreys).

Q: Without meeting the Kendals!
Merchant: Yes. Without meeting the Kendals.

Q: That is very interesting. We were under the impression that Shashi Kapoor started you off on this.
Merchant: Not exactly. The story which became *Shakespeare Wallah* was originally about a group of Indian actors travelling in India, performing English classics, that was the idea Jim had.
Ivory: But with Western classics not the English. Tennessee Williams and heaven knows what.
Merchant: So that was the basic idea. While we were making *The Householder*, Jim mentioned that he had something like this in mind and that it would be interesting and I said yes, it would be certainly very interesting. And then when we met Shashi Kapoor, Jennifer Kapoor, and Felicity Kendal and Geoffrey Kendal and Laura Liddell, we thought to transform the characters, because they had had similar experiences of going around in India, performing Shakespeare with Indian and English actors. It was much better because it had much more authenticity.
Ivory: And it was better for Mrs. Jhabvala. She was not terribly interested in the idea of highly westernized Indians, going round performing in small towns and that kind of thing. What really got her interested was the diary that Mr. Kendal kept in 1947, when they first came to India. That made the connection, I think. That diary (not that there was anything in *Shakespeare Wallah* that was from that diary) held this idea of a group of English people going round India, putting on Shakespeare and

sort of paddling remnants of English culture after the British Raj had really ended. This was what decided her and really sort of gave a central theme to the film.

Q: And you commissioned her to write the script according to this? She did not write the story?

Ivory: No. No. Listen. She and I, both in *Shakespeare Wallah* and *The Guru* collaborated together. We discuss the things we want and then the actual writing is pretty much done by Ruth. Sometimes I add things of my own. We were able to make *Shakespeare Wallah* really because we had sold *The Householder* to Columbia Pictures and they had given us a large balance in rupees.

Merchant: While we were making *The Householder*, we had many financial difficulties. You had asked how we got on after getting the novel. Well, between Jim and me we had some money and with the cooperation of the actors like Shashi and our cameraman, Subrato, we all sort of made the film.

Ivory: Then we got the investors. Soon . . .

Merchant: The investors came later. One of them is a Bombay exhibitor and the other one just a friend. They invested some money and that is how we completed *The Householder*. And once we showed it to Columbia Pictures, they liked it very much and bought it from us on a worldwide basis. They wanted to pay us in rupees which they had here, blocked, and we said, fine, that is a very good idea. We got the rupees and thought of making *Shakespeare Wallah* with it.

Q: Was *Shakespeare Wallah* also handled by Columbia?

Ivory: No. Several distributors.

Merchant: Apart from acceptance from the critics, and this was our first sort of experiment. *[The] Householder* was also accepted by major companies. There are many independent distributors in America. But to have a major company which operates all over the world was what we wanted and that was really quite a boost. So when we came up with *Shakespeare Wallah* and we won an award at the Berlin Film Festival, we thought there would not be any problem selling this film. But it was ten times harder to sell *Shakespeare Wallah* than *The Householder*.

Ivory: When we sold *The Householder* to Columbia there was a kind of wave (that was in 1963) when almost any foreign film, which was reasonably well made, could sell and attract an audience. By the time we got

Shakespeare Wallah, two years later; it was very difficult to get a foreign film into a theatre.

Q: But the better reviews . . . ?
Merchant: No. No. Jim. I don't think that is true.
Ivory: Oh, yes.

Q: There were better reviews for *Shakespeare Wallah*.
Merchant: No, the thing is that there are about six to seven hundred films brought to America every year, foreign films and independent films, and these films have to have outlets and markets. It is tremendous competition and New York City is the main test of a film. If it is success-ful in New York City, it is bound to play all over the United States. If it is a failure in New York City, it will never go beyond. When we finished *The Householder* there were about six hundred films lying without release in New York City, but *Householder* had a certain kind of appeal on a broader base because its problems are quite common to those of a married couple in New York, for example, or in France, England, or in Canada. The other thing which sells very much is sex. *Householder* did not have any sex as such but was a very sweet, gentle, and day-to-day depiction of a married couple. We were successful in giving it to Columbia who recognized the very good talent which then elicited a favorable response from the crit-ics as well as from the public. But financially, *The Householder* was not successful. Later . . .

Q: What do you mean by financially it was not successful?
Merchant: Well, financially it did not run very well in America.
Ivory: But did they cover the money they paid for you?
Merchant: Well, from the world market, naturally.

Q: You made *The Householder* in two versions.
Merchant: Yes, it was made in English and Hindi.

Q: What about the Hindi version?
Merchant: It's playing here.

Q: I mean, how did it fare, financially?
Merchant: Not very well. And you know people. When *Shakespeare Wallah* came it had ten times the reviews that *Householder* had, and still

in New York City we showed it to something like twelve distributors and nobody wanted to buy it. They said that it was too gentle a film, too gentle and too sophisticated. It was too this and too that, would not get the business which they want it to get and all that. Well, I said that is all a bloody lie and you cannot predict whether a film is going to be successful or not. Nobody can predict that. If it could be predicted there would be no question of hiring independent producers to make films because the major companies would themselves do so and would make millions of dollars for them. So we said we would distribute *Shakespeare Wallah* ourselves and this became my first experience as a distributor in New York. We took the risk and hired a theatre, laid out the premiere and did the advertising campaign. The film had an option from the distributor Walter Reade who loaned us the theatre. He said that if the film were successful in the first week then he would take the option and distribute our film. If it was not, there was of course no question. So the film opened and it was a tremendous success. I mean absolutely tremendous, with reviews, with finance, with everything.

Ivory: He did not wait till the first week to take up the option. I think he did not wait till the next evening. I think it was even before the film opened or the day the film opened or something.

Merchant: In London also it was a thumping success and on the strength of *Shakespeare Wallah* they bought *The Householder*.

Ivory: Yes. Columbia Pictures decided, well, maybe they could sell *Householder* in London, so it came out in London, really quite soon after *Shakespeare Wallah* and it had marvelous reviews in London too.

Merchant: It got better reviews in London than *Shakespeare Wallah*.

Ivory: Sometimes *even* more extravagant, considering that you know *Shakespeare Wallah* is a very nice film.

Merchant: And some of the critics *did* not know that *Householder* was our first film and thought it was [our] second.

Q: Yes, in *Sight and Sound*, *Shakespeare Wallah* was mentioned and noticed first and then *The Householder*. Did this pave the way for you with 20th Century-Fox?

Merchant: No. 20th Century-Fox had seen *Shakespeare Wallah* but they did not take it when it was shown in New York for the distributors' viewing. But there was one man who was in charge of foreign distribution. He liked a couple of things he saw very much and he wanted to see it again. So, when the film opened and it got such sensational reviews, and [became] financially successful, he took his own family to see it and then he told Fox what a foolish thing they had done not to buy this film and perhaps they should try and get the international rights. So they bought the European rights for the film.

Ivory: No, European rights were mostly held by Contemporary Films in England.

Merchant: Scandinavian countries . . . and then Fox took it for some of their African countries, Israel, and Middle East.

Q: During your distributors' viewing, did you make any effort to get in touch with Joseph Levine, because he is a man who is always on the look out for talent and . . .

Merchant: At that time Joseph Levine had a sort of come down. Every company and producer at some time gets all the talent but there is a certain time when . . .

Q: At one time he was picking up all sorts of people and I thought that you people might get to him. Anyway, coming now to *[The] Guru*, did you capitalize on Maharishi Mahesh Yogi?

Ivory: No. No. This is a bandwagon. It has been pushed onto us and has nothing to do with the film.

Merchant: Like in the beginning, you know, when again after *Shakespeare Wallah* we were planning to do another film in New York. Jim and I discussed it and we liked a property which we wanted to shoot in New York. That project fell through and while we were discussing it and while *Shakespeare Wallah* was being made, Jim and Ruth Jhabvala and I had discussed an idea, a musician and his disciple. That was in 1965.

Q: How did the idea come?

Merchant: Well, Jim had a friend.

Ivory: Who is a kind of slave to one of the great Indian Ustads. He is a foreigner and is sort of . . .

Merchant: The idea has to expand from an actual relationship which always is much more fascinating because it is truer to life. The relationship between two human beings, one a master and the other a [disciple]. Then Jim wrote something, Ruth Jhabvala wrote something, and the writing started back and forth. One day we decided that the project in New York was not materializing and we just wrote out a synopsis.

Ivory: Wait a minute. You are going too fast. Meanwhile we had written a whole script around this idea of the Ustad and a foreign disciple and the Ustad had two wives. Much of the stuff in *The Guru* was there in the first script. Meanwhile, George Harrison came to India to study with Ravi Shankar and this was like Mr. Kendal's diary. That was just the thing.

Q: This is surprising. You know, the way something turns up!
Ivory: So we thought why not make this central character a pop musician instead of just an ordinary disciple. We did that and of course we had to change the script a lot. Twentieth Century-Fox also liked it and let us make it that way. Later on, when the Maharishi was at the height of his fame, there were attempts by publicists and others to link up our film with the Maharishi and all that and to say that we were making a film about the Maharishi.

Q: It is really very interesting to note that all through the three films you have met certain loyalties. Ruth Prawer Jhabvala, Subrata Mitra, and even this music you like to have on the Indian side, and you even managed to get Satyajit Ray for two of your films. Who is the music director of *The Guru*?
Merchant: Dulare Lal. Well, I think this is like, for example, Bergman—Ingmar Bergman who has a repertoire of actors, cameraman, musicians—he has always used them in his films. Similarly Fellini and Antonioni, they have a group of actors, maybe they do not have the same scriptwriter. Similarly Jaffrey who played a part in *Shakespeare Wallah* and she is in *Guru* too. We had an actor Utpal Dutt who played not so big a role as the Maharaja in *Shakespeare Wallah*, is now the leading man in *The Guru*. We have a young man who is in all the three films of ours. Pincho Kapoor, he plays small parts in *Shakespeare Wallah*, *The Householder*, and *Guru*. Similarly Prayag Raj played in all the three films. We have had the same technicians. They understood your temperament and you understand theirs. And it is like a team work. Normally there is a producer; there is always an assistant and so on. In our team it is not so. I can become a boy who carries a cup of tea and technicians can do the same to me. So that is the sort of thing we understand. The basic thing is the respect for feelings, for work which we have in our organization. I think our strength is that everyone wants to do for the betterment of the film. It is not right where everybody is so impersonal; the director does not know what the assistants are doing and the assistants do not know what the director is doing. The cameraman and the director have got to be absolutely one. The music director and the writer are to be well knit together.

Q: Subrata Mitra has shot all three films?
Merchant: Yes.

Q: How is his color work in *The Guru*?
Both: Excellent.

Q: Now to go back to the film when you started first, why did you want Subrata? Is it because he worked with Satyajit Ray?
Merchant: When we came here we asked Satyajit. Jim knew him well. Though I never met him, Jim told Satyajit that we were planning to make a film and asked him whether it could be possible to loan his camera-man, Subrata, to us to make *The Householder*. Satyajit Ray suggested to Subrata to come down and talk to us. That is how it started. Satyajit has added a great deal of strength to our team. Just by being there he may not have directly to do with our films, but yet the man is there who is like a pillar of strength for us.

Q: But he directed the music for your second film?
Merchant: Naturally. Even if we make a film completely independent—like *The Guru*—Satyajit is still there, a pillar of strength to us.

Q: When do you expect *Guru* to be released?
Ivory: We are planning to have the world premiere in New York. After that it will be released here.

Q: What is your next project?
Merchant: There are so many. Actually the one we want to do in London is a sequel to *Shakespeare Wallah*, when the girl comes to England, what happens to her. Then we want to make a film called *Passion* in India. We want to do a film in New York, too.

Q: So there are several projects. [Mr. Merchant], you started as a director of *The Creation of Woman*?
Merchant: No. As a producer. Never as a director.

Q: Who was the director?
Merchant: Charles Schwer, another American. I do not have the patience of a director, I just cannot.

Q: You organize the whole thing?

Merchant: Yes, I like to organize things; I like to watch. I like to get the right subject, right actors, directors, but of course in this case, Jim knows his job well and I never interfere in anything what he does.

Q: Do you sit on script conferences?
Merchant: Well, there is no such thing as a conference. When the script is written I read it and I give my comments. There is very little in which I differ from Ruth and Jim.

Q: Now we want to take off at a different angle from what we were talking. Ever since Rudyard Kipling wrote "East is East . . . and the twain shall never meet," right down to Forster's *A Passage to India* and Edward Thompson's *An Indian Day* and J. R. Ackerley's *Hindoo Holiday* and all that, there came a stage when the question of India and the West together became significant—the problem of how they could meet. I think in this context your films have a definite place in the sense that you have tried to fathom the cultural and other relations between India and Anglo-Saxon civilization. But we find in your films you are avoiding certain points, for instance in *Shakespeare Wallah* after all is done the two people part, and I believe in *A Matter of Innocence* which of course we did not see, there is a similar ending, and in *Guru* from what I heard, the end is not a question of blending but again a question of separation. The pop singer comes; he and Rita Tushingham. And again they go back. These people stick to their civilization [. . .] Hadn't you thought, as an intellectual proposition, or as a creative person, that you could contribute something towards this problem, that you could give a definite turn and not take a non-committal attitude?
Ivory: I don't think it is non-committal. Not in *Householder*.

Q: In *Householder* the problem is not there.
Ivory: . . . in *The Guru* I don't think it is non-committal.

Q: Do you think that [as] these two belong to different cultures and two different traditions there cannot be much meeting?
Ivory: I feel that as far as India is concerned, the foreigners have either got to get submerged themselves completely in Indian life, I mean, really become Indian—they must marry and they must die and their children become Indians and their grandchildren become totally Indians. It is either that or it is nothing.

Q: You are an American. You come all the way from the States and understood India's past both in terms of *Sword and the Flute* and *The Delhi Way* and the present and you really have a very good grasp of our modes and our behavior and our problems. Now this itself is a very interesting thing, without your marrying an Indian girl or going on barefoot putting on Kurta or growing long hair—all gimmickry. You have made a good understanding of India and doing a good job. Don't you think that here could be better understanding between and sort of reconciliation of the two? Don't you think you could perhaps contribute something more difficult? [We] feel you both could perhaps find another subject and you could give another theme with a flavor of language—our language—and, well, be definite about it.

Ivory: Let me sort this out. You must think of the people who make a film. Apart from the producer and the actors, you must also think of the point of view of the people who are responsible for these films—Mrs. Jhabvala and myself. We are Westerners. She is European and I am an American. We don't have the Indian mentality. Of course, we may understand India to a certain extent as much as an outsider can and sometimes I think an outsider can understand a lot better about a country. But our point of view is really that of foreigners, of Westerners. So the films that we make reflect this point of view and even though Mrs. Jhabvala has been totally in India and to some extent my life is totally in India, you have got to think about our point of view as outsiders. We see things in a different way.

Merchant: A more objective.

Ivory: Not necessarily more objective. But we do look on India from the point of view of outsiders. And this is something that people here don't think about when they talk about our films. They often see our films as if they were made by Indians and as if the thought that was expressed was Indian. Well, it is not so.

Q: You are trying to do a good thing as far as you could. Forster, you know, says exactly the same thing as your films. Are you not tempted to film *A Passage to India?*

Ivory: I would never dream of it. That's too complex to become a film. It's too rich, too many characters. If it was to be made into a film it would be so coarsened and so much lessened. You cannot. There are certain works of literature that should not be made into films. And this is one of them.

Q: Did you see Santha Rama Rao's stage version?
Ivory: I saw it on the stage.

Q: Did you find it satisfactory?
Ivory: No. Not in terms of the book. I mean, it was enjoyable; I enjoyed it on the television later. Very enjoyable. Very moving.

Q: Same people and the same cast as on the stage?
Ivory: No. Well, Zia Mohiyeddin was in it. Everybody else was different. But it's not a book that should be made into a film, though there were plans for it some time ago. I say this passionately because I just finished reading it again about a month ago and, well, once I thought it to be a very good thing to be made into a film.

Q: If you are going to make another film in India, what aspects would you deal with?
Ivory: Well, I think we will have to make a film in which foreigners are involved, partly because of the language thing and also because it is easy to get finance for such films; you know if you have a foreign actor and actress, an English or American actor or actress, it is easy to get finance. We got finance for *Guru* really because I suppose we have Rita Tushingham in it.

Q: Yes, that way they are great at it.
Ivory: Not only through predilection but it is more practical for us in terms of money too to make films in which a foreigner comes to India or for some reason a foreigner is already living here, [. . .] as I have to make films in English. I do not want to make another Hindi film unless I could speak good Hindi.

Q: I believe you are both due to leave very shortly.
Merchant: Yes. We are going to leave, as a matter of fact next week and will be back after the release of *Guru*.

Q: Is the film now in the finishing stages?
Merchant: It is almost finished and we are now going to record the background music and then we have to do some printing and technical work in London.

Q: How do you find the working conditions in India, the laboratory and the workers and . . .

Ivory: Well, I think in some way the working conditions are very good here and in other ways they are not good. They are very good in that the people are extremely willing and optimistic about getting things done and try generally to help. But the mechanical facilities are not very good, there are all sorts of shortages and I don't like to say, shouldn't say really because they are so loyal to us, but people here are somehow not as well trained as they might be. How could they be, because there are not enough opportunities to use all kinds of new equipment that comes out. In the West they are constantly abreast of all the new equipment, they are constantly using and as soon as a new microphone is invented it is immediately brought into use and then discarded and another one is brought to use and all that kind of thing. Now because of the difficulty in importing equipment in India, people don't have the chance to use equipment here and to keep abreast of it. This is true in editing and true, well . . .

Q: These are limitations which are there and which we could not help.

Ivory: But they have a stunting effect on the technicians. Of course, that can't be helped; that is the way it is. When new equipment comes here some day then, maybe, things will be lot more improved.

Q: Your black and white films, were they processed here?

Ivory: Yes.

Q: Printed and developed and all. But this color film you have developed abroad.

Ivory: But I liked the prints of *Shakespeare Wallah* which they made here in India much better than the prints we made in New York. They were much richer, maybe because Subrata was sitting on their heads all the time!

Q: There was a foreign print that we saw was much too sharp and refined.

Ivory: I went to see *Shakespeare Wallah* the other day when it was in the Regal. I had never seen it with an Indian audience so I wanted to go and see what it was like and I did not like that print—grey, sort of washed down. Not those nice tones that you got in Famous here [Famous Laboratories, Tardeo, Bombay].

Q: It is flattering. And all these films you edited in India?
Merchant: Yes. Completely done here.
Ivory: Not the sound editing. Much of the sound editing of *The Guru* is going to be done in London because we are using magnetic tracks instead of optical. We can't do that here.

Q: What about your making Hindi films?
Merchant: Oh, certainly, I would like to make if I get good scripts, good ideas. There must be good writers. The writers who are here, their ideas are so corny and the characters so silly and absurd; they always want to do something escapist rather than the real, substantial. I think that there has to be a definite story; it may not have a plot as such because I do not believe in plots—there has to be a relationship between characters, a particular atmosphere, and a particular environment, something of human interest. If it is there I am here to back films up.

Q: What is your attitude as a filmmaker now? Would you stick to this sort of a film which microscopically looks at a small group of people or would you expand into historicals, or suspense story or . . .
Ivory: Yes. I would like to but I would still do it in terms of microscopically looking. I would like to do a suspense story. If I do, it would focus on characters, characters are the people. If I do a historical thing—I am thinking right now, Mrs. Jhabvala and myself, working on an idea on something that is set in the nineteenth century—well, still that would be microscopic [. . .]. I could not do something on a huge scale. I don't want to because I know I will be very bad at it. I don't think that is my *métier*.

Q: Since your films have Indian characters and Indian surroundings, why don't you make them in Hindi also, rather than in English only?
Merchant: A good Hindi film should be first made as a good Hindi film and shown abroad with subtitles. If in India you have a market, that's fine. If there isn't, that's fine too because our films do not depend on the Indian market. Because unless we have theatres which can support an art movement, for example like one in Madras, there is one I am told, similarly in Bombay, we must have such theatres in Delhi, in Calcutta and so on. For the last ten years people here have been talking about art theatres but nothing has happened. Our government who have been spending foolishly, absolutely foolishly, on actors, and people in films going out abroad, filming a song in Paris, while the director and the scriptwriter have never seen Paris and the script doesn't call for it, precious foreign

exchange is spent on that silly, stupid thing. Why couldn't the government with the help of some of these major companies, whose rupees are
blocked in our country, make out about at least five to seven art theatres
and these theatres could be of great help to people like you and people
like us because you want, you have Film Forum where there are many
members who want to see good films, Yugoslav films, Italian films, Scandinavian films, English films, *The Knack,* for example, should have been
shown here ages ago; it was never shown . . .

Q: Because the distributors here in India do not take these films.
Merchant: Because there is no market. The other thing is about the
censor. They are worried about the censors. Censorship laws should never apply to films like *The Knack* or films like *Blow-Up,* [or A] *Taste of Honey.*
There could be small three-hundred-seat theatres and the films could
run for two [or] three weeks in Bombay, Calcutta, New Delhi, Madras.
That's sufficient. One gets so dejected, all the times there are meetings,
there are committees, there are stupid conversations and cups of tea float
around and then in the evening everybody congratulates everybody and
goes home. And the Film Finance Corporation, which formed, well, why
has this organization been formed? To give finance to Dil Dekha Karo
or things like that? No, the Film Finance Corporation is a body, everywhere, whether it is in Italy, in France, or in England, everywhere, it is
formed to develop talent and to give money to people who really want to
do something different. Well no, it is not so here. A man like Mr. Kotak,
who was the chairman of the Film Finance Corporation sometime ago,
has never seen a film in fourteen years and these are the people whom
we make our chairman. It is too discouraging, the kind of people who are
involved. Unless you are so independent that well, I am going to do this
thing the way I think the best, and I don't give a damn about you people,
and this is how I feel and this is how I am going to do. There are many
multi-millionaires in this country who spend money on this charity and
that charity. Consider this also to be a charity, to develop the taste of an
audience. And so much land, just near the Napean Sea Road. I think,
some central government building is there; well, if central government
could have quarters for their officers to stay, well similarly a small plot of
land, may be in the same building on the top floor, or the ground floor
or even on the basement for a cinema movement could be given. Yes, in
the basement. Why not? A cinema movement could be in the basement
too with three hundred seats and two projectors and all. Now I think
we should get somebody who is really powerful, someone who is really,

solidly someone whose words really mean it who should say, well, to hell with the government, I am going to get it done, and he goes and digs a hole, makes a basement, gets projectors, gets the movement started, sells the tickets, doesn't pay the taxes, and that's how it should be done.

Q (Jag Mohan): Well. This should be the man (pointing to Arun Kaul). Well here is a mission Arun Kaul. Go ahead!
Basu: Are you getting nervous, Arun?
Arun: Not at all. Why should I?
Merchant: Well. I could. I could do it. I could dig a hole, I am sure, somewhere in this big city, perhaps in the Sachivalaya: let us go and dig a hole there and put in projectors: what are they doing in the evening? They come at 10 o'clock and go away at 5. I am very keen on it.

Q: When are you coming back to India for a larger number of months?
Merchant: Okay. I am going to be here and I am certainly going to start. I am certainly going to get two hundred businessmen and start with the theatre first in Bombay. I will give you a theatre.

Interview with James Ivory

Stephan Varble/1972

Originally published in *Interview Magazine*, vol. 2, no. 2 (1972): 15–17, 38. Reprinted by permission.

Since 1962, James Ivory's films have been produced by Ismail Merchant and written by Ruth Prawer Jhabvala. At the outset of this interview Mr. Ivory stressed the importance of their longstanding collaboration.

Stephan Varble: Well, I don't have a first question . . .
James Ivory: Then you'd better go on to the second.

SV: I suppose I should ask when you were born. Or is that pertinent?
JI: July 8, 1942.

SV: And then I was going to ask when you speculate your date of death will be.
JI: Oh, well, I won't answer that.

SV: But that would make interesting reading . . .
JI: Why?

SV: If you see it on a page after the date of birth, it might make people very curious.
JI: [*Tinkles ice cubes*] What shall we talk about?

SV: Well, there's a very serious thing I noticed about all your films.
JI: What's that?

SV: A thing that really disturbs me about them . . . a whimsical resignation to the impossibility of communication between two people.
JI: I wouldn't say that it was whimsical.

SV: I think it's also deadly, but faintly funny. It's the deadliest impossibility I've ever seen on the screen. It's deadly as Godard almost. I think this is why you have such a peculiar bunch of "stoned" fans.
JI: I wish I knew more about them. Where are they when my films are opening?

SV: And there is a kind of color cult forming about *The Guru*. There was an article in *Show Magazine* about a year ago.
JI: Yes, I saw it.

SV: So many have commented to me, and it was indicated in that article, also, about the extraordinary use of color in *The Guru*. It was beautiful and ultimately satirical. Rita Tushingham is the one who is there in India trying her best to be spiritually involved and yet Michael York is the beautiful, serene one. He comes across [as] so much more spiritually fulfilled than she does. But then again I wonder if his serenity isn't serenity at all, but a kind of narcissistic elation.
JI: There is a certain kind of narcissism in any kind of young idol. Michael York perhaps is one of those young leading men who has a kind of narcissistic quality.

SV: He reminds me a great deal of Catherine Deneuve.
JI: Really?

SV: If you got them together you might *really* have a star. I've begun to believe all great stars must be androgynous like Mick Jagger. His vacillations between being male and female are *captivating*. Have you seen *Gimme Shelter*?
JI: Umh . . . [*affirmative*]

SV: Did you like it?
JI: I liked it in some ways. I thought it was a vision of Hell and, because of that, terribly interesting.

SV: Did the androgynous aspect of Mick Jagger interest you?

JI: I thought he was demonic . . . he was like Satan up there and the most potent thing about the whole film was that nude woman trying to climb onto the stage, being constantly pushed back into a pit of Hell by all those people.

SV: People have spoken of your films as complicit in a literary sense. That is, that the characters, scenes, montage maintain a verbal inertia. Everything is colored in a verbal monochrome. But I'm not sure that these statements mean anything. Are you aware of any of this, as cryptic and remote as it may sound?
JI: I don't understand complicity.

SV: Everything of the same color . . . but I'm much more interested in the whimsical, though gritting resignation.
JI: But I'm very suspicious of that word "whimsy." It was always applied by critics to the films when we first started out. That there was always a wry whimsy or Mr. Ivory is, you know, something, something, something . . . Whimsy! My goodness! It's more than whimsical.

SV: But it's deadly, too. *Bombay Talkie* is so rigid and yet so funny. It made me feel as if I had raw knuckles.
JI: *Bombay Talkie* is a movie about things not working out, of how people can believe in all sorts of wonderful things happening in their lives. They can have money, appetite, so much vitality, everything: but still it doesn't work out. Life goes completely against what they want. *Bombay Talkie* is simply a demonstration of how things don't work out. All our films are like that except *The Householder*. But always in an Indian context and always in a context of foreigners in India, although that's less true in *Bombay Talkie*. But it's certainly true of *Shakespeare Wallah* and *The Guru*. Things cannot work out for these people. They don't belong in India. They shouldn't be. India wants to get them out.

SV: I love *The Guru* for showing the overwhelming power of India's beauty. The sunglasses of Michael York, as obvious as they are, become unforgettably transient in the wake of the environment. He is beautiful and serene and yet he has those sunglasses, an imperial contradiction. The scene where he leaves to judge the beauty contest dressed so modishly is another example.
JI: And goes away in the boat!

SV: They both become so absurd in the location. Everything that the film talks about is in that scene.

JI: That's true. It's so crucial. I can't understand why people in this country laugh then at Rita Tushingham. When she says to the Guru, "I belong completely to my Guru," she really declares herself. I can't understand why people laugh at that line. I don't think the line should be laughed at. Everybody knows all through the film what she's wanted and what she's after. She just wanted to live in a slavish way for the Guru. In that scene by the river she shows her soul and everybody laughs. I suppose it's a horrible failure on my part.

SV: I think I laughed.

JI: You shouldn't have laughed. Nobody should have laughed. It's very sad, particularly the brush-off the Guru gives her, such as, "Oh, it's time for dinner."

SV: Tell me about your budgets.

JI: The cheapest was *Shakespeare Wallah*, which cost $80,000 to make. We spent another $10,000 to $15,000 on prints and so forth. *The Householder* cost more because we made two versions: one in English and one in Hindi. It doubled the cost, which all in all was about $120,000, about what *Bombay Talkie* cost. *Guru* cost $800,000 and I've recently seen a statement from Fox which said *The Guru* cost more than a million dollars, which is shocking. That film could have been made for about what we made *Bombay Talkie* for, or a little bit more, because we traveled around a lot in making *The Guru*. *Bombay Talkie* was relatively cheap because we stayed in Bombay the whole time and there weren't any expensive hotel bills, except mine.

SV: Are you just as concerned with the mysteries of India as with the mysteries of film itself? Or is it for practical reasons that you go there?

JI: It's very complicated the reasons why I go there. First, I went there simply because I *wanted* to go there. Then I started going because the money was there in India to make films and no money was here, and also because I wanted to make *particular* films at that time in India. I wanted to make *Shakespeare Wallah*, for instance, and we had the money to make it. We had been paid all this money for *The Householder* by Columbia Pictures, but we had been paid in rupees and we had to use those rupees up so it was obvious we'd go make another film and that was *Shakespeare Wallah*. Then *Shakespeare Wallah* was a success and 20th Century-Fox wanted to make a film in India. All these big American film companies have frozen rupee accounts in the banks and they want to utilize that money in some way; and so there was the money and Fox wanted to make a film and we wanted to make a film like *The Guru*. We'd had that idea a long time so they said go make that film, and we went. *Bombay Talkie* came about through different circumstances. Money came from here for that. But it's sort of an economic necessity that makes us go there. It's also a desire to make a certain kind of film which I can't make anywhere else. I have an interest in India and in Indians and in the Indian scene and I think I understand it in a way. Subjectively it appeals to me for all kinds of reasons. But at the same time, mixed with my liking is a kind of dislike, a criticism, and even a kind of hysteria.

SV: I think *Bombay Talkie* is hysteria! Manic.
JI: It is.

SV: When Lucia Lane is in the taxi going home after a party she says to her escort that she has a headache. She explains, "It's all this bloody hair." That's the kind of ash you're capable of dropping, a total ash. One wonders where she can go from that point, how can she develop since she's burnt out. The movie is the playing out of a final act of hysteria.
JI: I hate that particular scene. When I saw the original script, Lucia Lane's part was far more hysterical, far more demented, than it is in the film. I thought I couldn't manage scenes like that. Too much! Too hysterical. Mrs. Jhabvala and I talked about it a lot and we toned her down and then I toned it down more in the performance. I don't know. Maybe I went too far in the other direction.

SV: There's a kind of restraint you have . . .
JI: Look! Just look at the characters in *The Householder*. Those are the most rampageous ladies you'll ever hope to see. I didn't shrink from that at all. I thought it was nice. It was just this particular role. I didn't think Lucia should be as wild as she was first made out to be.

SV: I didn't think Jennifer Kendal understood her role in the scene where she can't make up her mind, after having had a terrible argument with her lover, whether to have her friend, the writer, fetch him for her. She deliberates on some steps in a kind of cypress garden. For some reason I thought her lines were poorly delivered. There was a moment when I thought she didn't understand them.

JI: Sure she did. She stops her friend. Her impulse is to say, "Go and get him." Then she thinks, "No, it's wrong." Some pride is there and a certain amount of calculation. So she thinks a bit . . . she's thinking, "No, I shouldn't." Then she says, "Yes, do go." He starts up the stairs. Then she has another change of mind. She says, "Wait," and again she's thinking, "This is wrong," and then she thinks: "Oh, what the hell," and says, "Oh go on, get him. Do as I say!" She certainly knows what she's doing. I like it so much when she's climbing up those hot stairs, holding her purse. It's so hard for her to go up those hot stairs to her lover. She's carrying such a burden: Love! She's old. She becomes an old woman then. Pathetic. We've got lots of stair scenes in that film which some critics have objected to. I don't know why. I like it when people are running up and down stairs. They have such different ways of running up and down stairs. They are so useful to show how people are feeling.

SV: You give human beings the benefit of the doubt. Even in their silence you give them an important, valuable reality: A kind of glow. At least their reality is not diminished simply because they do not indulge themselves in introspective monologues. Michael York and the old man in *Shakespeare Wallah* are like concrete poems. They simply "are."

[*Pause*]

SV: What filmmakers do you like?
JI: Once Satyajit Ray said he does not like particular filmmakers. He only likes particular films and I think that's the way it should be. Still in all I can't help having my heroes, and he is one of them.

SV: He did the music for *Shakespeare Wallah*?
JI: Yes. He also did the music for *The Householder*, although people don't know that.

SV: He's not in the titles?
JI: No, but he composed the music and supervised the recording.

SV: The music of *Shakespeare Wallah* is lush, voluptuous. There's something earthen and wormlike about it. It has a strange texture . . . silken, fleshy, humid. Which reminds me, strangely enough, that there are so few animals and even fewer birds in your films.
JI: A few cur dogs.

SV: And those two monkeys in *Shakespeare Wallah*.

JI: I'm afraid both animals and children are sort of not seen in our films.

SV: Do you think there's any reason?

JI: Probably a good reason but I've never thought about it. Now, what else?

SV: Well, what do you think is important that we haven't talked about?

JI: There's so much. I'm like an iceberg. Only a little tip protrudes, sticks out above the water. Now what else? About my career? What else will I say? Hum? One thing I must say. I think when people here in this country—I don't know about England—hear that it's an Indian film or a film made in India, they just turn off immediately. They assume it's going to be depressing; that we're going to show horrible sights; that it'll be one of those long, slow, draggy oriental pictures; and they just don't go to it. I think so many people who would like our films don't go because there are all these built-in ideas about India. You know, a friend of mine here is head of the Indian tea board, which is a Government of India corporation that's responsible for the export of Indian tea. They did this survey, and it turned out that the survey discovered that the reason why Americans don't buy Indian tea more than they do is because they think it will be dirty and full of germs. That just shows what the popular idea about India is and I think this comes over into our films. People think our films will be dirty and full of germs and that's why they don't go to them. Even a film like *Shakespeare Wallah* . . . I mean you *can't* have better reviews than we got from *Shakespeare Wallah* . . . was a bit disappointing in terms of box office. Maybe it was the name that turned people off, but I think it was the idea of India. I don't know how to counteract that.

SV: Do you want to make a film here [in America]?

JI: Of course, I want to make a film in my own country. I've tried before. I almost made a film out of Lillian Ross's novel, *Vertical and Horizontal*. We were going to make it for Paramount. This was after the success of *Shakespeare Wallah*. Paramount told us at the beginning that they would support us through the writing of a script and then they would decide. So Lillian wrote a script and I kind of worked on it with her though she did most of the work. We went on for a good six months and they paid us and then Paramount decided not to make the film and meanwhile we had cast it; we had a cameraman who was to be Boris Kaufman; we had so many actors and actresses all sort of arranged for, and then Paramount just cancelled it. It was crushing. I always think of my films as being like a room and on the walls are a number of pictures all sort of done up and hanging up there but there is one space—a great large empty space where you'd expect to see something hanging—and that's *Vertical and Horizontal*, which isn't hanging there for the year '66–'67.

SV: Do you plan to direct this forthcoming film with Holly Woodlawn?
JI: *Sunny Side Up*? Sure.

SV: How much is it going to cost?
JI: $150,000.

SV: I guess everything will be an arrangement when you're talking in terms of $150,000.
JI: Right.

SV: It's not like *The Guru* where you had ample funds . . . ?
JI: Here I really want to go on record about *The Guru*. I've said it many times but never for anything that was going to be printed . . . that Twentieth Century-Fox, as far as my work was concerned, were gentlemen from the beginning to the end. They never at any time interfered in anything I wanted to do from the first moment they laid eyes on the script right down to the end when the film was released. They never, never threw their weight around, and they could have. They could have so easily. They didn't very much like the finished film, actually. Richard Zanuck and David Brown liked it very much and they said so and they seemed very happy with it. But when the distribution and publicity people in New York saw it, they didn't want to get involved with it. But as far as the studio ever bringing any influence on me or making me do anything whatsoever they never did that. People always just assume that we had to knuckle under to Twentieth Century-Fox [with] *The Guru*. We never did. Whatever is on the film is absolutely what we have put there. Whatever is not in the film is what we ourselves took out. I want to say this because I think that Fox in this respect was marvelous. I thought that we'd have all kinds of trouble. People warned me. I met a director who had made a film for Fox in Paris who was very, very disheartened with what had happened to it. But this never happened to me. So, I mean these big studios aren't always bad. They aren't always going to destroy a director.

SV: Where did *The Guru* have its greatest success?

JI: In England. It was in the top cinema in London. The Academy One, in fact. There was a lot of interest in the film because it was the first film we'd made since *Shakespeare Wallah*. I went on *Late Night Line-Up* and talked about making the film and there was great attention paid by all the critics. It wasn't a very successful run, though. I don't think British audiences like it anymore than American audiences did. In India it was reviled. It was a scandal. Editorials were written about it. It was so this. It was so that. It was considered an affront to the whole idea of the guru/disciple relationship, which is one of the basic foundation stones of all Indian society. Indians . . . certain Indians . . . thought that we were poking fun at that relationship, that we were dragging very sacred things down into the mud. But we weren't making fun at all. We were showing our guru as being an imperfect man and at the same time a great artist. Human, that's all he was. A great sitar player, Ustad Vilayat Khan, said that the characterization was extremely true and real and absolutely correct, but the Indian press just thought that that was the most awful, vicious, nasty, bad film and, as I said, that we dragged sacred . . .

SV: Probably because of those sunglasses . . .
JI: I don't know about that. It was a great sort of *succès du scandale*. Only it wasn't that much of a *succès*. You know in India a film that's *really* successful can run for about a year. These big Hindi films often run a year.

SV: Really? How long did *The Guru* run?
JI: In any big city if we get three weeks we're lucky. We sort of graduated from one week on *Householder* to two on *Shakespeare Wallah* to three on *Guru* and I expect *Bombay Talkie* will get four. Which, however, is quite a respectable run for an English-language picture.

SV: What about the English reception?
JI: Hasn't opened.

SV: When's it going to?
JI: June 16 [1972].

SV: You think it'll be a success there?
JI: No. I think people will object to the melodramatic story as much there as they did here, maybe more so. But they will get the character of Lucia Lane, the writer. I think they'll understand her better. Americans had no idea who she was or what she came from, or they didn't know from her

accent what kind of English woman she was. They simply couldn't place her, but I think English people will know exactly who she is and why she is, and appreciate everything she says and does. They will appreciate the *performance*. This is what I feel from talking to English people here who have seen the film in New York and who like Jennifer Kendal so much for all kinds of subtle things she's done.

SV: I don't think any of your films have courted mass audiences, have they?

JI: No, we've never *courted* any audience, but you should really always think about your audience.

SV: Who do you think are great actresses?

JI: Who do I think are great actresses? I always wanted to work with Vivien Leigh. I almost had a chance once, but she died before we could do it.

SV: Do you want to tell the story of her suit which she left behind in India? Perhaps you'd better. That's sort of why I asked you the ostensible date of your death. There's a whole whitewashed aspect about you of surreptitious morbidity.

JI: I'm half Irish, Irish people are always sort of brooding on their deaths, but I'll expect I'll be around past the year 2000.

SV: But what about Vivien Leigh's suit? That Kleenex, which always excited me . . .

JI: Kleenex?

SV: The Kleenex we found in her purse . . .

JI: She liked us; she knew lots of people, but I think that at that time in her life she didn't have the time or energy anymore to be really "fond" of very many people. I think you reach a time when you're kind of exhausted and you've been through a lot and you don't have much energy left to be really fond of people, except one or two. She had one friend she was very fond of and she was also very fond of her daughter. She certainly remained very fond of Laurence Olivier and had some other friends she must have been fond of; but I think you reach the time when you don't make many new friends.

SV: I'd like you to describe to me your feelings about those people whom you have known who have had international fame while also remaining

real to you. Your relationship to Vivien Leigh, though it wasn't particularly intense, nonetheless it was a real association over a period of a few months . . .
JI: Years.

SV: Well, I'd like you to describe her find of fame. Was it dehumanizing?
JI: I think famous people sometimes aren't aware of their fame. I don't think they have time to be. I don't think famous people always know what's going on. They don't realize that there's all this about them. There are charged moments when everybody's clamoring and they know they're the center of attraction and attention and all that, but after all they have to think of their lives. They have to practice a profession, whatever that is, and do the things that they like doing best. They just don't have time to think about all these people. But from time to time it does break in on their consciousness, for instance with Vivien Leigh: we went to a vegetable market in Bombay with her which is quite spectacular, called Crawford Market. It's a tremendous Victorian building with so many vegetable stalls . . . all the vegetables are piled up . . . it has such beautiful color, with the sun streaming in through some high gothic windows. It's a marvelous place and so we took her in there just to let her have a look and while we were standing there some school girls came up to her and one of them said, "Oh, Miss Leigh, could I have your autograph?" I thought that it was quite something that three Indian girls in the depths of the vegetable market of Bombay had recognized her and asked her for her autograph. If that isn't international fame I didn't know what is. She was casual about it because she had given her autograph so many times in other places, but I don't think she realized the uniqueness of this moment. In a way she was almost past her fame, she was past her moment of greatest success, at any rate. But those girls recognized her and came up to her and asked her for her autograph and she gave it, a rather mechanical giving of it and I think she didn't realize what it meant, but probably later on she did.

SV: I think fame gives one a particular kind of transfusion. It gives one a marvelous license with oneself. I wonder if you have feelings about it, strong ones or not.
JI: No, I don't.

SV: But hasn't this entered into your attraction to film? You're not aware of the extent of your audience, of those people who extol the opalescence of *The Guru.*

JI: What good is it if you don't see it? It might as well not exist.

SV: But you just said one never sees it. Vivien Leigh didn't grasp the significance of those three little girls in Bombay in terms of her audience. Anyway your major audience is yet to come, I think.

JI: I hope it comes around before I get too old to enjoy it.

SV: I think it's important . . . the timing of the release of films. I think it would be beautiful to see *The Guru* in April.

JI: It's going to come out again at the New Yorker. All four films. I don't know when though. I think from June to September.

SV: Well, I'm going to stop the tape recorder. I've just given my cadenza of adulation but would you be so good as to sigh for us into the microphone, so we might be left a bit of suspense.

JI: [*sighs*]

Merchant-Ivory

John Gillett/1973

From *Sight and Sound* 42, no. 2 (Spring 1973): 95–98. Reprinted by permission of the British Film Institute.

Savages has been nicely described by Penelope Gilliatt as "a glittering sarcastic fable [. . .] full of withering social comedy and a peculiar, erratic stateliness of style." Far too idiosyncratic ever to have emerged from a major studio, it was shot entirely at a big house in upstate New York, Edith Wharton country, among the furniture and books and portraits left behind by the owners when they finally closed their unmanageably large mansion. *Savages* builds on the associations of its setting; the house itself seeming like a great, grounded ocean liner of the 1930s. But at the same time, both the film's wayward, elaborately eclectic style, and the circumstances in which it was made, seem to reflect the offbeat enterprise and enthusiasm of its makers, James Ivory and Ismail Merchant. Their company, Merchant-Ivory Productions, is now just on ten years old. They began together with *The Householder* in 1963, went on to make *Shakespeare Wallah*, *The Guru*, and *Bombay Talkie* in India, and have now launched out on their first American-based film. At the same time, they have come up with three new or newish shorts, of which the longest, *Adventures of a Brown Man in Search of Civilization*, about the Oxford adventures of the Bengali sage Nirad Chaudhuri, had its first airing on BBC television last Easter.

First impressions might suggest that they're an incongruous pair. Ismail Merchant, who was born in Bombay and educated mainly in America, is an outstandingly ebullient example of the producer who really produces. Wherever one meets him—in London, Bombay, Cannes—he gives the impression of being on the way to something important: a distribution deal to confirm here, a cinema booking to be checked there. At

Cannes last year, he launched *Savages* with the sort of party Hollywood companies don't give any more, with all the food (Indian, of course) air-freighted from London. James Ivory, his partner, is a thoughtful Californian, a very quiet American, perhaps with temperamental allegiances to James and Fitzgerald (he's anxious to film books by both of them). He talks with the kind of detached, watchful urbanity which has characterized his outsider's view of some of the byways of an India trying to come to terms with Western styles.

Their seemingly contrasting personalities must cohere and play off each other during shooting, perhaps reinforcing an obvious desire to explore areas neglected by more hidebound studio partnerships. Unlike many directors, Ivory likes to have his producer around; and although Ismail Merchant takes no part in the actual filming, he acts rather as a distanced observer, putting himself in the place of the future audience. Merchant attends to all the preparations ("doing everything an assistant would do, and better," says Ivory), and may suggest additions and alterations to the director if he feels that the day's rushes miss out on any point of emphasis. Both of them seem a bit nomadic, wandering easily between continents; possibly because both of them are really living with their pictures.

The problems of setting up and financing their kind of independent operation would seem formidable. Even technically, because of the currency restrictions which make it so difficult to import new equipment from abroad, film-making in India tends to become more rather than less difficult as the old machinery wears out. Merchant, however, approaches the financial side of the business with an air of rather spectacular unconcern. "Most people going into films seem frightened of the idea of money, as if it is something that is going to defeat you. I never think of financing before the film is properly set up, otherwise it exhausts all your time and energy. It is something that will come automatically."

Ivory's description of how their earlier ventures came about suggests the mixture of luck and a special kind of acumen that has sustained their progress. "We got money for *The Householder* from an Indian businessman, plus some money from my own investments. When we sold it to Columbia, they paid us mainly in rupees. With that money, we made *Shakespeare Wallah,* which is still the most successful of our films. It keeps bringing in a little cash from TV screenings. Then Fox seemed interested in doing a film in India, and financed *The Guru* from their frozen funds there. After *The Guru* failed at the box-office we certainly didn't contemplate another film immediately; but thanks to Joseph Saleh, an

American businessman, we were able to do *Bombay Talkie* the following year. Saleh himself didn't much like the idea of *Bombay Talkie,* but he seemed to like us and he knew that was what we wanted to do. Now he has backed *Savages,* so we owe him a lot of gratitude."

After *The Guru,* both Merchant and Ivory were left with mixed feelings about working for major companies. "Fox were incredibly decent and nice during the shooting," Ivory says. Once the project had been agreed and set up, Fox left them alone to make the picture, remaining helpfully calm at the other end of a telephone line even at such moments of crisis as when the star, Utpal Dutt, found himself briefly imprisoned on a political charge. "All Fox did was to request a cast replacement if there was going to be a great delay."

All the same, the Merchant-Ivory type of picture probably gains from more specialized selling than a big company is likely to give it. Merchant prefers to look for his backing from Wall Street, private investors and merchant bankers, visiting prospective investors armed with a dossier detailing Merchant-Ivory's history and its films' reviews. "I always tell them there is only one chance in ten of making money, as films are something that either take off or they don't. But if the production is cheap enough, they are bound to see a return from TV sales and 16mm distribution; and if the product is good enough it will have a long life, like *Shakespeare Wallah.* This way, you hope to raise quite small amounts from a number of people. But when you realize that out of a hundred films announced these days only about ten are ever finished, it's not surprising that independent financiers are very wary."

Short films are even riskier, almost to the point of certain loss. ("If you spend between five and ten thousand pounds on a short subject, you might get back between seven and eight thousand at the very best"); but they provide an agreeable interlude between features as well as opportunities for further collaboration with friends and colleagues. The most substantial of their recent trio, *Adventures of a Brown Man,* was commissioned by the BBC, who put up £5,500 for two TV screenings. The other rights remain with Merchant-Ivory; and they themselves put up the finishing money from what they intriguingly refer to as their "reserve fund."

Produced by Merchant, written and directed by Ivory, with Anthony Korner as associate producer and photography by Walter Lassally (as on *Savages),* the film is a portrait of Nirad Chaudhuri, the diminutive, 76-year-old Bengali writer, stringent critic of his own country and of the West, and admirer of Kipling. To Chaudhuri, the idea of Westerners going to India for spiritual insight is as ludicrous as the yoga cult or the segregation of the sexes in Hindi society ("India is not 'the biggest democracy in the world.' So far as it operated as a government during the lifetime of Nehru, it operated as a dictatorship. The only person who did not know that it was a dictatorship was Nehru himself—all else knew it. He is now gone, and there is no government in India.") However barbed the comment, it is uttered with disarming sweetness of manner, and in a tone suggesting that its truth must be self-evident to all reasonable people. Chaudhuri, in fact, is one of those compulsive talkers who turn conversation into monologue. Boredom threatens; then, repeatedly, a phrase in his beautifully academic English or another waspish aphorism rivets the attention with its sense and sanity.

Ivory patiently captures all the maddening and beguiling aspects of this forceful personality, watching him being measured for a suit and later dressing up in Regency ruffles for an Oxford dinner party, over which he reigns supreme like some elderly latter-day Beau. In some respects, Chaudhuri appears as an extension of several characters in Ivory's (and Ray's) Indian films: a product of the British Raj and immersed in dreams of England, literature, and the European tradition, he has discovered the best and worst of both cultures and is very willing to offer us his conclusions. As he wanders around Oxford, oblivious in his talk to the pressures of traffic and people, he's clearly relishing playing the role of sage in this archetypal setting; and also happy to play tourist, feeding the ducks on the Thames and stretching out an imperious hand for the breadcrumbs carried by his wife in a paper bag. Ivory's cool, unstressed style, and Chaudhuri's apparent unconcern for the camera eye, combine to build up a portrait of a living, thinking human being; and there's a sense of a shared, ironically romantic reaction to Oxford by the American filmmaker and the Indian writer.

The finance for *Helen, Queen of the Nautch Girls* (directed by Anthony Korner, produced by Merchant, written by Ivory) and *Mahatma and the Mad Boy* (produced and directed by Merchant, photographed by Subrata Mitra) came from the earnings of Merchant-Ivory Productions in India. Merchant's policy here is not to keep money for the sake of keeping it, preferring to invest it in modestly budgeted shorts to help maintain the company as a continuously going concern. And the switching and mixing of roles involved also pleases Ivory, who enjoys working in cutting-rooms, watching over and helping to shape other people's material.

Helen is mainly a montage of production numbers from a few of the five hundred films to which this fabulously popular dancer has contributed since 1957; a heady potpourri of the real commercial Indian cinema, that extravagant, rigidly conventionalized world of mythological sagas and novelette-ish modern dramas where the action always stops for song and dance, and the numbers themselves give full rein to some astonishing fantasies. These numbers, often set in impossibly ritzy-looking cabarets, and becoming increasingly suggestive as the years go by, comprise a basic dream world for a vast audience deprived of any other direct sexual stimulus from the censor-bound local screen. For a Western audience, the snazzy camerawork and design, the high-pitched wailings of the playback singers and the often catchy orchestrations (taking in all kinds of pop and rock influences) induce a mood of bemused amazement.

Through it all cavorts Helen herself, looking like India's answer to Barbra Streisand: indefatigably agile, provocatively dressed, taunting a poor convict locked up in a cage, flirting with plumply lecherous leading men as the camera swings with her across a tinselly, flashing stage, and prancing on the giant keyboard in another section of that typewriter number in *Bombay Talkie*. Intriguing, too, to wonder how the plot comes out in the film where, while she's dancing, rats seem to be nibbling away in best Bulldog Drummond tradition at the ropes binding one of her audience to his chair, Seen in a dressing-room interview, Helen herself provides a charmingly matter-of-fact contrast, talking practically about her career and costumes and the journey from hard-pressed childhood to star status. She's obviously something of a phenomenon, and the film enjoys all her manifestations.

Merchant's own *Mahatma* is his first essay in direction (an earlier American short, *The Creation of Woman*, marked his debut as a producer in 1961), and was shot on Bombay's Juhu Beach, a glistening yet grey setting for a little parable about a poor beach boy and an eminently photogenic monkey, who become involved with a large official meeting pompously dedicated to Gandhian principles but blandly oblivious to the boy's plain need for food and sympathy. Although a trifle soft-centered (and with the boy himself looking too actorish for his role), the film has a distinctive atmospheric flourish, as the camera sweeps across a beach bleakly inhabited by practicing gymnasts, a few tired tourists, and the droning, white-clad speechmakers, all of whom are watched benignly by a bust of the sage himself, now silenced forever and protected behind a small enclosure of iron railings. Having made its point without too much repetition, and used its setting to the full, the film sensibly knows when to stop.

The three shorts were made quite separately, arising out of different ideas by different people, yet in effect they seem to comment on each other and could well make up a package program. Perhaps they are also the partners' last look, for a while, at the Indian scene. Both are now looking to the West as their main area of production, an expansion which is also a reflection of filmmaking realities. "For one thing," Merchant says, "American films have a much greater chance of being shown. India is still a far-out country for most people, with a totally different culture and background, so with any Indian film you start out at a disadvantage."

Ivory's main concern is the script now being written for them by Lillian Ross (another old friend, first encountered at the time of *The Householder*). It's about a community of rich Chinese who settled in Manhattan from about 1948, and are spectacularly Americanized in their pursuit of the "good life," with its attendant riches and power, while retaining all their close-knit family and national identities. "I haven't seen a word she has written yet. Of course I agreed with her on basic characters and themes, but my policy is then to let the writer go off and finish the script. Afterwards we get together and Ismail and I will make suggestions. But I have great respect for writers like Lillian Ross and Ruth Jhabvala in matters of characterization. In the case of the Chinese story, I have a good idea of the milieu and the types involved, but the basic story will be Lillian's. This is how I normally work, the exception being *Savages*. On that, we started out without a complete script and it turned out more of an on-the-set collaboration, with lots of changes. But that was the sort of picture where you could make the characters fit the actors."

Once the Ross script is finalized, Ismail Merchant will start making his rounds of independent financiers and perhaps some major companies, as well as exploring the possibility of TV collaboration. ("I might also try Chinese investors.") The project is owned entirely by producer, director, and writer; and although it will probably not be a big-budget picture, they are still faced with all the problems besetting a company without a fixed base or studio. Another plan, to make Turgenev's *Torrents of Spring*, would involve filming in Germany, with perhaps studio facilities and another tie-up with TV. As more distant projects, Ivory is thinking hopefully about Fitzgerald's early novel *The Beautiful and Damned* and about Henry James's *The Bostonians,* a subject perhaps given a fortuitous kind of topicality by Women's Lib. "I hope the James film won't be one of these dreams that you carry around with you until you are seventy. Then you finally get the money and are too tired to do it."

Merchant's own plans include another film to be directed in India ("although I don't want to jump into it right away"), and he would like to produce something for Jacques Demy and Satyajit Ray. (Incidentally, it is not generally known that Ray offered to help Ivory reshape *The Householder,* and it is virtually Ray's cut which we now see). If these plans come to fruition, could it mean that the company will soon be heading in completely new directions, and ceasing to be basically a "family" concern? "Making films with friends is marvelous, even though it has sometimes landed us in bad situations—perhaps we haven't always been ruthless enough. Now, when we want to do different things, it might be the right moment to bring in new people to enlarge our operation."

Whatever the outcome, these two resilient international optimists continue to plan and organize in the firm belief that the best is yet to come. Ivory suggests, half-jokingly, that Merchant is bound some day to have a really big financial success, "either from me or, I suspect, from someone else." Anything less would seem a betrayal of destiny. Meanwhile, having just completed editing *Helen* in a Wardour Street cutting-room, and caught the London opening of *Savages* (the Curzon earning high marks for concern about print and sound quality), they are off again to New York to see how the Chinese story has progressed, and to India for some more unfinished business.

The Merchant-Ivory Synthesizers

Judith Trojan/1974

From *Take One* 4, no. 9 (January–February 1974): 14–17. Reprinted by permission of Judith Trojan.

Director James Ivory studied for his Master's degree in filmmaking at the University of Southern California; producer Ismail Merchant studied for his in Business Administration at New York University. But East/West conflicts don't begin to end there. Ivory is an American from California; Merchant, an Indian from Bombay. Somehow, these two unlikely candidates for collaboration crossed paths at a screening of an early Ivory documentary, *The Sword and the Flute*, an art film on Indian miniatures, and the MIP logo was born.

Merchant, a flamboyant, passionate fellow with a penchant for promotion, had one successful film to his production credit. While Ivory, whose dream of set design blossomed into filmmaking, had several exquisite one-man documentaries in the can. Their resultant synthesis on film has run the agonizing gamut of contrasts—pulling their dramatically opposed cultures and lifestyles into a workable body of celluloid in both short and feature formats. Honored with festival and art house accolades at home and abroad, they continue to work, as independents, towards commercial success in both 35mm and 16mm distribution. They have only just completed their first "Hollywood" extravaganza, a true departure from their intimate Indian feature films of the past. Called *The Wild Party* and scripted by Broadway composer-lyricist Walter Marks, the film focuses on the tragedy and milieu surrounding a fading, fat, silent film comedian named Jolly Grimm (played by James Coco) and also stars Raquel Welch. If that surprise is not enough, the film has been picked up for distribution by that bastion of commercialism, American International Pictures, for whom it hopefully will be a departure.

Merchant-Ivory have also completed a film for NET-TV in the States, tentatively titled *The Autobiography of a Princess*, starring James Mason and Madhur Jaffrey. *Princess* apparently retains the seminal Merchant-Ivory conflict of East-West cultures coming face to face in the guise of a few strong, universal characters.

Hope for mutual understanding between disparate cultures and traditions may only be an unfulfilled dream in their scenarios, but the Merchant-Ivory team is a viable reality. Their Indo-American product is right for an artistic medium that bridges international language barriers and demands inherent character conflict for its success.

James Ivory and Ismail Merchant were interviewed in New York early into preparation of the final cut of *The Wild Party*:

Judith Trojan: How did you make the transition from 16mm shorts to feature films?

James Ivory: Ismail offered me the chance to direct my first feature; so, of course, I took *that* chance. It *was* a chance because we were making it in two versions, one in English and one in Hindi, and I didn't know any Hindi. I had never worked with actors before, so it was quite an undertaking. That film, which was *The Householder*, we then sold to Columbia Pictures. And that's how we really got started.

Trojan: Yours are independent productions?

Ismail Merchant: Totally independent. We work all the time developing our projects, getting the scripts, the writers, our own crew. And twelve years have passed, and we have done very well. Not that we have become millionaires, but *very well* in the sense that we have established an independent identity.

Ivory: We do seem somehow to find backing for films we want to make, rather than have to make films that somebody else wants us to make. We've been quite lucky in that way.

Trojan: Aside from the other close Merchant-Ivory collaborations, you have worked with only two cinematographers, first Subrata Mitra and now Walter Lassally, and also have used Ruth Prawer Jhabvala consistently as your screenwriter. How did you get involved with her?

Ivory: Well, I had met her before we made *The Householder*, but I didn't really know her. Ismail had read the novel, *The Householder*, and decided he wanted to make that into a film. So we wrote to her and went to see her in Delhi.

Trojan: What is her literary background? Is she Indian?

Ivory: No. She's Polish, brought up in England, married to an Indian living in India. She's written many novels, all of which were published here in the West, and writes all the time for the *New Yorker, Cosmopolitan,* and British magazines. She has written six scripts for us, five of which have been produced, which is pretty good!

Trojan: Do both you and Ismail have a hand in the scripting, or do you give her free rein?

Ivory: Well she, being the writer of the script, has pretty much free rein. But four or five of the six scripts that she's written were collaborations. The first film that we did together was *The Householder,* based on her own novel. She wrote that script straight out of her head without even referring back to the book. Then, I got the idea to do *Shakespeare Wallah;* she became intrigued with the idea and decided that she would write that screenplay. It's a collaboration in the sense that I suggest the kinds of characters, scenes, and setting, and she develops and enlarges that to a form that makes sense in terms of a story, plot, and characters. And then I work on it a bit more to add certain scenes of my own. But they're additions rather than being any major kinds of redoing; and later on with subtractions, because things happen in the shooting. The script, as it comes from her, is pretty much what we shoot. So that's how we worked on *Shakespeare Wallah,* on *The Guru,* and then on *Bombay Talkie.* And we also wrote a sequel to *Shakespeare Wallah,* which is called *A Lovely World.*

Trojan: And what happened to that?

Ivory: That was to be made in London, but we never were able to get financing for it. Now it's too late to do because the girl who was in *Shakespeare Wallah* is too old. It was to have carried on her life back in England. After *Bombay Talkie,* we made *Savages* here, which Ruth wasn't involved in. Then we did this film recently for NET (National Educational Television), starring James Mason and Madhur Jaffrey, for which Ruth wrote the script.

Trojan: What was the name of that?

Ivory: Well, we call it now, *The Autobiography of a Princess,* which is a very inexact title because the film is not an autobiography in any sense. It's really about maharajahs and court life. We used a lot of footage made by maharajahs in the twenties, thirties, and forties.

Trojan: Court life in India?

Ivory: Yes, but it's about other things too. It's about English people in India, what happens to them. The whole thing is really just two characters. Most of it was shot in London. A good deal of it was shot in India, too, but without actors.

Trojan: So you're once again zeroing in on an intimate group of characters who represent conflicting societies, lifestyles, traditions, et al.?
Ivory: They're usually symbolic characters who represent different attitudes and different cultures.

Trojan: And universal conflicts? What about *Savages?*
Ivory: Well, *Savages* is a special case in a way. *Savages* was—I know Ismail doesn't like me to say this—but it was really something of a joke and was not ever really meant to be taken all that seriously. And in this country, it *was* taken too seriously, which is a pity. In Europe people knew how to sit through something like that, without becoming bored or outraged.
Merchant: And also, it is too European in character. If it had been done by Bunuel or some European director, this snob appeal of American critics . . .
Ivory: Oh, I don't know!
Merchant: They would've gone and licked the boots of it and said, "Ah, what a great masterpiece has come our way!" But it was done from home ground, you know, like a prophet is never known in his country! In Europe, it has gotten the most fantastic reviews, and also did very good business.

Trojan: Where does it show successfully in America? What audiences understand and appreciate it?
Merchant: College students. This film is one of the most sought-after films in 16mm distribution. People just go and see and enjoy it. They laugh at the right places and they get the right idea. Wherever I have gone and talked and shown the film—Yale, Harvard, UCLA—there's been enormous enthusiasm for the film, which is very satisfying. One doesn't always have to get the so-called interpreters [*sic*], like critics, to take it upon themselves to interpret a film.
Ivory: There was nothing to interpret. It was just simply a humorous demonstration of the rise and fall of civilization, done within a particular context which was this house, with these mud people coming to it, becoming civilized, and then regressing to their original state. The only things to interpret were the various scenes in the film which stood for

various moments in time, of historical development, up and down the scale of civilization.

Trojan: For example?

Merchant: Like for example, the man who's drowned . . .

Ivory: And when they go and rob his body. That represents such a breakdown of society which has reached the point at which the dead are no longer respected or sacred, and the tombs are being robbed and despoiled.

Trojan: Those fantastic credit titles and title cards throughout were definitely a tongue-in-cheek throwback to silent films.

Ivory: Yes. Everything was supposed to be like something found in an attic. All those things, like the title cards, were supposed to be like it all had gotten mixed up; and they had, the numbers were all out of order. They had all been found and just used. But nobody appreciated that here. I mean, the people in the audiences did, but none of the critics did. They thought that was all pretentious, and silly, and "what were we doing!"

Trojan: When you make a film, do you think in terms of future audiences, or do you think solely in terms of what you want to do with the film?

Ivory: Oh, more what I want to do. But you *should* think of who your audience is gonna be. I don't want to make films for an audience of esthetes, just average people.

Trojan: Did you make *The Guru* to cash in on the George Harrison publicity?

Ivory: Well, "cash in" is not really the word. But that's what was usually written about it, that we had. It may have been 20th Century-Fox's motive, I don't know!

Trojan: Was it originally your idea to do *The Guru*, or did 20th Century-Fox come to you with the property?

Ivory: It was our idea.

Trojan: Is *Shakespeare Wallah* based at all upon the Kendal family's true life story?

Ivory: No. It isn't really.

Merchant: But it is like they are! They actually had toured around India performing Shakespeare as a family before the film came into existence.

Ivory: And went on doing it afterwards. But they look upon their life in India as a great success. We were using them as symbolic characters, to represent a decline of European values and the gradual disappearance of European civilization in India, which is what has happened. So the real Kendals aren't the same as their namesakes, the Buckinghams, in the film. And that's why we couldn't use the episodes from their life as scenes in the film. There's not a single scene in the film which is something that happened to them.

Trojan: But had you known them before you made the film? I mean, did knowing them or having seen them perform give you the idea for this film?

Ivory: Partly. Yes. Not completely. They had a big company at first. But gradually the audience disappeared.

Trojan: How have the Kendals felt about the Indian audiences turning away from theatre in favor of films, as was the basis of their downfall in the film?

Ivory: Well, not the films as such, but simply the interest in indigenous entertainment.

Merchant: Stage has limited appeal. You saw our film *Helen, Queen of the Nautch Girls*. Everything is done for entertainment, in the sense of escapist entertainment. You cannot have anything which is structured on reality. People want to get away from their lives, from the misery which they live in, from day-to-day hardship, like for example, during the Depression here in this country. All the Hollywood escapist films were very popular. Box office results were very high. India still has that same escapist value in entertainment.

Trojan: Are all indigenous Indian films musicals?

Merchant: Mostly. The majority of films which are made in India have eight to ten songs and dances.

Trojan: How do your Indian films do in India?

Merchant: They are seen. They are treated exactly like foreign films.

Trojan: And something like *The Householder* is treated as a foreign film?

Merchant: Yes.

Ivory: Only the English-language version of it, not the Hindi version.

Trojan: In several of your films, at some point, you seem to ridicule the whole guru phenomenon. . .
Ivory: I don't think I really ridicule the guru, as such.

Trojan: Well, they're sort of depicted as superstars with blind followers.
Ivory: They *are* superstars!
Merchant: You can see through them! A con man's success in America, in the West, is more than a con man's success in India because in India there are con men on every street corner and these are the gurus.
Ivory: But you should stress something on the positive side of gurus. In India, you can have all kinds of gurus. You can have a guru who's a master of political intrigue and manipulation. He would be a guru of politics; and everybody would go to him to get his advice on how to get somebody elected or how to swing a district. Or, you can have a guru in some form of art. He can be a dancer, a great instrumentalist, or a singer. And everybody goes to him because he is a tremendous exponent of his particular form of art; and they learn from him and they offer up their lives, in a sense, to the guru. But what they're really offering up their lives to is to the art itself. And their own ego is kept very much to the back and out of the way, while they learn the various forms which they've got to learn. Then, there's a religious guru, who has spiritual powers. He can help people attain a certain state that they want to attain, more peace of mind, whatever! But I don't poke fun at gurus as such. Our own guru, in *The Guru*, was presented as a great musician; he was always shown in his artistic guise as a very dignified person.

Trojan: But you do poke fun at the people who come to follow gurus from the West. The beatnik character of Ernest in *The Householder*, for example . . .
Ivory: Ernest and all those English people at that house in *The Householder* were very broad, and really caricatures. I knew nothing of such people, had never seen them, never met them. The casting possibilities weren't perhaps ideal. It was much more subtle as written than as it actually turned out because I didn't have the skill or understanding.

Trojan: What about Jenny?
Ivory: You've got two kinds of disciples in *The Guru*. You have the mindless kind of devotion, which Jenny has and which is partly sexual. And then you have the much more genuine attempted devotion of Tom, who is really there to try and learn to play the sitar. He comes as a profes-

sional musician to learn music from another professional musician. But, he is not prepared to go through the entire guru situation of casting out his own individuality and simply learning by rote. And that's one of the things a very high-handed guru sometimes desires. If he senses pride and other characteristics in a disciple that he thinks are going to keep that disciple from actually learning the music, or whatever he's teaching, then he's going to try and *rid* that disciple of that pride because it stands in the way of understanding. That's a perfectly legitimate thing to do. Of course, there are some gurus who want complete surrender, more or less for power reasons. That's a different kind of situation. In *The Guru*, it was a bit of both. He was supposed to be a *great* artist, but also a man with his own needs, interests, and vanities. That's not different from artists anywhere. Artists are not totally noble. They may make wonderful things, but they have a side to their character, which doesn't always bear close inspection. So, it was really *that* that we were trying to show in the film. But, of course, that was misinterpreted, in India especially.

Trojan: Your female characters seem to act as major catalysts or victims in the typical Merchant-Ivory conflicts—Eastern culture vs. Western culture, tradition vs. modernity, etc. How would you categorize your female characters?

Ivory: The Indian heroines *are* always shown *within* the framework of their own world. That gives them an added strength, and sometimes a dignity, that is denied the foreigners, who aren't Indian and who are cut off from their world, and only have really what they can carry on their backs and what they bring with them from their own cultures. But, of course, sometimes *that's* a great strength too. It was the strength of the girl, Lizzie, in *Shakespeare Wallah*. The parents thought that if she didn't get out of India she would lose her Western character. It would be submerged and she would grow older as a kind of exile: a dislocated person. And that's why they were urging her to go on to England. Whereas Jenny, in *The Guru* was someone who had *left* England without even a care, she thought, and had come out to embrace everything Indian. But, as it turned out, it wasn't all that easy for her. She gradually becomes fearful and wants to go home. The English writer in *Bombay Talkie* comes to India seeking new sensations, wanting new material for a book, and hopefully to find romance. She's escaping from a world that she's had enough of, *too* much of. She can't find what she wants in India either; but she couldn't find it anywhere. She's sort of a universal, discontented type.

Trojan: There will be many people who will make the obvious comparison between Jolly Grimm in *The Wild Party* and Fatty Arbuckle's Hollywood scandals. Is the film based at all on Fatty Arbuckle?

Ivory: No, it's *not* based on Fatty Arbuckle. It's based *rather loosely* on a long narrative poem by Joseph Moncure March called "The Wild Party," which was written in the late twenties.

Trojan: Was the poem based on another real-life Hollywood incident?

Ivory: No, it's a whole invented thing. In the poem, all the action takes place in Greenwich Village *at* a wild party, and it concerns New York theatre types—comics, ex-chorus girls, vaudevillians—rather than Hollywood types. Our scriptwriter, Walter Marks, took the story and set it in Hollywood of the late twenties. He made the central character of the poem into a silent movie star, played by Jimmy Coco. And because Jimmy Coco is *fat,* and because the film is set in Hollywood in the twenties, everyone just assumes that we're doing the Fatty Arbuckle story. But we're not. The Fatty Arbuckle story was sordid and tragic, and I don't think our film has that element of the sordid about it. It's tragic, I suppose.

Trojan: Were you offered this project or . . .

Ivory: I heard about it and went to see Edgar Lansbury and Joseph Seruh, the executive producers. We showed them *Savages*, which they liked very much. They didn't have a producer either, so they offered Ismail and me the jobs. We said we wanted to do it, but that we couldn't do it just as written because the script that was written was much too atmospheric, in the sense that there was very little actual plot or story, and very little character development. The characters were suggested, but they were types rather than real people.

Trojan: How did you go about integrating the songs and poetry?

Ivory: Poetry is easy, because it's either spoken directly to the camera by David Dukes or done in voice over. It's terribly interesting, and very theatrical. It works as a device, a sort of formal structure really: within the party itself, and at the very beginning of the film and at the very end. It's like a kind of narration that links everything together, sets the stage for various developing situations. The songs I'm not so sure about: we'll see! To me it's like an opera, where there are all kinds of superheated emotions, a lot of singing, wonderful arias, and sometimes rather implausible tragic events at the end. This film is a bit like that to the extent that it's not an absolutely straightforward dramatic story. It has these musical interludes and the device of the poetry. So, it isn't a *realistic* film in the usual sense. It's a heightened kind of view.

Trojan: Most of your films deal in some way with the film industry, especially in India. Now, you're doing your first Hollywood film and it's set in Hollywood's golden era. Since you were a film student, do you have a "Bogdanovich" reverence for old films, for the film industry per se?
Ivory: No, I don't. I'm not a nostalgia buff. My own nostalgia for things has nothing to do with films really. I make films about things that I know about. My life is making films, and so I show that world very often.

Trojan: In *Bombay Talkie*, which is a study of some characters who people Bombay's film industry, are you giving us an accurate picture of the stars and industry? Would Vikram be typical of Indian stars—the childishness, the egotism?
Ivory: Yes. He *is* typical. Oh, yes, absolutely! In fact, it's very much played down in *Bombay Talkie*. It's much worse than that, much more extravagant, much more foolish and destructive. It is just really hard to describe. I mean no one would believe it! That film was planned the way it was because I wanted to make a film about the Bombay film industry, as I had observed it. I had made three films in India and had seen that film industry up close. I just thought that was very good material.

Trojan: Will you be making more films in India?
Ivory: Oh, sure.

Trojan: Will you be making any more shorts?
Ivory: Sure, I like to make shorts. Except my shorts are very long. And this Princess thing just started out as a kind of documentary about maharajahs, and it gradually turned into this whole sort of, well. . . . Of course, it's not edited yet, but I think of all our films, that's the one where all the elements are in the most perfect balance.

Trojan: I read that you purchased Sylvia Plath's *The Bell Jar*. That's a very interesting rumor!
Ivory: We never did. That was a mistake.
Trojan: What about Lillian Ross's script for *Vertical and Horizontal*?
Ivory: We *have* an option and a screenplay on that. That film was originally going to be made by Paramount, and then they backed out of it. We didn't do anything about it for a number of years, but now we've come back to it. Maybe, it'll be made!

Hollywood versus Hollywood

James Ivory/1976

From *Index on Censorship* 5, no. 2 (Summer 1976): 10–16. Reprinted by permission.

One of the many grey areas in the practice of the arts is the influence of commercial pressures and the extent to which that influence can be qualified as "censorship." It is clear that some art forms are more vulnerable than others, particularly in the sphere of mass entertainment, and few are more vulnerable than films, but how does the pressure work and what are its effects? James Ivory, the American film director, here describes his experiences with The Wild Party *and explains how it is that his version of the film has still not been released to the public, one year after its completion, and probably never will.*

The term "the final cut" in commercial filmmaking has an ominous sound to the layman, who cannot understand how it is possible for the director of a film to have his work re-edited by others against his wishes. The final cut and who has the right to make it is an issue that has been fought over by the creators of films and those who have the controlling financial interest in them since the beginning of the film industry. Unless his contract protects that right, so basic to any kind of personal expression in films, the director will usually lose this last battle, though he may have won all the others in the course of making his film. Once he has done everything else satisfactorily, his masters may now decide they can afford to dispense with his services. Since few directors in English-speaking countries are ever powerful enough to demand and get the final cut, history provides many examples of mutilated works, major and minor.

When a director has been ousted from his editing room, all appeals to reason having failed, he may find allies among the powerful stars who have acted in his film. Or he can go to influential critics, who may be willing to take up his cause in the newspapers. But once the altered version of his film is before the public, there is little chance that it will be recalled in favor of the one acceptable to him, and it will continue to play, for better or worse, usually giving everyone a bad name: director, writer, actors, and—finally—the persons responsible for the mutilation.

This form of censorship, undertaken for commercial reasons, is in some ways as effective as any applied by totalitarian regimes to suppress dissent. And the men who carry out this work so eagerly are often, psychologically, like the petty functionaries the State employs for its purposes; former advertising executives, accountants, lawyers, agents turned showmen—frustrated "artists" who are thereby given a chance to meddle with the work of genuine artists. These latter, however, they often fear and hate, and treat with contempt—despite the show of deference due to the supposedly exalted position of film directors. Let a film be reviewed badly or, much worse, be a flop, and you will see that deference transformed into a gross contempt expressed, in some cases, by the physical destruction of the film itself. In the atmosphere of panic which is created whenever the investment in a picture seems threatened by an early, bad, (or sometimes merely contradictory) reaction to it, fumbling attempts to make it "work" are hastily made by the studio functionaries—who also scramble to get out of the cursed shadow of the failure as fast as possible. But this rarely manages to save a film or make it more palatable to the public.

Some films fail because they are bad. The public sees this at once and stays away. Sometimes, however, the public is put off a good picture because of an accident in timing: the appearance of a favorite star in a guise which is unacceptable; a directorial style which is not accessible to a mass audience; a story which has a depressing effect on people. No re-editing has ever saved either kind of failed film, good or bad, or turned it into a box-office success. Time alone works to redeem a distinguished failure, but too slowly to do anybody much immediate good, and certainly not fast enough to save the financier's investment.

Sometimes a case can be made for the studio presented with a finished film which really is too long, and might tax the patience of the public. One can certainly sympathize with the distributor without advocating hasty trimming. And many disciplined directors have coolly cut excess footage without regrets once they've seen how their film played. But this is a different situation from that of the filmmaker whose work is taken away from him and drastically altered; when the story line is changed so that the purpose and point of view of director and writer are made unclear; when material is removed that is needed to reveal the characters, while other material already discarded by the director is introduced to provoke easy laughs or prurient interest; in which the style and texture of the piece have been debased.

Such was the case with *The Wild Party*, which started out to be a Hollywood-in-the-twenties musical, and which, in its patched-together remnants, proves once more that you cannot effectively re-edit a picture and change its character in order, allegedly, to "save" it.

Selling Nostalgia

American International must have thought that if they backed a film called *The Wild Party* starring Raquel Welch, and let it be identified with the squalid Fatty Arbuckle scandal ("A Night of Gin and Sin, a Night They're Still Whispering About!"), they wouldn't have to do anything else: they could sit back and let the money pour in from small town drive-ins, as well as cash in on the current craze for nostalgia in somewhat more sophisticated places. They thought the film was nostalgic because it was set in 1929 and the extras wore a lot of beaded dresses and wing-tip collars and talked about the swell party over at Doug and Mary's. But did they *look* at that collection of bleary-eyed drunks carousing in a disheveled mansion and think they were selling nostalgia? Did they look at anything? When press agents dictated blurbs about Hollywood decadence, did anyone stop to ask: what decadence? In 1929, Hollywood was entering its Golden Age, and its citizens, who are presented in the film, were taking part in a gold rush, like pioneers. They were not decadents, but on the contrary, rather wholesome people, getting rich and having fun, as they invented both an art form and an entertainment industry. That is what the film is about; the story tells of a silent-screen actor's professional downfall and personal collapse. It was meant to be taken seriously—but not so seriously that there was no room for the songs and dances which are an outgrowth of the party's natural action and which were intended to lighten the mood. These carefully choreographed numbers were also casualties in the massive re-editing. How did all this happen? How does a film, carrying its loads of hope and gold, sink as easily as this one did?

The Wild Party is based on a blank verse narrative poem written by Joseph Moncure March in 1926. The action originally took place in Greenwich Village at a party thrown by a vaudeville comic in his walk-up apartment. When it was published it had a kind of underground success due to its frankness, but today the poem's charm lies in its jazzy rhythms and period slang. To try to make a film with American International out of such material would perhaps seem to many readers an act of madness. To accept money (but who refuses an offer of money to make a film?) from such a source might seem to be either calculating or an act of extreme innocence. But then, encountering the poetry in the script (the setting had been shifted to California, though the characters, in their Hollywood equivalents, were the same), which was sometimes to be spoken directly to the camera by the poet-narrator, and many other "artsy-fartsy" touches, as Sam Arkoff, the owner of American International put it, why go ahead and back the film at all, especially when it was to be directed by "that mystic"—myself? Arkoff is supposed to have said that he took up this dubious project because of its enticing sounding title, and because of the presence of Raquel Welch as Queenie, though he is also supposed to have said that the mystic would turn her into Doris Day. Yet one can plainly see that it was a fine and daring thing of American International to go into such a venture. Arkoff alludes to his involvement with some pride in a story about him printed in the *New York Times*. So what went wrong?

The Not-So-Final Cut

When the first rough-cut of the film was shown to American International, few misgivings were expressed about the picture as a whole. The film was too long, running two hours and a quarter and the pacing was erratic, but the mood at AIP's offices on Wilshire Boulevard was one of cautious optimism. After this first screening there was a "creative" session. We went down a list prepared during the screening by Arkoff's associates, who had huddled together in the dark scribbling comments down on a clipboard to which a little light had been attached. This light kept going on and off, signaling displeasure I felt sure, yet some of their suggestions were excellent. Others were merely frivolous, an annoyance, and the rest were bad. We went back to New York, where the film was being edited, determined to carry out the good suggestions, to ignore the others, and generally to do the things to it which we felt were necessary.

After a month, when the length of the film had been reduced to a little under two hours, we were again summoned to the Coast for another screening and another creative encounter session in AIP's boardroom. Now the mood had changed. Sam Arkoff was "disappointed." The film didn't *move*. There were further suggestions, each person putting forth his ideas about this or that scene. Edgar Lansbury, one of the executive producers, was also there, looking grave. Probably he had been taken aside and made to listen to doubts about my editing methods, which seemed not to be getting us anywhere. But as he had supported me through the turbulent shooting, I was confident I would retain control of the film's final form. We returned to New York and another list appeared a few days later. There were new suggestions on it, as well as all the old ones we hadn't taken seriously. Although this kind of interference is forbidden by an agreement, the major movie-making companies have with the Directors' Guild of America, to which I belong, I removed another ten minutes from the film. I was not unhappy to lose ten minutes; but American International was by now telling me *which* minutes, for example insisting that I shorten Raquel Welch's big number, *Singapore Sally*, and sending me detailed instructions to show me how they would do it if they were editing the film. Their demands were challenges. Not to combat, but to find satisfactory solutions.

When the film's running time was down to an hour and forty-eight minutes I decided that was as much as I could do to oblige American International. It was not only a matter of what was right for the film; their harrying us all the time was going to put us off schedule. The editor, Kent McKinney, was afraid we would never be ready with our sound tracks by the time of the re-recording, a date set months before. Arkoff sent two of his creative consultants on a quick trip to New York to see my "final cut" before the re-recording started. They didn't like the film at all. But Lansbury and his partner, Joseph Beruh, were getting fed up with all this meddling and they sent the Vice Presidents back to the West Coast unsatisfied. The film was mixed, the negative was cut, and the first prints were ordered. I felt the picture was substantially as I had wanted it. The battles of shooting, the sessions with AIP in Beverly Hills—all that was forgotten in the feeling of euphoria (short-lived, in this case) everyone shares when a film is completed and, one believes, completed well. Yet my presence at, or around, the delivered film was resented. When I went to Hollywood to be on hand while the prints were being "timed" at Movielab in the absence of the cameraman, Walter Lassally, who was in England, I was made to feel I was being humored in some last act of self-indulgence.

I knew what effects Lassally wanted—how light, how dark, etc.—and the grading man was wonderfully cooperative, but it was sometimes hard to get my recommendations carried out. American International's head of post-production always sat in the theatre. I would have to hear things like: "You have these fantastic sets, what do you want to make them so dark for?" They were afraid that, after more than a year on the project, after having brought it through several script re-writes, the casting, very difficult shooting, and the editing, the director would now somehow wreck everything. It was time, they felt, for the *real* professionals to take over.

Ismail Merchant, the producer, now wanted to show his new film to a few friends and to persons who could be trusted to write usefully about it. He wanted to be able to start promoting it, in his usual energetic way. But American International was afraid that he, too, would spoil everything. It seemed obvious to us to open the film in New York and Los Angeles in prestige theatres as quickly as possible, while there were the benefits of the considerable advance publicity to help the film, and before the other Hollywood period piece, *Day of the Locust*, made its appearance.

But this would have been a radical departure from AIP's regular and highly successful grab-a-buck-and-run distribution pattern: saturation booking away from the media centers and then, when the picture is in profit and it no longer matters whether the critics pan it or not, bringing it to the major cities. With the greatest misgivings, AIP turned over one of its prints to the producer and to Edgar Lansbury, who also wanted to elicit some opinions, and this was taken to New York. Simultaneously, they began to speak of a shorter version of the film, one playing for ninety-five or a hundred minutes. But we felt that if we could get a few powerful New York critics to come out for the film, AIP might be discouraged from tampering with it. However, our strongest ally was to be Raquel Welch herself, who was now shown the finished film. She was excited by it and by the response of critics like Arthur Knight and Judith Crist, who had seen the picture and found her performance a revelation of unsuspected—or at least up to then unrealized—talents for acting comedy and for singing and dancing. We held a general screening in New York for a hundred guests and followed that with a big party. Our reading of the audience reaction was that people had liked the film very much and this was backed up by the comments of the critics. We felt the chances for the film were good, given the right send-off.

In the same week (that of January 27–February 2, 1975), AIP held two "sneak" previews of the film, one in Santa Barbara, the other in San Diego. There are no attempts at advance secrecy any more when sneaks are held; ads are put in the local papers giving the name of the new film, which plays for a night on a double bill with the picture already running in the theatre. Cards are passed out to the audience to fill up. The questions asked of the audiences for *The Wild Party* in the two cities were: What scenes did you enjoy the most? What scenes did you like the least, if any? Would you recommend this film to your friends? If so, what particular scene would you relate in recommending it? How would you rate this film? (Excellent, Good, Fair, Poor)

Sex and age were asked, and there was space on the card for additional comments. Both previews turned out disastrously. The atmosphere in the theatre at Santa Barbara had been particularly frightening. The reaction to *The Wild Party* had been one of loathing. The audience was composed mainly of students from the adjoining University of California campus and they jeered at the film. Their most violent reactions seemed, judging from the cards they filled out, to be against Raquel Welch and the young leading man, Perry King. They wanted the old, slam-bang, camp Raquel, not the new, serious, vulnerable one we gave them, and they bated Perry King's sleek looks and immaculate evening dress and immaculate accent. The only things the students liked were the "orgy" scene—a kind of erotic musical number which was cut in Great Britain—and a fight. But in San Diego everything was reversed. *Singapore Sally*, at which the students had hooted, was the high point for this predominantly middle-class audience, and Raquel, who grew up in San Diego, was much praised in the cards. Not much else was. The "orgy" and the violence were disliked, and there were many walkouts, each one noted by an announcement made into a tape recorder brought to the theatre by an AIP executive. Joe Beruh had gone to California to be present at the two previews and to report back on what happened and on what AIP would do next. Both partners had a lot of money tied up in the film; it was important to get it in front of the public right away. But now, understandably, AIP was in no hurry to open the picture. The two previews had upset everything and were causing further confusion by being contradictory. Joe Beruh returned to New York with a message from Sam Arkoff: Did Ivory have any ideas how the film might be shortened?

I was glad to be asked my opinion at this late stage, but I felt I needed to look at the film with a different editor and I engaged Alan Heim, fresh from *Lenny*, to help me trim it. We worked for two days and managed to remove eight more minutes—but Heim did this so cleverly that it was very hard to tell anything bad had been done. From AIP's point of view this wasn't much help. It was the same film, minus some entrances and exits and bits of dialogue. No editorial magic had turned it into the film of their dreams. Meanwhile, without telling me, Lansbury and Beruh made up their own list of proposed cuts and sent it out to California.

They were getting itchy; they wanted—who didn't?—to get on to other things. We urged the distributor to release the film in New York before any more time passed. We were confident that it would find a following and that the New York press would support us, despite the debacle of the two previews. We pointed to all the hits that had been booed during their sneak previews. We were getting rather desperate. AIP was now talking about making Jolly Grimm, the main character of the film (played by James Coco), into a more lovable man. Audiences could not identify with someone so choleric they said. We begged for the film to be given a chance as made, but this only made them angry. Who were we to tell them how to market the picture? We withdrew at this point and I began to edit my next film, *Autobiography of a Princess*.

Raquel Welch now heard that the film was being totally re-cut in Hollywood by AIP's own editor. She instructed her lawyers to notify the distributor that she would do no publicity for the picture until she saw for herself how this new version turned out. They tried to reassure her: they told her she would love the new, exciting, Felliniesque version of *The Wild Party*. But when she saw it, she hated what they'd done to the picture and threatened to sue if they put it into release. More time passed, during which Lansbury and Beruh, followed by Walter Marks, who wrote the screenplay and much of the music, saw and approved the re-edited version, which ran ninety minutes—Sam Arkoff's magic number. People began to ask: Whatever happened to *The Wild Party*? It was going around that there was some problem with the picture. And when film festivals tried to show it, AIP refused permission.

Disastrous Reviews

In late spring 1975, there seemed to be a change of heart. Whether due to the pressure kept up on them by Raquel, or a negative reaction from exhibitors to the re-edited version of the film, American International decided to release my cut everywhere—that is, in the hundred-minute form Alan Heim and I had prepared. There had been talk of showing two versions, mine in the cities, theirs in small towns; preparations were now made for a kind of selected city approach. We were ecstatic, and threw a big party in New York so that the press could meet the stars of the film. But the question everybody asked was: When is the picture having its New York premiere? It had opened in Washington and was due to play in Boston and Denver; what about New York? During the party, a well-wisher sent us an envelope containing the first reviews from Washington. They were terrible. We did not show them to Raquel, but their import was ominous: she had gone to Washington to promote the film and the same papers that had carried her interviews and photographs now ridiculed her performance. And business was terrible, too. The same thing was repeated in Boston. Savage reviews, bad box-office. After this, the film was withdrawn from release.

It was now summer; six months had passed since the film had been delivered to the distributor. It existed in a limbo of rumor. No one could find out anything definite; the anxious co-stars were fobbed off with stories of an imminent opening which kept being put further and further ahead: 16 June; 26 June, then 26 July, etc. I was told nothing at all. But our fears that the re-edited version of the film would now be generally released—the Ivory version having been "market-tested" and found unsalable seemed confirmed by an event which seems like one of Fate's grand Coincidences. Ismail Merchant, in London in connection with *Autobiography of a Princess*, heard, as he was screening that film for some friends, the music of *The Wild Party* coming through the wall of an adjoining screening room on Wardour Street. He went into the projection booth to watch and to ask who was being shown the film. A delegation of Rank exhibitors was seeing the AIP cut of the picture before its release in England. When told of this I wrote to Sam Arkoff, threatening to take the whole thing up in the newspapers, but this letter was ignored, as all our others had been.

The English release of the picture was being handled by a company called Seven Keys, who showed it to the trade papers and monthly magazines in early August. This screening was presided over by Andrew Gatty, the head of Seven Keys, who spoke of bringing a new optimism to the British film industry; "entertainment" was to be the key word. Later, when asked privately by our solicitor whether he knew of the existence of the director's version of the film, he said, oh, yes, he had preferred it to the one being released, but Rank had turned it down. He had asked Rank to have another look and had only reluctantly shown them the AIP version, which they took. What could he do? Artistically, Ivory's was the version he liked, but he was also a businessman: if he hadn't accepted Rank's offer, *The Wild Party* would never have been shown in England at all. All I could now do was write to the British film critics to explain what had happened to *The Wild Party*. My letter appeared the day the film opened in London and brought the first communication I had had from AIP in months. It was a furious one, consisting of charges of having damaged the film's chances for commercial success by defaming it in print, and of deliberately trying to sabotage those chances, for which I would be held personally responsible. This was soon followed by a letter from Seven Keys' General Manager, James Robinson, who was "shocked and appalled" that I would take it upon myself to make such damaging comments about the film and, by inference, about Seven Keys, whose credibility as renters to the cinemas and as suppliers of the product to the public had been unfairly damaged by my irresponsible action. This, he said, had had the effect of associating his company with the "cheap attempt to over-exploit everything exploitable" with which my letter had charged AIP's editors. He wrote:

> We have spent a great deal of time, a great deal of money and a great deal of thought in the promotion of this picture not at all with a view to simple exploitation, but within the serious philosophy of our company of making sure that all our advertising and promotion work attracts the sort of person who, when he sees the film, will be in no way disappointed. We take great pains *not* to mislead . . .

Seven Keys required my assurance that I would immediately desist from writing all these bad things. They too were going to hold me responsible for the "devastating effect" my letter had on business. One could not help asking at this point why, if Seven Keys had spent all that time, money, and thought on the film's promotion, they had opened it on a double bill with an old Mel Brooks film, and at the Astoria, which John Coleman, in his sympathetic review in the *New Statesman*, called "that great graveyard on Charing Cross Road where celluloid white elephants go to die." Or why they had not bothered to invite the critics of the Daily and Sunday London papers to a press show, but had caused them to go out and buy tickets in order to see the film. But all this hullabaloo seems not to have had that adverse effect on the picture's chances after all, rather the contrary, and it had a perfectly decent run of several weeks. *Variety* reported business as being good.

Since then, the film has played here and there around the United States in the AIP version and on Home Box Office—subscription television. It has still to open in New York and so, *officially*, has not opened at all. It is becoming legendary, one likes to think. As it recedes in time from the days of expectation when it was being made, hopes for it fade for everybody who took part in it. For Raquel Welch, who, after her success in *The Three Musketeers*, wanted to do something challenging and unlike anything she had ever done before; for Jimmy Coco, who needed a grand, starring vehicle to show off *his* talents; for Merchant-Ivory Productions, who hoped against hope for an American-style commercial success; for Lansbury and Beruh, who wanted to make some money while enlarging the scope of their showmanship; for Walter Marks, whose dream *The Wild Party* was, and who, in his innocence, tried to make an expressionistic screen musical with sex, murder, and poetry; and finally for American International Pictures, who, despite all talk to the contrary, wanted to "go straight" and to do something they could be proud of.

Where Could I Meet Other Screenwriters? A Conversation with Ruth Prawer Jhabvala

John Pym/1978

From *Sight and Sound* 48, no. 1 (Winter 1978–79): 15–19. Reprinted by permission of the British Film Institute.

Massachusetts, early October. The author Ruth Prawer Jhabvala occupies a bare, modern room in an anonymous modern hotel in Leominster. The room seems to contain only a typewriter, a few papers, and a well-preserved copy of the Penguin edition of Henry James's novel *The Europeans*. She likes the hotel: it takes care of the domestic arrangements, not her forte, and the atmosphere is conducive to hard work. A few miles away at the Barrett House, across the state line in New Ipswich, NH, her colleagues, the producer Ismail Merchant and the director James Ivory, have just started filming her (and Ivory's) adaptation of *The Europeans*. It is their eighth film together in fifteen years. The budget, Merchant estimates, will be about £450,000, and the money, as always, is coming from various sources: individuals in Britain and the United States; the German production company Polytel; and the British National film finance Corporation. The crew is largely British, and all but two of the cast American: Lee Remick stars as the Baroness, and Tim Woodward plays her brother Felix. The house and its adjoining cottage, supposedly just outside Boston, are exactly the right period and positioned just as James described them. Sand is sprinkled on the road and we seem to be in the nineteenth century. Mrs. Jhabvala, however, prefers to remain in her hotel.

Born in Cologne in 1927 to Polish parents, she came to England in

1939. She had been writing in German since she was six, but almost at once switched to English. She took a degree at Queen Mary College, London University, and soon afterwards married an Indian architect and moved to Delhi. For some twenty-four years she lived almost wholly cut off from European society: she raised three daughters and at the same time wrote continuously. Her eighth novel, *Heat and Dust*, won the Booker prize for fiction in 1975. The debilitating Indian climate and the tensions of Indian life—tensions detailed in her novels—now compel Mrs. Jhabvala to divide her time between Delhi and a new home in Manhattan. In 1963, she began a fruitful, and until recently a virtually exclusive collaboration with Merchant and Ivory, which has resulted in a series of films—*The Householder* (1963), from her own novel, *Shakespeare Wallah* (1965), *The Guru* (1968), *Bombay Talkie* (1970), *Autobiography of a Princess* (1975), *Roseland* (1977), and *Hullabaloo over Georgie and Bonnie's Pictures* (1978)—all of which, with the exception of *Roseland*, have a European/Indian background. James's early short novel about the arrival of two "Europeans" at the home of their proper New England cousins and the genteel, faintly humorous disorder they create, seems tailored for Mrs. Jhabvala's gentle, ironic talents.

John Pym: Could you say a few words about how you came to screen writing

Ruth Prawer Jhabvala: Well, Jim and Ismail came to make *The Householder*. I was in India at that time. They bought the book from me and I wrote the screenplay. I had never thought of doing any screenwriting before, and I was so surprised when they said: "Why don't you try and do it?" But it seemed reasonable. I mean who else would do it?

JP: Had you previously been an enthusiast for the cinema?
RPJ: No, no, not at all. I'm still not; never have been. During all the years in India I hardly saw any films. I started coming out slowly in 1966, so I saw a few more . . . but I lived in India from 1951 to 1975 and really never saw anything. And that's probably why I am one of the few screenwriters who doesn't want to direct. All I supply are the things that a writer should supply, like the characters, the situations, and the dialogue. I'm perfectly content to leave everything else to other people.

JP: Is your approach to a screenplay similar to your approach to a piece of fiction, or do you write shot by shot?

RPJ: Not shot by shot, but certainly not like a piece of fiction. The process is quite different. With a novel or short story I have to do so much more. I have to do everything. With a screenplay, I make more of a plan. I know what each scene is going to be, although the scenes develop within the framework and sometimes come out not quite as I expected. I don't do this in a book. In a book I just grope about and hope for the best. In a screenplay I have got much more of an idea. Having the idea for a scene, I work towards it through the characters: mostly by means of the dialogue. I'm not really very visual myself.

JP: You don't picture the scene? The locations usually seem very important in your scripts. They seem to have been chosen quite specifically.

RPJ: No. Let me give you an example. I knew that the last film, *Hullabaloo over Georgie and Bonnie's Pictures*, was going to be set in an Indian palace, but I didn't know which one. I thought it might be Gwalior, which I hadn't seen. I knew Jodhpur quite well because we had done *Autobiography of a Princess* there. I knew lots of Indian palaces, so I knew more or less what the layout would be, more or less what I had in mind. Of course, in general, that's always there. The people are not floating around in space. But just as the characters in your mind look different from the actors who finally play them, so does the place. But you do have to have a place in mind, and all its ambience and atmosphere.

JP: Your literary style would seem easily adaptable to screenwriting. Do you feel that the cinema at all influenced your fictional writing?

RPJ: In the beginning that would be quite unconscious. Of course, I had written quite a number of novels before I wrote screenplays. I may have been influenced by the films I saw as a child more than I realized. The dialogue in my novels, however, is qualitatively different from that in the screenplays. That's always so, you can't transpose the one from the other. The dialogue in the novel has to carry all the inflections, all the intonations, everything that the speech of the actor will give it in the film. The actors put in the weight, they give it color. But in the novel you have to do all that yourself.

JP: When you were adapting *The Householder*, did you rewrite the fictional dialogue?

RPJ: Oh, yes, you can't speak fiction. This comes out especially with Henry James. It's marvelous, wonderful dialogue, but you can't speak it.

JP: You said you might have been unconsciously influenced by the films you saw as a child. Did you go to the cinema then a great deal?
RPJ: I think as a child I did. As much as other children, say once or twice a week. I used to see everything. This would be from about 1936 to 1951. When I left school, I didn't see so many films. I lost interest. I was reading a lot. During my last few years in England I didn't see so many. And then when the New Wave came in I was in India.

JP: Were you brought up on popular writers' films from Hollywood?
RPJ: I was born in Germany, where we weren't allowed to go to the cinema being Jews. Whenever I went to Holland, which was quite often, I used to see films, but they were then dubbed into Dutch. I think I must have seen my first American movies in Dutch. Then I went to England and from '40 to '45, I saw everything. I saw all the war films, and then after the War I saw some Ealing comedies, that sort of thing. I think the first European film that came my way was Rossellini's *Open City*. I did see those very strongly storied films of the thirties, very conventional, magazine stories at the center. I felt that films have to tell some sort of story. Now I live in New York and I see everything. I go just around the corner, I like it. I don't run, but I certainly see everything that everyone else sees, and I go to revival houses too. I have never actually met another screenwriter. Where could I?

JP: What was your background as a novelist?
RPJ: Just the usual influences. I started writing stories as soon as I could write, and I read everything there was to read. I wrote and wrote and had drawers full of unfinished novels, unfinished stories, and unfinished plays. And then when I was old enough, I started sending things round. My brother is very literary; he's Professor of German Literature at Oxford. He was always reading German classics, which I wasn't. I mean, I do have a certain literary background, but no actual writers in the family. I think the Jewish writer Sholem Ash is somehow related to me, or maybe only by marriage, but we certainly all came from the same town in Poland. I don't come from a background where writing would be anything strange. I was a student, and then I married, and then I went to India and then I wrote the first novel. The first novel that I actually finished and sent to a publisher was accepted. I went to four publishers and the fourth one took it. I was twenty-five when I wrote my first novel and twenty-eight when it was published. I wasn't ready to publish anything before then.

JP: Have you thought of writing screenplays for anyone other than Merchant and Ivory?
RPJ: Well, yes. I wouldn't mind. It's never come up, though. If anybody has asked me, they usually propose projects I'm not interested in. I haven't any plans to adapt any of my other works of fiction. Actually, David Mercer has adapted *Heat and Dust*. On the whole, I'd rather not do my own novels. It's not so interesting.

JP: When you finish your novels, you prefer that they be left alone?
RPJ: It's not that. I don't want to go back to them. I don't mind if somebody else does it, that's fine. I'd rather do something new. I haven't read Mercer's screenplay. That was the novel of mine which was most influenced by film. The way I'm now influenced by film is that I go into the editing room. I'm not altogether as innocent as I pretend. Now when I write a screenplay it's always with the editing room in mind. I was in the editing room from the first film onwards. I stay away from the sets. There's nothing I can do and I don't understand what's going on, I'm just in the way. I always trip over the wires. But I'm always in the editing room. Well, when they have the first rough-cuts, that's when I get interested.

JP: You are here during the shooting of *The Europeans*. Are you editing the script as they go along?
RPJ: I've been here for a week and I have been doing quite a bit. But I'll go back to New York and then come and go. I'm here now because I don't like being alone in New York. At the moment, though, I think it's a good thing that I'm here since I've been doing a lot of rewriting and seeing the actors and cutting scenes. I usually consult the actors, especially when I've made cuts, and they usually have something very interesting to add. I often make some change according to what they say. The particular danger with this script has been all this marvelous Henry James dialogue. I threw up my hands. It was awful. I put it down and then, after I had re-read it, I found that I'd still kept in too much. I mean you can't have people sitting and talking too much, however wonderful the dialogue is. You just cannot in a film.

JP: One of the nice things about the novel is the ending, the marrying off of all the couples. How are you doing that? With a voice-over?
RPJ: Eugenia and Acton is the one match that doesn't come off.

JP: Yes, but he marries a "nice girl."

RPJ: He marries a "particularly nice girl." Well we haven't got that, we haven't got the nice girl. But as Acton rides away from her house, leaving Eugenia packing, he sees the other couples dotted about the countryside.

JP: Have you changed the novel a great deal?

RPJ: I've certainly switched it around and changed the structure. I haven't changed the story, but I have changed the way the story develops. You have to build up to something central, something big. The novel is a succession of small scenes which don't build up to anything particular. We've added a ball at Mr. Acton's house to which everything builds up, and from which everything then comes down. Everything from various parts of the novel is pulled together here. Eugenia's visit to Mrs. Acton, which is an isolated incident in the book, is the center of that ball scene. And the way Eugenia feels when she comes out. She leaves Acton's house and feels she has been a failure, that's really the central part of this scene. Also Jim has to have a big party in his films: a big party and lots of meals. There were lots of meals in the book but there wasn't a big party. Henry James obviously rings bells for me. This feeling I had about Europeans coming to India, he has about Americans going to Europe. Everything he did has always struck particular bells.

JP: How did you come to *The Europeans*?

RPJ: The script was actually written three years ago, but we couldn't get money for it. We put it off from year to year, always thinking that we had to start in May, just had to start in May because that's when the novel starts. But this year Jim said, "Ah well, if we are not going to make it now, let it be the dead of winter, I don't care." That's why we're here among the fall leaves of Massachusetts. For a long time actually I thought about *Portrait of a Lady*, then about *The Bostonians* and *The Golden Bowl*. I would have longed to have done those, but they are very long and complicated and expensive. Jim just loved *The Europeans* and he loves this part of the world and he wanted to come home to America, so for him this was really the best thing to do. But I'd love to do some of the others, *Portrait of a Lady* in particular. They have found a house in Salem [the Gardner Pingree House] for Mr. Acton's house, though I don't think the ball is going to be filmed there. I think they've found another place for that.

JP: Would you like to do any other adaptations of classic American authors now that you're living in New York?

RPJ: No, I've always preferred to do original screenplays. I think I might do another film set in New York. I can't say much about this since I haven't really thought about it. It may be set among theatre groups, in lofts. I have to live in a place to write about it. I actually have to be there, to look out of the window and see the weather. Now I spend about three months of the year in India. I take with me whatever I'm doing and pretend I'm here. I don't look around in India. It's a great disability. When I think that a writer like Joyce carried Dublin everywhere, wherever he went. He unfolded it and unfolded it and it was always his interior landscape. I don't have anything like that, unfortunately. There is a storehouse of memories, but I want to be right there, to be triggered right there. I want to hear the speech rhythms of everybody round me. This is not true of the adaptations. *The Europeans* I did in India when I was still living there. The idea for the new film is a Jane Austen unpublished play. We did *Hullabaloo* for Melvyn Bragg [*The South Bank Show*, London Weekend Television], and he has the rights for the Jane Austen play. I think the play was bought by David Astor. The idea, perhaps, is to have this very advanced theatre group in New York do the play, and see what they make of it. I think there always has to be a bizarre touch to everything we do, otherwise we don't feel quite at ease.

JP: I was struck seeing *Hullabaloo* on a cinema screen how well it looked. It was, of course made for television . . .

RPJ: Yes, but, you know, whenever you have a really good film director and he makes a film for television that is a film and not a television play. I think that is the difference. I think a film director can switch, but not the other way round. We also did *Autobiography of a Princess* for television. Then I've written two television plays, one was done by Granada and the other will be done by the BBC next year.[1] I really don't think about the difference between TV and cinema audiences. But television plays are different from films; again you have to switch a bit. You can use much more dialogue. In a film, you can think much more about location, it opens up much more, the dialogue is not so important. Essentially, I think a television play is people closed up in a room talking.

JP: What about the Indian cinema?

RPJ: There's no possibility there for me. The only Indian cinema for me, as for practically everybody else, is Satyajit Ray, such a giant and so truly Indian. When I see his films, I know that I couldn't make the right film in India, because mine would only be a European view. It always seemed impossible to make our kind of films. I think the fact that we have been able to is entirely and absolutely due to Ismail. Once he has made up his mind he'll just go out and find the money somewhere, somehow. Everybody tells you it's impossible, but he's done it for years now. I just don't think about it any more. So who cares about studios? It would be nice to have some money for a change, and for him not to have to jump up and down like that and really go through such terrible things to make the films. It would be nice to have some backing, it would certainly be restful, but if that doesn't happen he'll go on doing it. He's never failed once. I think I must have the highest average in the world for screenplays that have been made. I must have written, I can't remember exactly, eight or ten—I think it's ten—and of those eight have been made. That's entirely because Ismail makes up his mind that he is going to do a film. If he wants to do a film, he'll do it.

JP: Do you feel that you are writing for a dying art?
RPJ: Good heavens, no. Have you seen the queues outside New York cinemas? For instance, *Interiors* and *Days of Heaven* are playing in New York now, I think, to absolutely packed houses with long lines outside. I think they are both very, very superior films that anybody would have been proud to make. We are always hoping that one day we will be playing to packed houses. You can't tell, it just happens that you may tap the right note. Meanwhile, our films seem to be known all right, they are shown. What more can we ask? Some very cheap films have done extremely well. It's just striking a chord somewhere, and I believe one shouldn't think about it either. You can't start off and say I'm going to do this to get a huge audience. You just can't think like that. You have to do exactly what you want to do, which is the thing that you can do best. Then if nobody comes to see it, well, too bad, try again.

JP: The two unproduced screenplays, are they just waiting for the right moment?
RPJ: No, I'll tell you exactly what they were. One was about—this was about 1966, just after *Shakespeare Wallah*—the girl, Felicity Kendal, coming to England and trying to get into acting. It was about how she got on

and was in fact her story. It was at the time of "Swinging London." We brought in a lot of that, but of course by the time we failed to raise the money "Swinging London" was over. And we got money for *The Guru* instead. Then, by the time we'd made *The Guru*, it was no longer possible. The other script was about spiritual groups in America. But by the time we didn't get the money for that, the spiritual groups seemed to be over. Anyway I think that Ismail was never really interested in that. If he had been . . . I think he really didn't like it much.

JP: Have you any other New York film projects after *Roseland*?
RPJ: I do write an awful lot for myself. The stories I'm now writing are all set in New York. That's how I get to know a place, through writing. I think that if I didn't write for myself, if I didn't do novels, I just couldn't do the screenplays. I wouldn't have, I don't know, the knowledge, the strength of background. Sometimes the two—writing fiction and screenplays—go on simultaneously; I try themes out, for instance *Autobiography of a Princess* and *Heat and Dust* were written straight after each other and the same themes were in my mind. The novels, of course, are just mine, but the films are Jim's. I think if I only wrote films I'd feel frustrated. It's only in recent years that a screenwriter gets mentioned at all. I know when I first started nobody even thought to mention me. None of the reviewers, I think, mentioned who wrote the screenplay of *Shakespeare Wallah*. And I had written lots of novels by then. It's only in recent years that people say: "Oh, yes, somebody must have written the story."

As I have always worked with the same director, I know more or less what's going to happen. They have made other films, but of course when they made a film in India I was the only person. Jim doesn't like working with amateurs. We had a lot of trouble in India, where it was very difficult to get good Indian actors who spoke English well enough. He took amateurs, and they were usually terrible. He is a director who really wants everything polished. He doesn't improvise. Something like the orphan choir in *Hullabaloo*, you know that's going to be there, you find them in every Indian town. It wasn't improvised. You know it's going to be there, just as you know a Howard Johnson's is going to be in Massachusetts. I don't discuss with Jim each day's shooting; in fact, I usually don't know what they are shooting. There aren't usually many major changes at this stage. In *The Europeans*, for instance, most of the changes that are made are due to the weather. The scenes that were to have been outside, I have to take inside, and that sort of thing.

JP: You're working on *The Europeans* now; are you also working on something else?

RPJ: While I'm writing a screenplay I do it all the time, and an original screenplay usually takes between two and three months, but now that my work is really finished and I only have to do bits, the bits I do mainly in the afternoons and in the mornings I do other things.

JP: You try to sit down every day?

RPJ: I don't try, I sit. I don't know what else to do. I don't put off—I know there are some who do—but I'm not like that. It's like practicing the piano. I mean, if I played the piano I would play it every day, and know if I didn't play one day that I'd play worse the next. It's like that with writing. I think it was all those years in India that really got me into it, because I didn't have anything else to do. I didn't really know anyone outside my family, so I was alone the whole day. When I came out, I found that there was nothing else I wanted to do. Henry James was only an inveterate diner-out when he was young, afterwards he couldn't stand it. He used to have these visits from Edith Wharton. When he was younger he could take it, but later he would go crazy. She would swoop down and take him out in her big motorcar. He used to dread those visits. All he wanted to do was to get back home. I see that with other writers, too. After a time that's all they want to do.

JP: I believe that Leon Edel cast his eye over your screenplay and pronounced it fitting, but that this carried no weight with the National Endowment for the Arts in Washington.

RPJ: Did Ismail tell you that? Yes, Jim wrote to the National Endowment and asked them what projects they had approved, since they'd turned down Henry James. The projects were all by people who hadn't made any films at all. Then he asked for the reports of the committee on *The Europeans*, and they were all written by academics. They said, oh, *The Europeans* isn't a good novel. Literally one of them said that.

---

1. Never done. *Jane Austen in Manhattan* (1980) was written for London Weekend Television.

Ismail Merchant:
Snowballs to Eskimos

Charles Newman/1984

From *AIP & Co.* 56 (July 1984): 23–29. Reprinted by permission of the estate of Charles Newman.

There is a thread which connects Bombay with Cologne, Berkeley in California, Leamington Spa, and Russia. Difficult to be too precise, but it's the same line that links films like *The Europeans, Heat and Dust,* and *Savages.*

Of course, the line is Merchant-Ivory Productions. The places all feature in the biographies of the three central personas in the company; they all help explain a little here, a little there. And the films are just some of the MIP catalogue. In twenty-one years the catalogue has grown fast—sometimes on shoestrings—to more than twenty features, shorts, and TV films.

Ruth Prawer Jhabvala was born in Cologne in 1927 to Russian and Jewish parents. She escaped in the thirties to a strange Britain and escaped again, through marriage, to India. There she is at home. She says it might be something to do with the oriental element in her Jewish background. She writes most of the scripts that MIP produce.

James Ivory directs. He is from the US West Coast, a prosperous timber background and Irish/Louisiana French parents. His first film was about Venice, completed after a comfortable two years US national service. It was his interest in India that led to a meeting with Ismail Merchant in 1961.

Ismail Merchant was born a Muslim in the predominantly Hindu world of Bombay. His parents were prosperous supporters of the nationalist Muslim League with professional ambitions for their son—the only boy in a large family of girls. Like almost everyone in India, Merchant was obsessed with cinema from an early age. At first it was strictly Hollywood. Then, after university in India and a business course in New York, he turned from Hollywood to European film. Then, relentlessly, back to India. Ismail Merchant is the producer.

Mr. Fix-It

Merchant started life in films as a committed Mr. Fix-it. Surely the only thread that draws his own father, a dozen or so Wall Street bankers, Volkswagen USA, and a wealthy Oregon timber family together is the fact that they have all, at one time or another, financed Merchant's films. And then there are the film companies themselves—Merchant has worked with Fox, Rank, Hemdale, The National Film Finance Corporation, London Weekend Television, Channel 4, the BBC, New World Pictures, Gaumont in Paris, American International Pictures, and Columbia.

"No deal is easy with more than two people involved although most of our work has been financed that way," says Ismail Merchant. "It's never easy to have to deal with three or four sets of lawyers, each with their own pattern of thinking. Sometimes you have to know when you can push them, and just how far. That's difficult. But we're very clear about one thing. We make our own deals. We don't compromise on anything creative." Of course, that's what they all say, but Merchant's success—commercial as well as creative—is built on independence.

"For us each film is our own; we have a very close intimate relationship with each one. We want to give each one the best possible chance—so we give it the best marketing, we do our own campaigns, our own posters, our own brochures. Did you see our brochure at Cannes? It was the best. Better than anything EMI or Goldcrest could do. For most distributors films are commodities. We can't take that approach. We aren't big enough to be able to afford to do that. We keep every one of our film—nineteen of them—alive and off the shelf."

The commitment is complete. Ismail Merchant is an entrepreneur and he believes that that's essential to the success of Merchant-Ivory Productions. "We keep it small out of choice," he says. "Get too big and you lose contact with your product, you start to sell it like just another commodity—and you can't do that with films. They're all different and they all need different treatment." He believes that the presentation of a film in the eyes of a potential audience is a key factor in success. And, over the years, especially in the UK with his association with Wingate/ Curzon, he's managed that.

Entrepreneurial Style

Although his last release, *Heat and Dust* [1982], boasted production values markedly higher than previous work, Merchant believes that keeping a very close rein on the purse-strings is a necessary condition of an entrepreneurial style. "We've grown considerably in the last two years with offices now in New York and London as well as Bombay and we have expanded our personnel. Budgets have increased too. *The Bostonians*, due for release in September in selected venues in the US, London, and India, cost $3.5m—expensive by our standards, but every penny went on the screen. We don't like expense accounts and expensive cars and all that sort of thing."

Keeping Merchant-Ivory product alive is an important job for the company but—and the number of Merchant-Ivory retrospectives in the last few years are a testimony to this—it pays off. Titles like *Shakespeare Wallah*, dating from its first showing in 1965 still pop up some time, somewhere in the world. The important cultural themes that run through much of MIP's work help. And theatrical exposure is only a small part—although an important one—of the various revenue sources exploited. "We go for a selected theatrical release, typically grossing between 20 and 30 per cent of income, then cable operators—HBO and Showtime bought *Heat and Dust* for example for around $1.4m—then to video after a year, then into syndication." And then, once more, back into selected theatrical release.

And Ismail Merchant is a salesman too. "My principal at college in New York told me that I could sell snowballs to Eskimos," he remembers, and, as he sits there, elegant, assured, smiling, you can begin to see the potential for a big market up there on the ice flows. But Merchant is not just a salesman—he has an important creative input into the products that he sells to his financiers and, ultimately, to the audience. "Jim and Ruth have the ideas," says Paul Bradley, Ismail Merchant's London man, "but it's Ismail that catches the spark and fans it into a flame."

The Merchant-Ivory catalogue is long, and probably more varied than most would expect. First was *The Householder* which was premiered in October 1963. Then *Shakespeare Wallah* which put the new company on the art-house map. It cost $80,000 and gave Felicity Kendal her first film role (the film was loosely based on her family's adventures bringing the word of the Bard to benighted India). It was funny, sad, deep enough to be taken "seriously," ambiguous, and idiosyncratic. All good box office—in a small box office.

Then came *The Guru*, which benefited from a certain topicality (this was April 1969) although it centered on one of the company's characteristic themes. Cost: $86,000 from Fox. Apparently, Merchant wasn't happy with the way Fox promoted the film, thus leading to his future insistence on retaining marketing functions for his company's work. The UK film crews shipped in for *Guru* hated India, the male lead was arrested for being a communist (true life starts here in India), and, perhaps, the whole thing was not one of Ismail Merchant's happiest projects. After that came *Bombay Talkie*—centered on the huge world of the Indian film industry.

Wall Street Finance

It was an expensive film by Merchant-Ivory's standards—$110,000—but it was financed by a large clutch of individual Wall Street financiers that Merchant had managed to put together. He wasn't prepared to run the risk of big-film company finance if it meant that MIP would lose control.

Bombay Talkie starred one of the Merchant-Ivory regulars, Shashi Kapoor. Others that owe their exposure in the West almost entirely to Merchant-Ivory include Madhur Jaffrey and Zohra Segal. It was the strange strengths and paradoxical artistic achievement of Indian film and filmmaking that was to be the subject of a Merchant-Ivory TV documentary about *Helen*, a superstar entertainer in India which was shown in 1971. Before that came another TV program, *Adventures of a Brown Man*, shown on BBC2 in 1970.

Savages was a relatively successful art-film based on muddy aliens evolving into high, East Coast Vanderbiltesque society and marveling at it all. Merchant handled the distribution at first, four-walled it in New York after which it was taken up by a group of sub-distributors. Merchant lost all the extant prints. Only the negative was rescued from oblivion (just). Some more lessons learned. Now the film is a strong part of the Merchant-Ivory catalogue.

A short called *Mahatma and the Mad Boy* and *Autobiography of a Princess* followed; the latter for US television and underwritten by Volkswagen. Next was *The Wild Party* with Raquel Welch and James Coco in a period piece about—a wild party. Merchant-Ivory were hired for the film by the producers, American International Pictures. What happened to the film after it was made is too complicated to bother about. It must have been a relief to produce *Sweet Sounds*, something about children making improvised music.

The next period of Merchant-Ivory activity represents a transition from a company that had produced a couple of interesting art films to a real production house. Ivory instigated *Roseland*, an American story, albeit with special elements of culture-confrontation. *The Five Forty-Eight* was written and financed for US television, followed by *The Europeans* (NFFC, May 1979), and *Jane Austen in Manhattan* (1980), which was a TV film, at least partly financed by London Weekend. Previously the company had made *Hullabaloo over Georgie and Bonnie's Pictures*, also financed by London Weekend for the *South Bank Show* to the tune of £250,000. It was screened in September 1978. Then came *Quartet* about the relationship between Ford Madox Ford and Jean Rhys and financed by French Gaumont, Fox in London, and New World Pictures of Los Angeles. Last, but by no means least, and not last either for that matter, was *Heat and Dust*—certainly the most widely seen Merchant-Ivory film in the UK at least.

Two Films a Year

There is no shortage of future projects—the company is hoping to produce two films a year from now on. *The Bostonians* features Vanessa Redgrave and Christopher Reeve in the Henry James story and will open in London, New York, and Bombay in September. *Comrades*, about the "Tolpuddle Martyrs," the British trade union pioneers, directed by Bill Douglas is due for release next May. *The Deceivers* is an Indian-set film based on John Masters's novel and is due for autumn of next year, and *Twins of Three Continents*—again, set predominantly in India—should open later in 1985.

James Ivory: An Interview

Pat Anderson/1984

From *Films in Review* 35, no. 8 (October 1984): 478–80. Reprinted by permission of Roy Frumkes, editor.

Tall, handsome, mellifluous voiced, James Ivory has traveled far from his native California, teaming up with Ismail Merchant from India and Ruth Prawer Jhabvala (from Germany and England) who is married to an Indian. From this collaboration have come some marvelous and marvelously diverse films. The only thing they all have in common is a meticulous attention to detail, with every object (even the tiniest) perfect for its period and every setting completely fitting the subject.

I talked with James Ivory while he was in the midst of editing *The Bostonians*, for which he is finally getting the popular recognition he deserves. He said he had never read Henry James until Ruth Jhabvala brought this quintessential American writer to his attention. "The first book she gave to me to read was *The Europeans*, then I went through them all. But it's very hard to get financing for a Henry James story. I spent many years trying with *The Europeans* and finally got the money from Britain. And the same with this one: a little American money but, again, the English came up with most of it. Henry James just isn't box office here, apparently. He's more appreciated in England."

The Ivory, Merchant, Jhabvala collaboration has lasted twenty-three years, is still going strong, and has recently received a retrospective at the Museum of Modern Art. Of course they have their differences. "Ruth and I wouldn't push something on Ismail that he didn't really want to do. But he pretty much leaves us alone. He doesn't involve himself in the writing at all. Occasionally when he reads a script, he'll make some suggestion—like 'Couldn't you develop this character or this or that scene?' But he doesn't obtrude himself.

"There were times when he's suggested actors for parts that I have felt weren't absolutely right. He's insisted that they would be right and gone over my head and cast somebody in a big part. And those people have turned out to be fantastic! For example, he was convinced that James Mason was just *the* person for *Autobiography of a Princess.* We went through a whole bunch of people like John Gielgud, Ralph Richardson, Michael Redgrave, I mean a whole series of them. None of them could do it. He kept saying 'James Mason, James Mason. Oh, he'll be good. You must try James Mason.' Ruth and I kept saying we weren't sure. Finally he just cast it. He sent Mason the script and he cast him anyway. When we heard about it we were very alarmed, but from the very first moment that Mason worked on the film he was perfection.

"The same thing happened with Maggie Smith on *Quartet.* I had mixed feelings about her. I don't know why. I hadn't really seen that much of her work, but I felt she just wasn't the right person. Again, as with James Mason, I accepted Maggie Smith. After all, she is one of the great, great actresses—and it was one of the most wonderful things that ever happened to me. On one or two occasions, however, Ismail has wanted a particular actor but when I've told him if he insists on casting that actor the film will be ruined, he's withdrawn.

"But again, Ismail wanted Vanessa Redgrave very much for this film. I wanted as much as possible to have a completely American cast. But we were never able to make that work out. We couldn't get a suitable American actress to play that kind of part. So we sent Vanessa Redgrave the script, and she's marvelous. So I accepted her, English though she is with an English accent. In the thirties and forties they used to hire English actors all the time for American films to play upper-class parts, remember? So I suppose I accepted her on that basis.

"I was very keen to do something of Jean Rhys's, but Ruth felt that Jean Rhys was too low-spirited and that there was something depressing about the material—that it wouldn't really make a good film, but I kept after her. I had always liked *Quartet*, and eventually Ruth agreed that, okay, she'd adapt it."

Asked how much he or Ismail Merchant were involved in Mrs. Jhabvala's novels, Ivory responded, "I wouldn't say at all. She has certain ideas that she follows and thinks out for herself as a writer that have nothing to do with us, except that because of the films we've made together she's been taken out of the world she was in when we first knew her, which was India and only a particular part of India. We've taken her out of that world and into all kinds of other worlds she had never seen before. And because of all the time Ruth's spent in editing rooms in the course of our films, she does say that first, she's picked up subject matter and become acquainted with places and people that she never would have otherwise, and second, that certain techniques of writing have suggested themselves to her from the process of editing films. In that way Ruth's scriptwriting and filmmaking have had an effect on her novels and her short story writing."

On the subject of their pictures that have been successful without being star vehicles, Ivory said: "If we're lucky to get the right star, I mean the right star for the right part, then, of course, it's a great bonus. So far I think we have not been in that bad situation where we have had a star who turns out to be someone who is utterly wrong; all of the people we've used are very good. I think one of the reasons is that we don't so much present them as stars as we treat them, or use them, as actors, which they respect. A good example of this was Christopher Reeve in *The Bostonians*. It made him happy to be working with the other people— not in a star-like situation where he was the dominant person and everything revolved around him, but rather as part of the ensemble. And he went along with that very, very well and he did a really terrific job. He's marvelous. And another great thing about it is that he's the master of the spoken phrase. People don't know that. People will see in *The Bostonians* he's extremely gifted."

For the last twenty-five years James Ivory has made his home in New York, though he misses California and would like to make films there. As a young man on the West Coast, Ivory enrolled as an architectural student at the University of Oregon then switched to Fine Arts. At that time he had no special reason to become interested in India. "It wasn't as thought I had a childhood preoccupation with India. It was completely accidental and was based on my seeing *The River* and later on seeing a group of miniature Indian paintings. And then, most important, seeing the films of Ray, the Apu trilogy. That's what really got me started—a combination of things spread out over a period of six or so years. But as a child I had no interest in India as such. And the fine arts courses I took were always concerned with Western painting: Italian, Spanish, principally. No Indian, Persian, Chinese, Japanese. Nothing. Something just clicked but why, I don't know. Mysterious. Maybe you just up and grab something and try and make it your own."

There is no desire on the part of this gifted director to act or direct for the stage. "I think maybe I don't have that kind of patience. Though the making of films is a long dragged-out process, you do get some immediate gratification. You don't when you work on the stage, having to check what you do with the actors and analyzing the script with actors and so on. You get results a lot quicker in films. It's instant gratification. I accept the fact I might have to work over six or eight months to prepare a film, but I don't think I'd have the kind of patience to create successful stage performances. That's what strikes me. When you're making a film and got your location, you can look through the camera and see it all. It all takes form quickly right in front of you. It comes together, of course you have to keep doing that over and over for each different shot. But it's quicker, it's more fun. The other seems laborious to me. I'm sure that's a completely wrong personal impression. Any stage director would say that's nonsense, but that's how it seems to me.

"I hope after *The Bostonians* to do a modern story that takes place here and a little bit in India. It's a marvelous story that Ruth's working on. She is writing it as a novel rather than as a screenplay. Sometimes screenplays are just sort of pasted together. Even quite good writers get caught up in this superficiality, rather than in the definition of character and situation. So we'll see what it will be."

The Trouble with Olive: Divine Madness in Massachusetts

James Ivory/1985

From *Sight and Sound* 54, no. 2 (Summer 1985): 95–100. Reprinted by permission of the British Film Institute.

Ask any director and he'll tell you there's actress A, B, or C (it could also be actor X, Y, or Z) he's crazy to work with some day. Vanessa Redgrave was at the head of my list, and when Merchant-Ivory started to think seriously about *The Bostonians*—or as soon as there was a script—we got in touch with her. She was our first choice for the part of Olive Chancellor, but she turned it down. This was the spring of 1981. Since we were in London we asked her to dinner in order to talk about it, even though we knew she felt negative about the project.

It was not the first time we had gone to her. We had offered her the part Lee Remick played in *The Europeans*, and there had been much going forward and backward then. She liked the part, but when we were ready she decided to stand for election as well as to appear in Ibsen's *The Lady from the Sea*. Later, not knowing we'd already shot *The Europeans*, she wrote me a letter saying she would like to play the Baroness Munster if we ever did that film. Something like that happened with *Quartet*, until the part of Lois Heidler was offered at last to Maggie Smith, who snapped it up, whereupon Vanessa announced that she was free after all, but by then it was too late. So this time after she'd said no I wrote to ask if she were *very* sure. She came to dinner at Anthony Korner's flat in Cornwall Gardens where we were staying, to tell us her reasons, trudging up the four flights as she must have done hundreds of times in other tall English houses, campaigning or gathering names for some petition. She was wearing tweeds and sturdy shoes and her glasses.

She had little to say about Olive that night; it was as if she had already put her out of her mind and wanted to go on to other topics. Olive Chancellor wasn't a woman she could identify with easily, or that she had any feeling for. She didn't see herself as that character. Because Olive was a rich Boston bluestocking? She would not be pinned down.

We then ate dinner. During the salad she began a monologue, not looking at us but staring at the wood of the tabletop, her face half in shadow. To give a better idea of her here I will quote E. M. Forster's description of Charlotte Bartlett in *A Room with a View*: "... as she spoke her long narrow head drove forwards, slowly, regularly, as though she were demolishing some invisible obstacle. . . ." This harangue, delivered in a low, hollow-sounding monotone, like the prophecy of an oracle sitting in a cave, and mainly about the forces of evil generated by most governments, went on for some time as we—her obstacles?—nervously plucked string beans out of a bowl. What we could not appreciate was that the style of this piece would be duplicated in every gesture and intonation three years later as Olive Chancellor, with head bent and eyes lowered, reproved the worldly if ill-informed Mrs. Burrage in the following scene from *The Bostonians*:

> Olive: You seem to think that I control Verena's actions and her desires, and that I'm jealous of any other relations she may possibly form. I can only say your attitude illustrates the way (demolishing object) that relations between women are still misunderstood and misinterpreted. It is these attitudes we want to fight. With all our strength and all our life, Miss Tarrant—Verena—and I.

The climax of this somewhat dismaying evening (dismaying in that one could not help thinking, "Oh where is the quicksilver Vanessa Redgrave of our dreams, the Vanessa Redgrave of *Blow Up* and *Morgan*, the valiant creature that was *Isadora*?") came when she asked my partner, Ismail Merchant, for a very substantial donation for the *News Line*, the paper of her Workers' Revolutionary Party. The paper's cost had to be raised five pence per issue, putting it out of reach of many; our contribution, a kind of subsidy, would help make up the printer's losses. The buck was passed to me and I told her some narrow-eyed Yankee lie about seeing what I could do. After this, she left.

Many months later, during a blizzard in London, she called Ismail to ask him to come out and march against Ronald Reagan's Central American policies. He lay in a warm bed, drowsily watching a movie on TV.

The wind roared, snow blew about, the windows had iced over, while Vanessa's armies were gathering in—I think—Kensington High Street. This made us sad. Brave, noble, wrongheaded being!

Thus ends the first phase of our relationship with, and a way of thinking about, Vanessa Redgrave. We did not do *The Bostonians*, we made *Heat and Dust* instead, while at about the same time she was getting into difficulties with the Boston Symphony Orchestra over—apparently— having so openly championed the Palestine Liberation Organization. We sent our script out to other actresses for their consideration. We did not have much success with it, which seems strange since Olive Chancellor is certainly one of the great Henry James characters and one of his most fascinating women. Forty years ago Katharine Hepburn could have played the part, but the suggestion of lesbianism within the central triangle of the story would have kept Hollywood away.

At the beginning of the novel James describes Olive's first encounter with her enemy, Basil Ransom: "... a smile of exceeding faintness played about her lips—it was just perceptible enough to light up the native gravity of her face. It might have been likened to a thin ray of moonlight resting on the wall of a prison." She is last seen by him (and by the audience of the film) in her dash to the platform at the end: "[It] might have seemed to him that she hoped to find the fierce expiation she sought for in exposure to the thousands she had disappointed and deceived, in offering herself to be trampled to death and torn to pieces. She might have suggested to him some feminine firebrand of Paris revolutionaries, erect on a barricade, or even the sacrificial figure of Hypatia, whirled through the furious mob of Alexandria. . . ." In between there are fierce confrontations between Olive and a gallery of adversaries—scenes in which good actresses (and even some mediocre ones) may shine; scenes of passionate avowals to a cause and to love, and scenes showing how that love is manipulated, as well as a whole range of jealousies to find expression. Who would turn down such a role?

Directors like to think that any role they offer an actor is an irresistible one, and when it is turned down it is often the actor who seems to them to fall short of the mark, and not the part. Directors are in the position of powerful if importuning lovers; rejection hurts, because in offering a part to someone a director has taken an important step, has said in effect, "I trust you." Therefore the rejection of a starring role based on a great figure of our literature seems incomprehensible, a perversity. The analogy to a spurned lover is not inexact; depending on how attracted you are, you continue the pursuit, or you move on to someone else. The first of these was Blythe Danner, who turned down the part; then Meryl Streep, who also turned it down. We hit on Sigourney Weaver, at that time being groomed by her agents at International Creative Management to be a "big, big star." She kept us dangling for a month while she fretted. Wasn't Olive a bitter old maid, a probable lesbian, and a man-hating spinster? Wasn't she dowdy? And dried up? Could Sigourney's dashing new image that was being refashioned out of the approving reviews for her film *The Year of Living Dangerously* accommodate all those bad words? She was being hailed as the 1980s Vanessa Redgrave.

Christopher Reeve, in agreeing to play Basil Ransom, had consultation rights in the casting of Olive and Verena. He now suggested Glenn Close as a potential Olive. I'd never seen her work, but I liked the way she looked and spoke when I met her. I went to see *The World According to Garp* and felt encouraged by the material she'd chosen. In that film she played a virulent man-hater; compared to this, Olive Chancellor's views on that subject seem almost benign. But then it turned out that Glenn Close was also having image problems. The tragedy for actresses in both the United States and Britain is that by the time they have established themselves, they're often no longer young—or they don't *feel* they're really young anymore, so everything they do after thirty is seen in terms of the "right career move" and of enhancing their image as a saleable commodity.

With Glenn Close, who proved later that she could be winning on Broadway in *The Real Thing*—could be soft and feminine, that is—the risk was in doing another castrator. Wouldn't she be typecast? *The Big Chill* hadn't come out—and influential people hadn't seen her in it yet. I began to read her hesitation as resisting me. *Heat and Dust* was screened for her. We presented it to her beforehand as a film with complex characters, a film in which people are seen in varied lights, good and bad, and still manage to come across as sympathetic. After the screening we had this conversation in Ismail's office:

> Close: I had some trouble with *Heat and Dust*. I felt you were sort of removed from your characters.
> Ivory: Me? *(getting red in the face)* I reject that . . .
> Close: *(shrinking down inside her raincoat)* I'm sorry. I only meant . . .
> Ivory: *(looking over the top of her head)* reject that totally.

She said she needed a month to think about our offer, but meanwhile terms were gone into and some provisional dates were set aside. We left for Cannes with *Heat and Dust*. What we didn't know was that her agent, Clifford Stevens, was in negotiations for her over *The Natural*, starring opposite Robert Redford, and for a lot of money.

Meanwhile Vanessa Redgrave came back into our lives. As Glenn Close debated in New York, Ismail, who can't stand indecisiveness in any form and feared we would lose more time if she ended up saying no, sent *The Bostonians* screenplay to Vanessa, whose career seemed to have stalled because of the fall-out over her PLO and anti-Zionist stands. She read it and came right back: she wanted the part very much. Ismail cautioned her that Glenn Close had also been offered the part and was hesitating; she hadn't definitely turned it down.

Now Clifford Stevens had a brainstorm. Why couldn't his client play *both* parts, and commute between Boston and Buffalo, New York, where *The Natural* was to be shot? She would only be needed in Buffalo for ten days; if we agreed to this, she would play Olive Chancellor. Used to these kinds of arrangements in India, we said we'd try to work it out. Glenn Close still had many reservations about who and what Olive Chancellor was—she wanted to read the revised script before she *really* committed herself—but she said she'd go to London for costume fittings. Vanessa, somewhat irritated by now, waited to see what would happen, while the production managers of the two films tried to work out a schedule. Such situations are a nightmare for low-budget films. A single episode of an airport being fogged in would cost us thousands of dollars. The more comfortably financed film would be able to absorb losses like that without difficulty.

Glenn, back in New York from the fittings for *The Bostonians*, now read the new script. It did nothing to allay her fears and if anything intensified them. So I, from Boston, set up a meeting between her and Ruth Jhabvala. On that same day Clifford Stevens escalated his demands for more shooting days for his client on *The Natural*, saying that it was "*vital* for Glenn to work in that film." The ten days became fifteen, and that might not be the end of it. If we wanted Glenn, he told Ismail over the telephone from New York, the "bottom line" was that we would have to release her not only *when* she wanted to go to Buffalo, but as *often* as she wanted to go. At this, a furious Ismail, acting in the imperial style of the Hollywood czars of yore, gave orders from London to an underling to fire the leading lady and, rapidly passing on to more important matters, set about replacing her with Vanessa Redgrave.

While all these telephone calls were being made, Glenn Close was making progress in Ruth Jhabvala's Manhattan apartment on an under-

standing of Olive's character. Every obstacle had been overcome and actress and screenwriter had passed on to fictitious projections of Olive's
future: how that tragically disappointed lady, once she had climbed
down from the lectern in the Music Hall, would catch some slow, wast-
ing disease and soon die, etc. All fired up and ready to start work, Glenn
Close made her way to her agent's office, and in the midst of reporting
that her problems with the script had been settled, the telephone rang.
This was the MIP underling—if one may call, for the purposes of this
tale, the dignified production manager Ted Morley an underling. He was
calling from *The Bostonians* Company in Cambridge, Massachusetts. The
unexpected news was relayed. I knew nothing of this drama; while it was
going on I was in an airplane. When I reached La Guardia Airport, Ruth
Jhabvala told me what had taken place. That evening in London, Vanessa went to Cosprop, the costumiers, for fittings. When it was found possible to sew a foot or so of cloth on to the hem of Glenn Close's dresses,
which were far along by this time, that was done and other things were
packed which Vanessa had worn in *Wagner*.

There is a moral in all this, I think, for agents who use too peremptory
a tone with the prospective employers of their clients: it may happen
that a preferred first choice for a part is suddenly available. And though
Glenn Close rendezvoused successfully with Robert Redford in Buffalo, I
sometimes felt her ghost hovering over our shoot. I felt—I still feel, perhaps illogically—that I owe her a film.

II

In April 1982 Vanessa Redgrave was in effect fired by the Boston Symphony Orchestra without notice when a series of performances of *Oedipus Rex* at Symphony Hall in Boston and Carnegie Hall in New York
were cancelled. She had been engaged to narrate the Stravinsky work.
No official reason was given for the Symphony's action, but it was widely suspected that her well-publicized sympathies for the PLO made her
unacceptable to the Symphony's Jewish trustees and fund-raisers. There
had been unsubstantiated rumors of threats of uproar and violence by
the Jewish Defense League if she were allowed to perform and the Symphony management was thought to have panicked, justifying their action to themselves on the grounds of public safety. News of all this—or
just some bad rumors—had a sort of domino effect in New York and she
lost a Broadway part because of the cancellation. For fourteen months
after that she did no work.

She decided to sue the Orchestra, alleging that she had been denied her civil rights under a new and still untested Massachusetts statute, and asked for damages. Her going to court was no small thing. As it developed, she was taking on the Boston establishment. At first only she took her suit seriously, and it was dismissed as having merely a nuisance value. Boston's artistic community took sides and in time the Boston Museum of Fine Arts, the Athenaeum Library, and the Fogg Museum at Harvard all lined up behind the Orchestra, declining to host benefit premieres of *The Bostonians* because the star of the film was in litigation with their "sister organization."

Influential members of Boston's Jewish community were saying that the cancellation of *Oedipus Rex* had been a disgrace to the city; old friends weren't speaking to each other any more. In this atmosphere we arrived in Boston with Vanessa to make *The Bostonians*.

We stayed long enough there to have rehearsals and then the unit moved to Newport, Rhode Island, our first location. Some of us—Vanessa, Christopher Reeve, Madeleine Potter, and Merchant-Ivory-Jhabvala—put up at "Richmere," a turn-of-the-century Newport "cottage" that was being run as an executive retreat. Life seemed to center around the kitchen, where Vanessa did a lot of the cooking. We were doing night shooting next door at Château-sur-Mer, and she prepared herself every afternoon with large servings of steak tartare. This kitchen was the scene of heavy script conferences. Strengthened by years of polemical discussion and doubtless by her steak tartare, Vanessa began to bear down ideologically on *The Bostonians* and on Henry James, who was not there to defend himself, and on Ruth Jhabvala, who had imagined that all this sort of thing had already been gotten through.

Was not the reactionary Basil Ransom a "nigger-beater," Vanessa asked? Was he not deeply evil, and should he not therefore be made to seem more satanic? Had Ruth showed this clearly enough? Hadn't she made Basil much too *sympathetic*? Shouldn't he be shown in his true colors so that she, Olive, by contrast could shine forth—not be seen just as a hysterical eccentric, but as a figure of righteousness? That being the case, added Madeleine Potter, she—Verena—didn't want to be put in a bad light by *loving* Basil, she was only there to *reform* him. Since Basil was so villainous, wasn't her attraction to him suspect? There was about Madeleine Potter and Vanessa Redgrave's relationship throughout the film a similarity to that of a mama bird and a baby bird: the mama bird flies down with a worm, the baby bird goes Cheep, Cheep and opens its beak; the mama bird puts the worm in.

It hardly needs saying that Christopher Reeve knew nothing of these discussions, had no idea they were going on; but when Basil and Verena were out on one of their rare dates together—at Harvard, or walking by the sea at Marmion—it seemed to him that Verena, the character, wasn't having as much fun in his company as she should be. Why was that? Why at first did she wear a look of such concentration, frowning down at the path and kicking at stones when she should be smiling up into his face? Why did she seem so often to be on the verge of tears?

Some people said that Vanessa too was often on the verge of tears, because she was forced to spend so much time in enemy territory, i.e., Boston, a place that had shown itself to be hostile to her, and that the strain of being there made her tense and unhappy. Furthermore, she was helping to prepare her case for trial, which caused her to spend a lot of time on the telephone with her New York–based lawyers, adding further to the strain. These things may have been true, but the principal impression she made on most people was that she was having a good time in Boston.

There were no threats, no pickets, none of the disruptions which were supposed to take place when she appeared in public as a performer. She was always visible and accessible, in a way Christopher Reeve could not be. She carried requests for autographs in to him and when he'd signed she brought them out again to distribute and posed for photographs. She did not try to push her political views on her co-workers, as we had been told in England she might try to do. Some people said she elected herself the shop steward for the actors and extras hired for the film; others that nobody else wanted the job and somebody had to do it. Every morning she went through the *New York Times*, the *Boston Globe*, and the *Wall Street Journal* during hair and make-up time, reading aloud articles which interested her and puffing on a cigarette. When she arrived on set, all corseted, her petticoats rustling, murmuring to the throng, the feather on her hat high above other people's heads as she passed through, she was a queen by natural right and in everything she did or said.

But it seems to me that her recent identification with the People, meaning the underprivileged and disenfranchised, has perhaps had the unconscious effect of politicizing her portrayals of members of the Privileged, so that she can make them seem the monsters her propaganda says they are. Thinking of herself for so long as a People's Revolutionary, in her playing she has effaced some of her natural *noblesse oblige*. In her mind perhaps she has become a Woman of the People, who never possessed that quality, and who cannot easily introduce it when called on to be a fastidious great lady thrown among the nasty proletariat—as during the scene of the Tarrants' tea party in *The Bostonians*, at which she made faces and noises to indicate ostentatious distaste.

This led to our only real row, but when I tried to tone her down a bit she refused to take my direction; for the only time in my life I left the set, saying I'd come back when she agreed to do it my way, without all that sneering. In the lunch line by accident I hit on the key word that would bring her round: I told her that her morning's work had had the unfortunate effect of making Olive seem a little *common*, and after we went back she was more in character again. This episode is strange, because you could say Vanessa Redgrave's whole life of idealism and generosity to others (though not to Zionists) is a lesson in *noblesse oblige*, carried sometimes to lengths of real deprivation for her and personal sacrifice for the causes—mostly unpopular—she supports.

There were other scenes like these. When are there not, on a film set? She could be as stiff-necked as Olive out of a sense that she was right and the rest of us deeply wrong. On a bad day this could be carried to ludicrous lengths, when a detail—any detail: a line of dialogue, some bit of action, a prop, a piece of costume—seemed to her to be invested with the full weight of the entire enterprise, an absolute moral weight, so that if she did not get her way everything would be compromised. If I had said to her, "Vanessa, you *cannot* wear that dresser scarf around your neck," her mood might have been spoiled and the scene reduced. These eccentricities seemed a small price to pay for the performance I could see she was giving. In the end we parted as friends and collaborators. This was the second way I learned to look at her and to think about her, in the course of the intense relationship, tinged with lunacy, that a film shoot forges between director and star.

III

She went back to England—to a successful production at the Haymarket Theatre of her father's adaptation of *The Aspern Papers*, opposite Christopher Reeve and Dame Wendy Hiller; to Cannes, with *The Bostonians*, where the French seemed almost desperately grateful to see her, and ready to admire her in the film; and finally back to Boston for a WGBH production about the Salem witch trials, and to her own suit against the Boston Symphony Orchestra. Meanwhile, *The Bostonians* opened in America, where it became a popular success and, for her, a critical triumph. No one picketed outside Cinema One in New York. And not one critic commented on her English accent. I attribute people's acceptance of her as an upper-class Bostonian to a kind of holdover from Hollywood films of the 1930s and 40s, fed by television and revival house re-runs. An "aristocratic" American woman always had good diction in those films, sounded distinctly Anglophile if not English. It was a speech convention; American actresses were trained to speak well then (and they got some first-class lines to deliver also). Bette Davis, of course, but also Myrna Loy and Mary Astor. We remember the cultivated Mid-Atlantic accents of Olivia de Havilland and Joan Fontaine. That's how a lady talked (and anyway, there's a popular belief in the United States that a Boston Brahmin sounds like an Englishman).

When Vanessa Redgrave finally took the witness stand at her own trial in October 1984, this impression was enhanced for those of us who could remember films like *The Letter.* She was a very distressed lady whose good name has been dragged in the mud, speaking, the *Boston Globe* reported, in "a clear and carrying voice." The paper also commented that she played her voice "the way Rostropovich plays the cello." Was this consummate performance to be her greatest? Or had she dragged her own name in the mud?

The issues of the case were tangled and the positions of both sides were seen to be compromised in the course of the testimony. Vanessa Redgrave was asking for damages, but not solely for breach of contract. She held that, because she had been fired by the Orchestra, she had lost much other work by having become the victim of blacklisting. She also maintained that her Civil Rights had been abridged. The Symphony set out to demolish these arguments. They now stated that the official reason for the cancellation of her contract was that her presence was an invitation to disorder and possible violence. At the least, no music would have been played, none of her fine words spoken. In addition, members of the Orchestra threatened a boycott if she appeared, though they were reminded by the Symphony management that their contracts had a No-Strike provision.

The trial was full of these murky reversals. Oppressed workers were also her oppressors. But the sight of the completed jury must have reassured her: other workers (of whom only two had ever attended a concert at the elitist Symphony Hall), a self-employed electrician, a furniture restorer, a clerk, a janitor, etc. When they heard testimony of the kind of money she would make from her films before she was blacklisted, their eyes grew round: $250,000, $350,000, $400,000. What she'd managed to eke out since didn't sound so bad either: more than $200,000.

There are countries where a jury might not feel much sympathy at hearing the beautiful lady on the witness stand describe how she had lost a million and had to console herself with a couple of hundred thousand. But in a country where so many people are hooked on the endearing antics of the rich shown in serials like *Dallas* and *Dynasty* and *Falcon Crest*, she would not be the subject of envy or censure. She hadn't even *inherited* her money, she'd made it for herself. It would only be right to try to console her, which the jury subsequently did. Her attorneys, Daniel Kornstein and Marvin Wexler, argued that what was at stake in this case was a fundamental American principle: "to keep your job even if they don't like what you stand for." Their courtroom manner was restrained, their questioning of witnesses seemingly tentative, matching the tone of super-politeness set by Vanessa Redgrave.

One of the principal witnesses for the plaintiff was the twenty-seven-year-old Peter Sellars, who was to have directed *Oedipus Rex*. He gave his reasons to the court for wanting her as narrator, citing, according to the *Globe*, her "fiery directness" and the appropriate timbre of her voice. "She has the ability to deliver flat unequivocal statements that build to the height of tragedy." He thought of his narrator as a dispassionate television news anchor, "bringing us the bad news." When, in the hours of panic and muddle before the cancellation, it seemed to the Orchestra management that there was a danger of violence, Sellars suggested that the Boston police ring the stage, but the Orchestra general manager, Thomas Morris, and Seiji Ozawa, the conductor, wouldn't agree to the fittingness of that as a metaphorical comment on *Oedipus Rex*. "Society," said Morris, "was not ready for this living theatre."

Ismail Merchant was called as a witness. He was indignant that the Orchestra in a pre-trial motion for Summary Judgment had represented the shooting of *The Bostonians* as something of a small affair in an attempt to play down the evident lack of animosity to the actress in the city. He set the record straight. His star had been the Toast-of-the-Town, at the highly visible center, with Christopher Reeve, of a large-scale operation which went all over Boston for months without incident, dispensing smiles, autographs, *keema* and *dal*, and generally brightening people's lives. He was asked by Wexler how *Variety* had referred to the film on its release. "It was 'boffo' and 'socko,'" said Merchant. The Judge and Jury laughed, and the Defense declined to cross-examine the too amiable and possibly volatile witness.

Vanessa Redgrave's contention that she began to lose work in the wake of the cancellation of *Oedipus Rex* was reinforced by the testimony of Theodore Mann of New York's Circle in the Square Theatre, who had approached her to star in *Heartbreak House* with Rex Harrison in the fall of 1982. Mann told the court he was afraid to hire her after the BSO cancellation because if the Symphony feared disruption by people opposed to her, he also had that fear.

But everything else that was submitted to try to prove that she had been blacklisted was thrown out as hearsay. The manner of Robert E. Sullivan, the defense lawyer, contrasted with Kornstein and Wexler's: brisk, aggressively self-assured, he tried to undermine the Civil Rights part of the case by citing an instance of her own belief in blacklisting. Had she not presented a motion for consideration by British Actors Equity urging that British actors should not perform in Israel and that British film and television projects there should be cancelled? "I would never suggest a ban on Israeli artists and films," she testified. "Never. Israeli artists are welcome to come to Britain to work, but I do say that British artists should not go there, the way we say that they should not go to South Africa."

Sullivan tried to show that far from being the victim of blacklisting, she had turned down job offers with substantial salaries because she hadn't liked the material submitted to her, to which she replied that these had not been *serious* offers, with financial backing. He tried to show that she had not been forthright with the Orchestra, who were naive about her history of political notoriety, and had not warned them, when they offered her this job, that she hadn't worked in the States in several years and had provoked bomb threats when she recently worked in Australia. Witnesses called for the Orchestra during the two-week trial sometimes made an unfortunate impression. It had always been the assumption by people interested in the case, on both sides of the issue, that Vanessa Redgrave had been dumped because of pressure brought on the Orchestra by its rich Jewish backers who couldn't stand her, and this was confirmed by the testimony of an Orchestra trustee, Irving Rabb, who said he feared the loss of Jewish subscribers. He admitted phoning the Orchestra's General Manager and asking, according to the *Boston Globe*, "Is there any way you can get out of it and not have the performance?" The telephone log-books of the Orchestra were read into the records: "Miss Redgrave is a disgraceful person. She should perish," one caller said; another that she was "an accessory to murder."

There were dozens of protest calls, many from people who identified themselves as subscribers and patrons, who said her hiring was an "affront" to the Jewish community, and that it would be a factor in their future support of the Orchestra. But there were many calls of support also, the log-book showed, urging the management not to give in to pressure. The log quotes Arthur Bernstein, a subscriber and contributor, who also identified himself as founder of the Massachusetts Chapter of the Jewish Defense League, as saying, "You will have nothing but bloodshed and violence." (On the witness stand he later denied saying this, and that he had merely promised to picket.) The Artistic Administrator, William Bernell, telephoned Vanessa in England to tell her about these calls and letters, and to ask her if she feared disruptions. She told him it was her belief audiences would prevail over hecklers. Supposing she were shot at? She was sure the Boston police would apprehend her killer, she said by way of reassurance.

It was Seiji Ozawa's suggestion that Redgrave withdraw from the program. In testimony it came out that, like most of the jurors, he had never heard of the actress; his wife told him (approvingly) who she was when the furore began. "I disagree that politics and music must live together," he stated during the trial. "Music must remain neutral, in order to stay alive as an art." Kornstein asked Ozawa for his opinion of the philosophical and political context of *Fidelio*, an opera Ozawa has conducted ten times. Ozawa replied that he and many people thought its libretto was "stupid." He told the courtroom the opera has a "happy ending" because "the good man comes to save people from the bad king." He told Kornstein, "Don't waste time talking about *Fidelio*, it has nothing to do with this case." Sometimes the trial seemed to degenerate into a wrangle between some prosperous, willful, and dynamic oriental gentlemen over how best to serve old Boston's civic interests. And sometimes it seemed that Vanessa herself, whose long-necked profile in the witness box suggested the wavy-haired figurehead of a ship, personified Truth riding triumphant above the fray.

The Jury, in a commonsense, if split, decision, found in her favor. The Boston Symphony had not cancelled the concerts for causes and because of circumstances beyond its reasonable control, but had bowed to community pressure. They did not agree that she had been denied her civil liberties or that she had lost her job because the Orchestra disagreed with political views she had publicly expressed. She was awarded $100,000 in damages, plus the $27,000 contract fee.[1] Both sides claimed victory. Vanessa, leaving for Moscow to play Peter the Great's sister in a CBS Television Special, sent a "message" to the Boston Symphony: ". . . Not for the Management but for the musicians I had hoped to work with. My case was not brought against them. In fact, my defense is theirs, for it means that their jobs, too, can be secure. . . ." This merges uncannily with her impassioned statement on stage at the Music Hall at the end of *The Bostonians* and, like it, might have been set to martial music:

> I say we will be as harsh as truth; as uncompromising as justice. On this subject, we will not think, or speak or write with moderation. We will not excuse—we will not equivocate—we will not retreat a single inch. And we will be heard!

One could say that this trial, widely reported by the American news media, was her finest hour, if one concedes that an actress can have hours finer than those spent in front of a camera or on stage. No one will deny that her fight was well worth making, or that the stand she took was anything but admirable, with larger implications than a mere breach of contract. Whether she won or lost it would cost her dearly in legal fees, in valuable time, and in energy. The case might be a future irritant. Still, she fought it, often in a cuckoo world with the memory of voices crying, "She must perish!" Had she lived in Massachusetts three hundred years earlier, she might well have been branded a witch—or at the very least, an extreme trouble-maker—and been hanged on the village common.

---

1. Redgrave appealed against this decision. In February 1985 Judge Keeton revoked the Jury's award: she received only $27,500, and was liable for the Orchestra's costs. She contemplated appealing once more, but decided against it.

Interview with Ruth Prawer Jhabvala

Michael McDonough/1986

From *San Francisco Review of Books* 11, no. 4 (Spring 1987): 5–6. Reprinted by permission of Ronald E. Nowicki, founder and editor.

In the following interview with Michael Mcdonough, which was conducted in New York in 1986, Jhabvala discusses her screenplays and her novel In Search of Love and Beauty, *which she considers her first American novel, having written it after moving to New York City.*

Ruth Prawer Jhabvala was born to Jewish parents in Cologne, Germany, on May 7, 1927. Her father, Marcus Prawer, came to Germany to escape military conscription in Poland; he met and married Eleanor (Cohn) Prawer in Cologne. Ruth Prawer's grandfather was the cantor of the largest synagogue in that city and prided himself on his friendship with Christian pastors; her grandmother studied at the Berlin Conservatory of Music and played the piano. Her family identified with Germany and celebrated all national, civic, and Jewish festivals and holidays. She was raised in this solid, well-integrated, civilized atmosphere, surrounded by life-loving aunts and uncles, and the fragrance of her grandmother's tea cakes.

Ruth Prawer started school when Hitler came to power in 1933; then, one by one, all her relatives emigrated—to France, Holland, Palestine, and America. In April 1939, she and her immediate family became refugees and moved to England. She studied at Stoke Park Elementary School, Coventry; Hendon County School; and Queen Mary College, London University, where she majored in English Literature and earned her Master's degree in 1951. She married the Parsi architect C. S. H. Jhabvala that same year and moved with him to Delhi, India. While there, Mrs. Jhabvala wrote eight novels and four volumes of short stories.

American film director James Ivory and Indian producer Ismail Merchant met Ruth Jhabvala in Delhi in 1962 and asked her to script their version of her novel *The Householder*. Their next work, *Shakespeare Wallah* (1965), was based on her original screenplay. Other Jhabvala-scripted films followed, the most popular being *Heat and Dust* (1983), and, most recently E. M. Forster's *A Room with a View*. Her adaptations of Henry James include *The Europeans* (1979) and *The Bostonians* (1984).

Ruth Jhabvala left India and came to live in New York City in 1976. Her ninth novel, *In Search of Love and Beauty*, appeared in 1983. Mrs. Jhabvala winters in Delhi where her husband runs an architectural firm and teaches; her brother Siegbert Salomon is professor of German literature at Oxford; her three daughters are grown and have independent careers.

In March of this year [1987], Ruth Prawer Jhabvala won an Academy Award for screenwriting. The following conversation took place in 1986 at Mrs. Jhabvala's Upper East Side apartment.

Michael McDonough: Your writing is not novelistic in the sense that most stories simply put up the machinery of setting; your characters seem more intuitively related to the setting—
Ruth Prawer Jhabvala: I'd like it to be that way. I'm not writing a literary exercise. If something doesn't matter, if it isn't real, then I want nothing to do with it. I'm not interested in anything made up.

MM: But then the stories themselves, though they feel real, don't appear to be autobiographical.
RPJ: No, they're not autobiographical, but on the other hand I like to make the situation personally authentic, as though it could have happened to me, if my responses had been those of the character in the story, like a sort of vicarious living, I suppose. I want it to be almost like nonfiction, fake biographical, fake autobiographical, but on the other hand I also want it to have form and a kind of beauty.

MM: Intuitive structure seems important in your work. The scenes and episodes flow into each other as in *Heat and Dust* (1975), though my first experience was with *Travelers* (1973), where you had these little panel-like stories which seemed to interrupt and form a larger picture at the same time, yet you weren't aware of the structure except that it fit and was natural.
RPJ: All this is, as you say, intuitive, because I can't think it out, if it doesn't happen it doesn't happen—I set up the situation and follow along slowly and see what happens.

MM: How did *Travelers* start?

RPJ: *Travelers* was at a time when I started meeting girls who were traveling all over India in buses and trains, everything that I must say that I myself have not done. I used to look at them quite enviously for traveling this way in India which is a difficult place that they had chosen to travel in.

MM: Did you meet them in passing or were they introduced to you?

RPJ: They were introduced to me. They were friends of friends—someone would say, "When you're in Delhi you must look for Ruth," so they would write me, and I was eager to meet them. And then at one point I lived next door to one of those American programs that bring people to India for a year and that was very interesting and had a lot to do with it. One of those girls got involved with some guru and there was a sort of secret report that I managed to have a look at which concerned this girl and how she got involved with this guru and got very sick, and then her family tried to get her back, and then they tried to hush it up, and that spurred me on and crystallized everything that I saw happening there in the mid-to-late sixties.

MM: The theme of search on a very basic level seems to be a common thread in your work.

RPJ: Yes, that started off quite unconsciously but now it's more conscious. Usually it's a search for something higher and better. There are so many frauds who really want to take advantage of this really rather noble streak, I mean there were these girls who had come to India and were very open and wanted to make themselves better, and then there were those frauds who took the most horrible advantage of them in every way. I've seen that happen again and again, not only in India but everywhere. So many people seem to get trapped by the ignoble. So that's becoming a quite conscious theme also connected, I suppose, to obsessive passions for unworthy characters. I see something noble and beautiful in that search that's dragged down to a workaday level.

MM: People seem to be looking for something beyond the material world, especially Americans.

RPJ: I don't think Americans are particularly materialistic, I mean look how they came here in search of religious freedom. That sort of thing always seems to be with them, but in the meantime they made so much money that the society became materialistic. There seems to be this split between the altruistic soul and the desire to increase their wealth.

MM: This search becomes explicit in *In Search of Love and Beauty* (1983) in which a fraudulent guru who has been donning and shedding guises for years uses his charm to start a spiritual community.
RPJ: I think the guru there is more worked-out and interesting than the one in *Travelers*.

MM: He's had more transformations within the world than Swamiji—
RPJ: transforming himself into what a particular generation wants.

MM: In *Heat*, Anne is looking for her great-aunt Olivia—
RPJ: And also "looking for herself," as people do nowadays or did then.

MM: I read the character as trying to escape a materialistic world—
RPJ: But most people come to India not only to escape a materialistic world, but their boring English background too.

MM: The characters in your novels seem both physically and socially displaced.
RPJ: The European characters do: that's why they came to India in the first place.

MM: There isn't that mystical tradition in Europe and America that there is in India with all the religions, the sense of rebirth and transformation, because things are in a way more set.
RPJ: That's part of the boringness—religions are set because so many of them are no longer alive and people can no longer find the living fountain, they're so sealed up that they can't get anything out of them. I'm writing a new novel which is concerned with search more than ever; the working title is *Three Continents*: it's about two nineteen-year-old American twins who are very rich heirs in search of something nobler and higher and who get caught up in a world political movement which is also partly financed by smuggling drugs, paintings, and art objects.

MM: Events in your writings are framed and presented so clearly that the reader can discern how the characters relate to one another.
RPJ: I go along completely ignorant of what's going to happen.

MM: Do you re-write much?

RPJ: I have to polish, and if a thing isn't working well, I feel it's a kind of warning to stop and try something else, but I can't change the direction or the meaning except on the more superficial stylistic level of how to present the scene such as maybe someone else should be talking here. But on the deepest level you can't force a meaning into or out of a story or force a character into something that they're not naturally growing into. The same with a situation: if it's not developing along then, too bad. For one successful story you have to write a lot that don't work.

MM: Are you a strict critic of your work?

RPJ: I'm a bad judge and can't tell for a long time—I have to distance myself—but when the writing's really going well, then I know.

MM: Does a story ever write itself in the sense that something you've thrown away comes back and finally happens?

RPJ: Something I've thrown away sometimes comes back in a different form as if it had been a practice work.

MM: Some of the stories in *Out of India* seem to be studies for your novels.

RPJ: *Heat* was almost a companion piece to the film *Autobiography of a Princess*—both had the same sort of themes—and all the guru stories went finally into *Travelers. How I Became a Holy Mother* (1976) was after that but I've been going back again and again.

MM: How did you go about adapting *Heat* with James Ivory?

RPJ: I had to do something I hate doing—I had to reread the book which was published in '75; and in '81 or '82 I wrote the script. So I reread the book and did what I always do—I put the book aside and tried to find a completely new form to present the story—of Anne coming to see the only survivor. I had to find a way to tell the two-level story—that was the major problem. And the novel itself was written in a very strange way. It wasn't laid-out sequentially because I wrote big chunks of 1923 and big chunks of present time and then afterwards I cut it all up and thought what scenes of present and past would best set each other off, complement or contrast with each other, so I juxtaposed them—edited them in relation to each other—more like a film. I didn't do that much juggling in *In Search*.

MM: That's a sort of Central European-American novel. Did you feel you were getting back in touch with your roots with that?
RPJ: Absolutely. New York would have been the place you'd logically come to from Europe, so when I came here it was what should have happened in 1939. The first time I came to New York was in 1966 when I was here for ten days and I liked it, because it was like a cosmopolitan European city, so when the question came of leaving India, I came here. I was also keen to write something not about India, something closer to my own background and this was the background I could write about so that's how *In Search* came about; I consider it my first American novel.

MM: It's remarkable.
RPJ: I'm glad you liked it because all that time I was writing in India no one was taking any notice. The reviews of *In Search* said my Indian work was better and I should go back and write about that and this after twenty years when nobody cared a damn about what I was writing in India. My first American thing was my script about the New York dance-hall, *Roseland*, for the film with the same name which we did in 1977, and then there was *The Europeans* in 1979.

MM: How did that come about?
RPJ: I always thought that Henry James would be good for James Ivory because they had a lot of things in common—the way James viewed the world, and the characters he admired was a lot like Jim himself—so I thought they ought to get together. But the film we really wanted to make was *The Portrait of a Lady*, though that would be very expensive, whereas *The Europeans* was much simpler—a smaller cast of characters, more restricted American locations, and easier to get financing for. Then *The Bostonians* (1984) was actually started by WGBH who wanted to do a whole series on the James family and one American-set feature film, but the funding for our part of the project fell through, so we got our own funding for *The Bostonians*.

MM: Ivory was quoted in the *New York Times* as saying that your new project, *Three Continents*, would be similar to *Portrait*.
RPJ: There's something very peculiar about that. Somebody said he would finance a film for us and he said what do you want to do and we vaguely had an idea about a modern *Portrait*—what would a modern

American lady do—she wouldn't go to Europe but maybe to India on a quest in search of herself, but somehow I had the idea of nineteen-year-old twins, and so the man said okay, go ahead, but Jim said why don't you think of it as a novel and work it out in detail before you present the finished script. So I worked it out into a novel which moves from America to England to India and I'm so glad to have written what I suppose is my second American novel which is a sort of stepchild to my other work. Now, after all these years, the Indian novels are getting more attention, but *In Search of Love and Beauty*, the new path I've turned onto seems not to have been recognized, so I suppose it just does take twenty years for the work to be known and then it's there and you go on to something else. I think the film *Roseland* and some stories I wrote then were the beginning of a move away from India, but I hesitate to call these in any way American novels because I'm not an American though America's a mixture, as I am.

Dialogue on Film: Merchant and Ivory

American Film Institute/1987

From *American Film*, January/February 1987, 13–15, 54. Reprinted by permission of the American Film Institute.

The films of producer Ismail Merchant and director James Ivory have often revolved around a newcomer's changing perceptions of an alien culture, whether it's *The Europeans'* New England, *Heat and Dust's* India, or *A Room with a View's* Florence. Their twenty-five-year partnership has produced many works of social commentary, but the messages are conveyed through subtle performances, great artistic detail, and well-crafted dialogue. Ignoring Hollywood trends, the filmmakers have instead selected material of widely varying periods and styles, often turning to novelists such as Henry James and E. M. Forster.

Merchant-Ivory Production films are usually shot on location with sizable casts of both well-known actors and screen newcomers—almost all on budgets of less than $3 million. This paradox is made possible by Merchant's ceaseless fund-raising and the willingness of stars like Maggie Smith and Christopher Reeve to work at reduced salaries, plus percentages.

Ivory, a California native, was making a documentary about Delhi, India, when he met Merchant, born in Bombay and educated in the United States, who was then another budding filmmaker. Their first project, *The Householder* (1963), was a comedy made in both English and Hindi. The screenplay was adapted by Ruth Prawer Jhabvala—born in Germany, educated in England, married to an Indian—from her novel; Jhabvala has since written original material or adaptations for nearly all of Merchant and Ivory's films.

Shakespeare Wallah (1966), a poignant drama of a failing theatrical company, is considered a classic and the best of their early Indian films.

After making *Savages* (1972), an allegorical comedy-drama of primitives in a mansion, and several other highly original but commercially unsuccessful films, they tackled *The Europeans* (1979), the story of a conservative Massachusetts family disrupted by foreign cousins. Two films later, Merchant and Ivory returned to India with *Heat and Dust*, an ambitious work that depicts two Englishwomen's parallel discovery of India: Greta Scacchi plays the wife who abandons her husband for a sensual Indian prince; Julie Christie portrays an unhappy woman wandering through the country sixty years later, trying to understand her great-aunt's decision—and her own desires. The film won critical attention and international audiences, but was not widely seen in the US because of distribution problems.

The filmmakers are perhaps best known to American audiences for their two most recent films: *The Bostonians* (1984), a Jamesian love triangle that garnered Oscar nominations for Best Actress (Vanessa Redgrave) and Best Costume Design, and *A Room with a View* (1986). Critics say this latest film represents Merchant-Ivory's greatest critical and commercial achievement (made for roughly $3.5 million, it grossed more than $1 million in its first sixteen weeks at just one New York theater). All of the trademarks are present—the screenplay captures Forster's gently satiric tone, the Florentine and English locations are lovingly photographed, and the performances by both veteran actors (Maggie Smith, Denholm Elliott) and newcomers (Helena Bonham Carter, Julian Sands, Daniel Day Lewis) are humorous and touching. Twenty-five years after the two filmmakers became Merchant-Ivory Productions, their work is reaching its largest audience yet—without compromise.

Q: Can you talk about adapting a novel into a script and the sacrifices you have to make in narrowing it down?

James Ivory: They do seem like sacrifices, but later on in the editing room, if you've been indulgent at all, then you find you've got to trim it down anyway. And it's extraordinary how, during editing, one line or even one word can seem too much, and can spoil the rhythm of the dialogue. So you can imagine how much we have to get rid of with someone like Henry James! It seems while you're doing it that you're making everything crude, and in a way you are: You're making everything much more obvious and broad. It seems that you're doing a disservice to the writer, but that's in the nature of doing an adaptation of any great book. We try to be true to the spirit and to what the writer is trying to say; we try to get his or her tone.

You do your version of the novel—it's no longer a novel, it's a film. Ruth Jhabvala herself, being a very, very good fiction writer, is not down on her knees in awe of these masters. She approaches their work as another novelist and a craftsman with a problem, the problem being how to reduce all of this. And she can see ways to do it that somebody who is not already a good fiction writer wouldn't be able to do so well.

Q: What intrigued you enough to choose *A Room with a View?*
Ivory: The first and main reason was just the kind of story it was—something light, but in the best sense, a lighthearted, funny, youthful kind of story. Another reason was that it gave me a chance to go back to Italy; I hadn't worked there in twenty years.

Q: How did the visual look of the film evolve in your mind?
Ivory: If it's an adaptation, very often the visual look is suggested by the writing itself. And that is particularly true of E. M. Forster, because he is a very visual writer. As soon as you find your locations, you begin to imagine how you will do the scenes and how they're going to look. I don't really do that much visual planning at the script stage. It's all very well to sit in New York and write a script set in Florence even if you haven't been there in twenty-five or thirty years. But when you actually get to Florence, you find that all those lovely, calm places where the couple is supposed to walk along the Arno River are crowded with thousands of cars and Vespas and buses full of tourists. We had to rethink everything, and the thing that really had to be rethought was the room-with-the-view scene itself; that was the hardest of all because Forster's view was looking across the Arno toward the San Miniato, and we couldn't do that because of all the traffic. There was no way to stop it.
Ismail Merchant: The producer is the one who has to stop traffic and I don't speak very good Italian. It was extremely difficult. We were shooting that scene. On the south of the Arno, it sort of arches out and there's shops around and we had to dress it from the outside. Maggie Smith was sitting in one of the shops—she was buying some bags because she was leaving for London. I saw this woman and didn't quite realize who it was. She was peering out of the shop all the time, trying to see how we were managing. So I'm rushing down to pull her out of the shot, and I look at her and say. "Oh, Maggie, I'm so sorry." She says, "Darling, don't worry about it at all, just get the shot. I can give you the Academy Award for it because I've been watching what a dreadful time you're having."

Q: Whose idea was that beautifully done and very romantic last scene?
Ivory: It was written in a different way. We sort of rearranged things a little bit. I didn't tell Julian Sands how to take that bite out of her breast, that was his own idea—he just got into it. Generally in love scenes you really can't tell people what to do.

Q: Once you have the locations, how do you rehearse the story?
Ivory: We don't have that much rehearsal, because we can't afford to. That's one of the ways we make films for $3 million. And, well, some actors refuse to really rehearse properly. They are not going to show you what they are going to do. The best example of that in my experience was with Isabelle Adjani in *Quartet*. She would just sleepwalk through the rehearsals of her dramatic scenes. When we were actually shooting, she was just superb. But the rest of the time it was the drabbest, dullest kind of rehearsal, which was sort of off-putting to the other actors, Maggie Smith and Alan Bates, because their rehearsals were good.

The way I do rehearsal is sit the actors down, read through the script, and find out whether there are places that don't sound right. Perhaps the line is wrong, it's awkward—whatever. Then the whole thing is blocked out on location. Now, the locations have a lot to do with the way the scenes are acted. Because if you're working with real locations—say, just a room—and the actors have to move around in that room in a convincing way, they may have bits of business that take them here and there. They've got to feel comfortable. What I do is go through the scene from beginning to end, and just let the actors show me what they'd like to do. You see if things are going to work, and gradually the scene falls into place. Once it is blocked, the cameraman can get on with his lighting. When you come back to shoot, you have proper line rehearsals and you work everything out in fine detail.

Q: How did you deal with one location and two periods in *Heat and Dust?*
Ivory: It was a headache. We had Julie Christie and the modern cast out there first and then the 1923 cast. We simply had to do every location twice. It had to be prepared for modern times and then be completely redone.

Everyone feels more moved by the period story. But in the book, the modern story is very interesting and the book's single most dramatic moment happens in the modern story. It was something we attempted to shoot and it just didn't come off.

In the story, the beggar dies a very peaceful death in the arms of the woman in white with Anne [Julie Christie] as witness. To read it just stops your heart, but in the film it wasn't that good. For one thing, the actress could not keep her eyes from moving underneath her closed eyelids. And then, the woman in white wasn't wearing the right shoes. She should have had some kind of cheap sandals on; instead, she had on some kind of clog-type shoes. I don't know why. It was a terrible thing to think that the wrong shoes could ruin the most dramatic scene, but these things happen.

Q: In many situations, the distributor decides about cutting scenes. How do you two resolve such decisions?
Ivory: I might as well explain that, contractually, I have the final cut, but the film must be a certain length. We decide how long a film can be at its maximum, and then that's sort of my limit. We knew that *A Room with a View* would be a fairly long film, so I was given more time—two hours. The financiers are not going to put up money if they think the director will hand them a three-hour film. They will go along with a two-hour film, and within that time I can do what I want, though I can't trample roughshod over everybody's feelings. But I can occasionally be convinced that, for the greater good, I ought to give something up.
Merchant: We have bitter fights! I never go during the editing of the picture to see what's happening day to day. The picture is entirely edited by Jim, and then we are all there at the screening—Ruth Jhabvala, myself, Jim and the composer. If we find something not quite right, we have to convince Jim to eliminate or shorten or change it.

Q: Is it much easier now for you to find financing?
Merchant: Fund-raising is never easy, particularly if you want to do something of your own. If you want to do rubbish, it's very simple. But if you want to do something good, you really have to knock on doors and convince people about what you are going to do. We give back our investors the money plus a 15 to 20 percent return. But with this film [*A Room with a View*], they are going to get a 300 or 400 percent return.
Ivory: Let's hope.
Merchant: I think money-raising is obviously an important factor to a film. But we have never, never stopped our work for lack of money. We have always gone ahead if the project is there. *The Europeans* went ahead with actors and everybody without all the money. We never think that

you have to have your budget in the bank or the finances there in totality. We've never worked like that.

Q: How have your films done in India?
Merchant: *Heat and Dust* was more successful there than *A Passage to India*. *Heat and Dust* played in major cities. You know, the Indian cinema is a very healthy one—about eight hundred movies a year. But mostly they are song and dances and musical numbers.
Ivory: None of our Indian films, with the exception of *The Householder*, have ever been that popular in India, because they almost always have to do with foreigners in India and their point of view, and that's not of great interest to Indian audiences. *Shakespeare Wallah* was a kind of nine-day wonder; it came to India with prizes and wonderful reviews from abroad. But that didn't really make it that successful after its initial run in Bombay. People went to see it because they had heard about it, but it wasn't a mass success.

Q: Looking back over the body of your work over the last twenty-five years, what distinguishes it from the product that emanates from Hollywood?
Merchant: Hollywood is what you would call a giant conglomerate of different people who are shuffling all the time from one place to the other. It's like a round table conference: Today there is this executive, tomorrow that executive. And for the director or producer who wants to make a commitment to his work, studios are really accountants and lawyers. There is no personal commitment.

For example, Universal loved *Heat and Dust*, they wanted it, they took it for distribution in this country and Canada. And then they no sooner got it and opened it in cooperation with us, than everybody at Universal was fired or left. The film was in a kind of limbo and you couldn't even get anybody on the telephone to talk about it. It was impossible to discuss any further ad campaign or play dates at all. There was nothing we could do. *Heat and Dust* should have been more popular in this country: The timing was right, people were interested in India and in our work.

As Hollywood as an entity is concerned, films are made purely for the sake of money. And of all the films that you see in one year, I would say about four or five are good. The others make money, but there is nothing to hold onto.
Ivory: I'd say that with our films, we've pretty much done exactly what we wanted to do. And this has made our films rather cranky and indi-

vidualistic, and not particularly marketable. And perhaps not of great interest to many, many people. But they have at least the merit of being ours and reflecting our own preoccupations and our lives as we've lived them in different parts of the world. The films as a group are kind of a joint autobiography of the three of us.

A Film of Two Halves

Graham Fuller/1990

From *The Listener* 124–25, nos. 3195–96 (December 20–27, 1990): 62–63. Reprinted by permission of BBC/*The Listener*.

Joanne Woodward as the Kansas City country-club matron India Bridge—the fussing, ineffectual spirit of unemancipated, middle-class femininity, her dawning hopelessness waylaid by an arch gaiety—is, in James Ivory's *Mr. and Mrs. Bridge*, a sight to make one want to write immediately home to one's mother. Thirty years of anticipation (and perhaps, thirty years of parenthood) went into Woodward's performance, the most wrenching she has given in a film that stars her husband, Paul Newman.

She had first envisaged playing the part when Evan S. Connell's novel *Mrs. Bridge*—117 terse chapters calibrating the emotional abandonment of the gentle, unworldly India by her undemonstrative husband and their three self-absorbed children—was published in 1959. "I think that somebody said that Evan Connell wasn't interested in having a film made of it," Woodward recalls, "so it went by the wayside." Later, an adaptation of the book by O'Connell and *Kojak* writer Abby Mann failed to arouse any interest in Hollywood; then, in 1969, *Mrs. Bridge*'s discrete companion volume *Mr. Bridge* was published—141 episodes in the life of Walter, a conscientious lawyer and man of fixed views and habits, not unkind but morally strict and barely conscious of his sexual desires for his oldest daughter, Ruth.

Ivory had picked *Mrs. Bridge* up in a Charangee Lane bookstore when he was in Calcutta to show a rough cut of *Shakespeare Wallah* (1965) to Satyajit Ray and there recommended it to his producer partner, Ismail Merchant, who didn't have time to read it. Twenty-five years later, Merchant, Ivory, and their closest collaborator, Ruth Prawer Jhabvala, dined with Newman and Woodward in New York. Says Ivory: "Joanne thought it would be interesting to make a television film out of *Mrs. Bridge* only, and I said, 'Why not make a feature film out of both books?'"

"At first, she didn't really plan, I think, on having Paul do it. We met at a restaurant—I had never met the Newmans before—and I said I was sure Ruth would want to write the script, although I wasn't sure of that at all. And Paul said, 'Well, if she writes it and I like it, I could play Mr. Bridge.' And he did like the script, and he did play him."

The genesis of any movie is convoluted, but that of *Mr. and Mrs. Bridge* takes on the bizarre appearance of an off-Hollywood *Dance to the Music of Time* when Merchant relates an anecdote about how—as a business student and star-struck stage fan newly arrived in New York, on a snowy night in 1959—he had visited Newman in his Broadway dressing-room after a performance of *Sweet Bird of Youth*, and been given a lift home to Greenwich Village by the actor on his motorbike. Three decades later, it was the casting of Newman that enabled Ivory to clinch a $7.3 million budget for *Mr. and Mrs. Bridge* from Cineplex's Odeon. It was stretched to $7.5 million during filming in Kansas City, New York, Toronto, and Paris (where, on the eve of World War II, Mr. Bridge takes Mrs. Bridge on a sightseeing holiday, an interlude that only emphasizes the hibernatory quality of her daily life).

Connell has based the two novels on his memories of growing up in Kansas City, and had loosely modeled the Bridges on his parents. The books, though, are fascinating less as an affectionate semi-autobiography than as a searching critique of the dystopia of upper-middle-class society. Written in a spare, uncluttered prose, each chapter is a parable about the misunderstandings, sacrifices, selfishnessess, reticences, and occasional comforts of life on the home and social fronts.

To his mother's grief, Douglas Bridge (played by Robert Sean Leonard in the film) is too embarrassed to kiss her during his Eagle Scout inaugural ceremony. Mr. Bridge finds his daughter Ruth (Kyra Sedgwick) having sex on the living-room floor in the middle of the night. Feeling unloved, Mrs. Bridge asks Mr. Bridge for a divorce, but he gives her a glass of beer instead. Many of the chapters are rendered with dry wit, but their cumulative effect is to leave the reader with a sense of almost existential despair.

How do you forge a coherent movie narrative from 258 short episodes—most of them concerned with thought rather than action—without disrupting their slow but steady throb, or resorting to tableaux or, for that matter, offending their author? Although he says he feels guilty that he hadn't seen any of the Merchant-Ivory-Jhabvala adaptations of Henry James or E. M. Forster, Connell had a gut feeling that "they would do an honest piece of work. I am fatalistic about filmmaking. I find there is considerable distortion in most of the films based on books I've read, so I just assume that's what usually happens. If you sell the rights to a film company, you simply hope for the best. But I wasn't concerned about the episodic structure; I was uneasy that maybe the characters would be twisted all out of shape. In fact, that doesn't seem to have happened."

Ruth Prawer Jhabvala admits the screenplay was a complex business. "There were so many scenes in the books, and they weren't really structured ones, like in James and Forster, where people talk and something happens. So it really was a question of never using just a single bit, but of condensing several scenes together. With James or a more traditionalist novelist, you can take a scene from a novel and work it out dramatically. This isn't so in these books—and in fact, I don't think it's so in most other modern novels, either.

"Nothing was really invented. It's all there or it's indicated in the books. For instance, the scene in the bank vault where Mrs. Bridge asks Mr. Bridge, 'Do you love me?' comes from a different part of the book to the one in which he advises her not to sell her shares. But I combined the two to enrich the scene. You take things from here and there; you have to be somewhat uninhibited. However much you love a book, once you've read and enjoyed it, you shut it and put it aside. I don't know that you even think of its *spirit* all that much. You take a book because you feel a harmony with it, and there you try to express it in your own way."

The period luster and social setting of *Mrs. Bridge* and *Mr. Bridge* must have warmed the Merchant-Ivory team after their ill-fated movie of Tama Janowitz's *Slaves of New York*: akin, one would have thought, to following a badly mixed Manhattan with a good, strong cup of tea. Not that *Mr. and Mrs. Bridge*, for all its surface domesticity, is redolent of angel cake and antimacassars, or that the Merchant-Ivory milieu should be pinned—as it frequently has been since the success of *A Room with a View*—to what unappreciative critics have disparaged as the "Laura Ashley" or *Masterpiece Theatre* school of tasteful classic adaptations. The fourteenth film that Jhabvala has written for Merchant-Ivory in a partnership that began in India in 1961, *Mr. and Mrs. Bridge* continues their exploration of emotional and sexual repression, and the fogs of miscommunication that nullify relationships—themes as central to films like *The Bostonians* and *A Room with a View* as their visual stylishness.

As in those earlier films, it is the things that aren't said in *Mr. and Mrs.*

Bridge that echo loudest. "The thing I loved about those relationships," says Woodward, "was something that doesn't exist any more—the game of silence that both the children and the parents played. These days, your children are inclined to tell you everything they do."

Scenes with younger actors playing the Bridge offspring as children were shot but discarded, partly, says Woodward, "because I was too old to play the mother of these young children"—partly, says Ivory, because "the film was just too long." Jhabvala adds that "our own interest wasn't in children; it was more in adult life and in character."

Accordingly, for a film that might at first be regarded as passionlessly genteel, *Mr. and Mrs. Bridge* seethes with corrosive longings, Oedipal and otherwise, that Ivory's camera seems tacitly to acknowledge rather than bluntly state. A close-up of daughter Ruth's legs "greets" Mr. Bridge when he returns home from work on a summer evening and, having spied on her sunbathing from his bedroom window, he gently forces his wife on to the marital bed: Julia, twenty years his secretary and a spinster, makes him take her for a drink, but he remains oblivious to her needy flutterings.

It is simple yearning, and the array of emotions that stifle it, that threads the film together as much as the consistent characterization and the lambent *mise en scène*. Ivory denies, though, that it was their repressed ways that particularly attracted him and Jhabvala to the Bridges.

"It was the entire way they were that interested me. This was a world and a kind of American family I knew a lot about. Paul, Joanne, Evan, and I all came from families more or less like the Bridges, though in different parts of the country. American families of that type were the same everywhere—except possibly on the Eastern Seaboard, where it's more sophisticated."

If *Mr. and Mrs. Bridge* is flawed, it is only in the end titles that have been added to it, at the behest of the US distributor, supplying a spuriously optimistic resolution to each of the film's disparate lives. Unrelated to anything Connell wrote, they pander to the notion that the American audience is unable to cope with a little bit of sadness.

Unlike Paul Bowles, who plays a small but significant role in the film of his novel, *The Sheltering Sky*, the modest Connell—an author only now being recognized as one of America's finest—does not grace the film in which, in theory, Robert Sean Leonard plays a version of his younger self. But he was an eager spectator on Ivory's set.

"He liked watching. But I could never understand how he could stay around much, because watching a movie being made can be very tedious," Ivory says. "I always felt that he, particularly, would think that what we were doing was crude in relation to what he had written, and that it would be almost unbearable for him to watch the actors speak the lines and do the actions that he'd once written. But he seemed to love it."

Watching the shooting ushered in unusual feelings, Connell confesses, "to the extent that I could not judge the film objectively. I thought I would be able to, but I supposed I'd lived with the characters for so long that I couldn't. But it was the books [that] reminded me of my own childhood. Gale Garnett, who plays Mrs. Bridge's friend, Mabel, in the film, made a very interesting comment on the set. I said that my only reservation about Paul Newman playing Mr. Bridge was that he's just as handsome—and, after all, your basic attorney does not look like Paul Newman. Gale, after seeing him at work, said "He has thinned himself inside and out"—and I thought that was a remarkable way of expressing what he had done to change himself.

"He shows the kind of severe expression and manner that was characteristic, not only of my father, but of many men of that generation in the Midwest. There's an image of Newman seated at the table at the country club, with his glasses on, exactly the way my father sat at a table.

"The only thing that troubled me is that Mr. Bridge wears suspenders [braces]. I complained about that to James Ivory, and he was a little surprised, because where he grew up under similar circumstances, the men did wear suspenders. But I can't remember many of the professional men of Kansas City wearing them. Of course, the only people who will notice it are people who lived in Kansas City at that time."

A Truly Flourishing Plant

Michael Simpson/1992

From *What's on in London*, April 29, 1992, 17–18. Reprinted by permission of Amco Agency Limited.

This year marks the thirtieth anniversary of Merchant-Ivory Productions, a fact already celebrated by the publication of Robert Emmet Long's glossy book *The Films of Merchant-Ivory* (Viking). No less a cause for rejoicing is the fact that this occasion coincides with the release of their highly successful adaptation of E. M. Forster's *Howards End*. It opens in London this week, and the screening is by the writer who completes the triumvirate, the novelist Ruth Prawer Jhabvala.

When I met Ismail Merchant in London last year, he was already looking forward to the anniversary year, and not least because he would be making his first full-length feature as a director, Anita Desai's adaptation of her novel *In Custody*. This venture will take him back to India.

"We are enjoying the freedom of making the films the way we want to, on three continents. And we each come from a different continent. Ruth's European, I'm Indian, and Jim's American, and fate has brought us together. We come from different worlds, yet our thinking is the same. You benefit a great deal from this cross-cultural maneuvering, and for us it's a process of learning all the time. And each experience is a turning point. So, one is blessed that this has happened to us."

If it has been a learning process, this factor has played its part in making *Howards End*, the third of their films from the novels of E. M. Forster.

"If one were to ask among these three adaptations whose films they were, I would say that *Howards End* is Ruth's. *Maurice* was Jim's because he felt it was an underrated, understated novel, and *A Room with a View* was mine. But right from the beginning, even before we did *A Room with a View*, Ruth wanted to do *Howards End*. But it's a very complex novel, not as straightforward as *A Room with a View*, and not light in the sense of being frothy, beautiful, and romantic. It has so many levels, *Howards End*, and we thought that we were not really quite ready to do it at that time. I'm talking about ten years ago.

"After *A Room with a View* we were approached by every Hollywood company to do anything we wanted to do, but under their umbrella. As much money as we wanted to spend. But what is interesting for us is the independence. We cannot work in a corporate structure. We just cannot. It's like a plant which, under certain circumstances, can flourish, but which would die in other circumstances. In a corporate structure, we would die.

"Of course, we want as much distribution as possible for our films, and American studios put in a lot of effort. But their philosophy is that they make things which operate like a slot-machine. We don't, we make films painstakingly, with an emphasis on a good script, and on characters, relationships, atmosphere. These films say something about our life, and we can't make mindless movies. It's just not possible for us, even if they make billions of dollars. I'd rather make small sums of money but make films which will be remembered and talked about; films which will give a satisfaction of mind and soul as opposed to something which is just temporary.

"So after *A Room with a View*, we decided to do *Maurice*. That in itself shows that money is not the issue here. Then we went and did three American films, *Slaves of New York*, *The Ballad of the Sad Café*, and *Mr. and Mrs. Bridge*. *Howards End* was still in our thoughts, and it was just the right opportunity to make it, after spinning around in our minds for ten years. I've seen rushes and some edited passages, and I think it's the most accomplished thing we've done.

"It's a very definite kind of film—the images are strong, and it's more stark and more punchy. And as for the relationship between Helen and Margaret, the two Bohemian sisters, well you find the same characters in our lives today. So it's not that Forster is something that is past: Forster is of the present and the future."

Although we spoke before Ismail Merchant had seen the fully completed film, he was already enthusiastic over two players new to Merchant-Ivory Productions.

"Prunella Scales's son, Samuel West, who's playing Leonard Bast, is just remarkable. There were lots of people considered for the part. But when we met Sam, we both focused on him and felt he'd be wonderful as Leonard. And then there's Emma Thompson. There were many actresses for Margaret Schlegel, but you just go by your feeling. You meet some-body and there is something that strikes you. This is what you want. So you jump at it. Most of the time we just go by our instincts, I think."

As for the choice of material, it's no secret that Merchant-Ivory favors adaptations from literature, but Ismail Merchant picks out another line.

"Good writing is what we are attracted to, be it a short story, a novella, or a novel. And writers like Forster, Henry James, Jean Rhys—they are a rare breed. There's something in common, because to some extent they are all expatriates, often writing about other countries. Forster has writ-ten about Italy and India, Henry James about France and England, and Jean Rhys about her own experiences while living in France.

"And similarly, Ruth Jhabvala's *Heat and Dust* and *Three Continents* which we are going to do. If you take a good literary work, you want to bring the essence of it to the screen. These novels are all very visual. And they are also complex. But Ruth, herself a fiction writer of great esteem, can take the essence of Henry James or Jean Rhys or Forster and create something. She adds something of her own, which is very difficult to distinguish from the original writer. She does this very cleverly, bringing the novel into perspective and into the right focus for the camera. And Jim, as a visual artist, knows what scenes are wonderful to bring it into camera. So this has been a very happy association with a writer of great distinction, and with a visual artist like Jim Ivory."

No less happily, Merchant-Ivory are not short of future projects, in-cluding *Jefferson in Paris*, an original screenplay by Ruth Prawer Jhabvala.

"It's about Thomas Jefferson when he was ambassador to the French court and we plan to do that in France. And there are other things which have been brewing in our minds for some time. Ruth wants to do anoth-er James, *The Golden Bowl* or *The Portrait of a Lady*. So it could be a trilogy of Forster and a trilogy of James—which it would be good to have. My goodness, who could not be proud of all these?"

Buttling Under

Brian Case/1993

From *Time Out*, November 3–10, 1993, 20–22. Reprinted by permission.

One of our greatest exports to Hollywood has been the British butler, with wing-pole collar and tray. Sir John Gielgud won an Oscar for his Hobson in *Arthur*: "I thought it was rather vulgar when I read it. I turned it down three times and each time they put the money up, so naturally I became reconciled. I was enchanted when it was so acclaimed." But he wasn't tempted back into the striped trousers for *Trading Places*, and Denholm Elliott, possibly acting on the old knight's advice, turned that down twice until the money doubled and Concorde came into the contract. He hadn't got on with his screen master, Eddie Murphy: "I hardly talked to him and he hardly talked to me. He did praise my mobility of expression. I tried to get a much closer relationship with him first of all because I like blacks, get on with blacks very well, and I was playing his butler, but he regarded that as being absolutely not on." Despite offers of bags more buttling over there, he came home.

Now there is talk about another Oscar going to Anthony Hopkins for his butler, Stevens, in *The Remains of the Day*. Based on the Booker Prize–winning novel by Kazuo Ishiguro, and made by the Merchant-Ivory team, the film depends almost entirely on his performance. Stevens's life is governed by his concept of service, order, calm, and restraint. Great butlers inhabit their roles, he believes, and will discard them only when alone; lesser butlers are pantomime performers. The first person narrative of the book presents a subtle psychological portrait of a man in denial, a man who doesn't understand his feelings, but who leaks insights to the reader without realizing. Denied the narrator's voice, the actor has enormous problems communicating the human being buried alive beneath the glacial reserve.

"Absolutely right," says Ismail Merchant over the phone from LA, where the première found a wildly enthusiastic audience. "One of the great things about Anthony is that he is an actor who can do a twitch on his face and you can register a mile of emotion. One is grateful that there are such actors who can bring that novel into life. To do this very interior film you need an actor who doesn't have to explain or shout, a man who can twitch an eye and an audience will see and feel what is happening so far as his emotions are concerned. It's all bottled up." In fact, an exploding bottle of vintage wine is requisitioned to explain Stevens's emotional turmoil when he is told that the housekeeper, played by Emma Thompson, is leaving to get married. He loves her but fears a declaration would put their relationship on "an inappropriate footing." Merchant is vehement. "*Of course* the bottle exploding is a device, but everywhere else it is done by the slightest gesture. When he says 'My congratulations to you,' the side of his eye is twitching and he's almost about to burst into tears, and he conveys that to you."

The romance alternates between bickering about dustpans and shared cocoa evenings in her parlor. He dislikes her invasion of his monastic butler's pantry with flowers, refuses to share his feelings—"Why, Mr. Stevens, why, why, why do you always have to *pretend*?"—and when she coquettishly corners him and tries to see what he is reading, he simply freezes. "Anthony and I talked about that earlier on, and he said he admired the character because he had such dignity. People would say, oh my goodness, get off your butt and do something! When she asks him if he's reading a risqué novel and tried to take the book away from him, and they're both by the curtain and the light is there, and the audience is feeling—Grab her! Do something!—the way he looks at her is so moving and poignant, you know."

The sexuality of butlers—What the Butler Saw!—has been examined before. It seems quite a can of worms. Dirk Bogarde as the Mephistophelean Barrett in *The Servant*, panders to James Fox, until the chap's moral pinnings collapse; it is a perversion of J. M. Barrie's *The Admirable Crichton*, which saw the roles reversed on a desert island. Erich von Stroheim wore the white gloves for Max von Mayerling, Gloria Swanson's butler—and incidentally ex-director and ex-husband—in *Sunset Boulevard*. Emasculated by the role, he writes her fan mail and wanted to be filmed washing her knickers and frisking with her bra but Billy Wilder rejected the notion. Stevens's affections elsewhere are equally baulked. His father, now aged, had been a great butler, and Stevens gets him taken on as under-butler, but their relationship remains formal. Although his father is dying upstairs, Stevens still has the household to run and rises above considerations to serve the port to Hitler's appeasers gathered at Darlington Hall. But Hopkins does communicate affection in little ways—his eyes seem to police the listeners below stairs as his father, Peter Vaughan, tells an interminable yarn about a butler's *sang froid* in the face of a tiger in the study. At the deathbed, his silent whistling speaks volumes. "And when you see their hands together when Hopkins is trying to remove Peter Vaughan's hand from the trolley where he has fallen, their hands have such a resemblance! This man's entire attention and concentration is on little things—gestures are what they will do for the character." Merchant chuckles. "As a matter of fact, in Badminton House where we were shooting, there was a son who had succeeded the father and the father had become the under-butler."

It's a dying breed, the Stevens butler, reduced in number from fifteen thousand in the heyday of the great houses to a contemporary eighty. "And you're a genuine old-fashioned English butler, not just some waiter pretending to be one?" someone asks Stevens, who dates his interwar generation of butler from the central position afforded to silver polishing. Butlers should be attached to distinguished households run by gentlemen of moral stature, and, by contributing to the agreeability of the setting, contribute to history. It has been Stevens's bad luck to spend his salad days serving Lord Darlington—James Fox again—whom history had judged a Nazi sympathizer. Unlike Jeeves, though also shimmering in and out of the presence "with as little uproar as a jellyfish," few would say of Stevens that "from the collar upwards he stands alone."

Butlers knew their place to varying degrees. Jeeves, technically a valet, steered Bertie Wooster away from "sudden" checks and shirtings—"not uniformly successful, sir"—and confided once that "employers are like horses. They need managing." Nigel Dennis in *Cards of Identity* attributed much of a butler's essence to his name. "We begin with the premise that every butler believes he was born to command a fleet," he writes, and tries Nelson, Camperdown, Anson, Beatty, and Mountbatten before settling on Jellicoe. "A bellicose, echoing, challenging suggestion discreetly balanced by an opening syllable indicative of a nature congealed and wobbly." Bultitudes and Bullivants abound in Ivy Compton Burnett. The oleaginous, bowler-hatted Charles Laughton was Ruggles in *Ruggles of Red Gap*, delivering the Gettysburg Address, reducing the owlshoots in the Western saloon to shamed silence. British Eric Blore established himself in Hollywood with *A Gentleman's Gentleman* and *Top Hat*, and subsequently buttled snippily for Preston Sturges.

Is there a suggestion that the transatlantic trade has moved the other way? Critic David Thompson [*sic*] wrote of "a rather unobtrusively tasteful diffidence" about James Ivory's work. Pauline Kael, reviewing *A Room with a View*, found him "essentially a director who assembles the actors, arranges the *bric-à-brac*, and calls for the camera." She was harder still on *Maurice*: "Ivory was a stylist in all the subsidiary ways. You feel that the table settings are right and that he would jump if a fork were out of place." Both seem to be within a whisker of damning the director as a sort of butler himself to our great publishing houses, ensuring the seamless continuity of the literary tradition through celluloid, and generally buffing the decanter.

But rather than viewing *The Remains of the Day* as Ivory's most personal work, it's more pertinent to note the continuing theme. Stevens, like Mr. Bridge in *Mr. and Mrs. Bridge*, is a man who has failed to observe Forster's dictum, "only connect." "No, Stevens didn't connect," agrees Merchant. "What Forster meant was that we let our lives pass by and we never see beyond a certain thing because we are so absorbed in what we're doing. We never allow side winds to enter our lives. It's a kind of blindness." And it leads to the last scene in which Stevens faces what Forster calls "the shamefaced world of precautions and barriers" to realize that a lifetime of small incidents has rendered dreams irredeemable. He has wasted his life.

Despite Stevens's definition of greatness in his calling as a sort of Method affair, the actor was refreshingly pragmatic about his abilities, demonstrating the "unseemly demonstrativeness" of the Celt even on that melancholy shoot. "When we were doing that scene in Weston-super-Mare near the end where he and Emma go to the pier and sit down together, it was crazy weather. We were having a storm and it was very difficult to light, raining constantly, and the wind was blowing the lights away. It was a Friday night and I was cooking away"—Merchant is a celebrated cook and columnist—"and Tony loves Indian food with a passion and he'd heard that I was cooking. He suggested that we break and eat the dhal and rice before continuing so that the weather could calm down and our stomachs could calm down and we could continue with the work. He rushed to the catering van and pushed me aside from where I'd been cooking for hours and started serving the crew. 'I'm here now! I've prepared these fine dishes.' Then we went back and finished the shoot. That spirit you know is so important."

The Elegance of James Ivory: 1994 D. W. Griffith Award Winner

Carolyn Hill/1995

Permission to reprint this article from *DGA News* 20, no. 2 (April–May 1995): 26–27, 30, 32, courtesy of the Directors Guild of America, Inc.

Director James Ivory joins an impressive group of directors as only the twenty-fifth filmmaker to receive the D. W. Griffith Award for distinguished achievement in motion picture direction. A Guild member for more than twenty years, Ivory accepted the award, the DGA's highest honor, during the Beverly Hills ceremony on March 11, 1995, at the annual Directors Guild of America Awards.

Most recently known for directing elegant period pieces, Ivory has been working within the Merchant-Ivory framework for thirty-five years. The result of his collaboration with producer Ismail Merchant and writer Ruth Prawer Jhabvala has been such acclaimed films as *Remains of the Day, Howards End, A Room with a View*, and *Bombay Talkie.*

On the eve of the recent release of his latest film, *Jefferson in Paris* [1995], Ivory spoke with the *DGA News* about his style of directing, the three-picture deal with Disney, and how his career evolved over the years.

Questioner: How did you react when you were told you were receiving the D. W. Griffith Award?
James Ivory: I felt humbled—especially when I saw who the other recipients of this award have been, and for the fact that it is for all of my work.

Q: What was the turning point of your career?

JI: The turning point was meeting Ismail Merchant. I was already a director, but not a director of features. I suppose sooner or later I would have become a feature director. Meeting Ismail and Ruth Prawer Jhabvala, it all came about so naturally and so swiftly.

In a way, it happened before I was ready for it. I didn't know anything when I first started out. After attending the University of Oregon and then going on to do graduate work, I was working in documentaries. I was making the third one, *The Delhi Way*, which was about New Delhi, when I met Ismail and then Ruth. I met her through him; she had written *The Householder* and Ismail wanted to make it into a movie. Ismail and I went to see her. She was very dubious. People had approached her before about making books of hers into movies or plays—and they never materialized.

Q: How do you choose the subject matter of your movies?
JI: Most of our movies are not based on novels. There were a whole slew of movies before we started doing novels. I don't know—it just happens. I don't read things in order to make movies out of them. I make a movie out of something that I like. I am not searching for books to do.

Q: Is Ruth usually the person who brings up ideas to you?
JI: Sometimes. She steered me towards certain writers. An example of that is Henry James. I had not read much Henry James. She was aghast that I knew so little about him, so she started giving me some of the simple novels to read. I did read them and enjoyed them. Then of course, there are Ruth's own books.

Q: What is Mr. Merchant's role in Merchant-Ivory?
JI: He keeps everything in place and makes things happen. It all works because he is there and it wouldn't work otherwise. I have always thought that the three of us are a bit like the United States government—I'm the President, Ismail is the Congress, and Ruth is the Supreme Court. That's how we operate and how we get our business done. I think that defines our functions.

Q: Tell me about the Jefferson film. What happened when you got the call from Disney?
JI: I was really happy because it was a project that we have been developing for quite a while. We first started developing it in France and we had a modest grant from the French government. It seems amazing in the

United States to imagine the government putting up the money to write scripts. The French government liked the idea about doing a film about Jefferson in Paris.

In 1986, we took it further with TriStar and Ruth wrote a script. Then TriStar broke up and everybody left. We tried to interest people in financing it, but nobody wanted to. Then [former Disney chief] Jeffrey Katzenberg telephoned us in London to say that he had just gone to see *Howards End*. He liked it very, very much and said he was interested in the *Jefferson* script, so we sent it out to him. He got back to us in two days and said that he liked it, let's do it. That led to our three-picture deal with Disney. The Jefferson film is outside of that—it precedes the deal.

Q: Is it going to change your filmmaking in any way? Will you get more money for your films?
JI: Well, a bit. But I don't think it will change the way we do things.

Q: Did you know that the average price to make a movie is $30 million in 1994?
JI: Really? Well, *Jefferson in Paris* was made for half of that [$14 million]. We're able to do it because we have good people working for us.

Q: Why a film about Thomas Jefferson in Paris?
JI: In a way, the Jefferson film was like one of those projects you could never get off the ground. I've been thinking about it and dreaming about it for years. As a child, I was very interested in pre-revolutionary France. It was something I read about endlessly. I was also very interested in the American South before the Civil War. In the Jefferson story, those two strands are intertwined—the old regime and the French Revolution. That was very much in the times of American slavery. If I hadn't done *Jefferson*, I would always regret not doing it. It is the film I always wanted to make and never could. Now I have, and it seems to have turned out [well].

Q: Nick Nolte as Jefferson seems like an odd choice . . .
JI: People think so because of the perception of him; there are so many Nick Nolte parts that are a certain kind of American man. After seeing *Lorenzo's Oil*, [I felt] that he was a very thoughtful and deep actor. Physically he was right for the part in the sense that he was well over six feet tall, the right coloring, the right age. He was the right type. We just called up his agent and sent him the script.

Q: I was reading a *Forbes Magazine* article from 1987 about Merchant-Ivory and it said that for actors, "Merchant-Ivory Productions has established itself as the place to go to make quality films." Do you agree?

JI: I don't know that we are the only place to go, but we certainly make quality films. We find actors or they find us, they do find us. The girl who plays Sally Hemings in the Jefferson movie—she found us. I didn't know about Thandie Newton, she had the script because she has the same agent as Nolte. She came to our office in New York and, luckily, I was there. She didn't make an appointment, she just came and she read for me. I knew it would be. There's something so compelling and graceful about her.

Q: When you're casting, is there a certain feeling or vibe you get from an actor?

JI: Yes. With any actor, you want to find what I consider an individual distinction of personality and looks. In other words, they can't just look like everybody. I look for something that is special and theirs. I like them to look different as well. It has nothing to do with doing period films because you can dress people up and fix their hair. Anyone can fit into any period. I just like to get a look that's individual so they look like real people.

Q: How did you feel when Emma Thompson won the Oscar for *Howards End*?

JI: I figured she would. I felt when we were making the film, that her performance was something extraordinary—I had never seen anything like it. It was of the highest, highest quality. I also knew there weren't that many good women's roles, and this was such a wonderful role. So it wasn't that much of a surprise.

Q: How did you come to work with Anthony Hopkins?

JI: I had known of his work, but hadn't really thought of him as one of our actors.

Q: What do you mean when you say "one of our actors?"

JI: The kind of person who will be happy working under the Merchant-Ivory set up. It's a smaller, closer-knit, intimate organization and we have to have people who can live within that and not swallow it. There are actors who would swallow it—demanding all sorts of extraordinary powers, causing trouble with temper tantrums. We have had people like that. They last the whole film and then you never work with them again. When actors misbehave, it gets out. Very soon people won't hire them any more.

Directors talk all of the time. I've always wondered why these actors and their agents don't figure that directors get together. They suggest a certain person to be in a film, and you already know that this person is a nightmare.

Q: Tell me about working with actors. There's such wealth in the performances and yet, you have a reputation for not being the fiery-headed director.

JI: Well that would be distracting. They don't do their best work [under those circumstances]. You have to be outside of it somehow. The process is theirs: They are the ones who develop the characters. You have to leave them to do that and then see what they are going to come up with. It may not be quite what you have imagined. You may want to change it or you may not.

Sometimes what they bring to you is so far beyond what you could have imagined that you don't want to disturb the process. And then sometimes they're not quite on track and you have to poke them a bit. I'm never off the set. I never go away. I'm not someone who sits and watches the whole thing on the monitor. I stand behind them and whisper in their ears.

Q: How do you know if the chemistry is going to work between your principals?

JI: You don't, you just have to hope. It doesn't always, you know. We always have a reading. The one for *Jefferson* we did at the Ritz Hotel in Paris in a suite. For big scenes, there is usually a reading involving the whole cast.

For instance, in *Jefferson*, we had to rehearse the "Head and Heart Letter" scene very, very carefully. Ruth was present for that and she really didn't like the way it was turning out. She thought that there was something wrong with the way she had written it, and she rewrote things to make it better. It was about three times longer. We had to rehearse a couple of scenes, but other than that we don't rehearse, except on the set. We just jump in.

It was different with *Mr. and Mrs. Bridge*. We rehearsed that for two weeks before we started shooting. But that was because we could get the cast together in New York. Normally, you can't get the cast together. So there's no point in having rehearsal.

Q: Your films have been called "elegant." Do you think that's an accurate description?
JI: I would like to think they're elegant, but that the elegance is a mental one. The elegance is first found in the script—and not only as just an adjective. The script is well thought-out and has been well written. I think that's where elegance shows in a movie. You can have people in all sorts of fancy clothes and have the most elegant big cars, but if it's a lousy script, you're nowhere. The script is where elegance starts in a film.

Q: How do you choose a location?
JI: We really stick to about five different countries: the United States, England, France, Italy, and India. That's where we have filmed. I know enough about them to work there. I could probably work in Pakistan also. There's really no time, in my career, to film a whole bunch of new places and to try to learn about them. It would be sort of false. How long am I going to be directing movies? I hope for a while.

Q: What happened in Florence when you had to clear the Piazza della Signoria for *A Room with a View*?
JI: In Florence, you rent a piazza for various functions. Those piazzas are enormous meeting places for all of the people. So you can rent a whole piazza or a half or quarter of one, for a whole or half a day. When we rented Piazza della Signoria for the big scenes in *Room with a View*, there was a group of women protesting bad housing. They came with all of their banners and placards and such, but we got them to go away.

Then another day there was a real foul-up. We had rented another square and so had the local Communist party. They were building this enormous platform in the middle of the square where they were going to have their speeches and all that. We got them to move it out of the way and put it in a different part of the square. All of their people and our crew got into it and picked up this incredibly heavy iron and wood platform and moved it to get it out of camera range. I can't imagine what it weighed.

Q: You seem so un-Hollywood. Do you ever go there?
JI: Yes, all the time. I enjoy going to Los Angeles. I have lots of friends

there. How can I think of Hollywood as bizarre or strange? There's been a connection with Merchant-Ivory and Hollywood since the beginning, film after film. Most people don't know that.

Our first film, *The Householder*, was distributed by Columbia Pictures. That gave us the money to do our next film, which was partially distributed by Fox. The next film was made by Fox. Then there was involvement with United Artists and on and on. It's not that we feared corruption from Hollywood. There's not a script we didn't send to the studios. Usually they turned them down—in the seventies, anyway. Then, with *A Room with a View*, we became very popular.

Q: Any final thoughts from this year's D. W. Griffith Award winner?

JI: I'm glad I'm still working. I'm glad I haven't stopped.

Ismail Merchant:
The Maker of Dreams

Shahrukh Husain/1995

From *Index on Censorship* 24, no. 6 (1995): 34–36. Reprinted by permission.

Ismail Merchant was only seven years old when his passionate affair with cinema began. From his first film, the boy was gripped by the magic of Indian movies.

"It was *Mela*, starring Nargis and Dilip Kumar," he recalls. "The stars were so handsome, the story so painfully beautiful . . . and when they sang the song," he muses, quoting extensively from its most famous lyric, "I cried."

Other films followed, classics of Indian cinema and its stars. There was *Jugnu*, starring the singer-star Nur Jehan and many others, including the great Raj Kapoor movies, *Aag, Andaaz, Awaara* with their lavish sets. V. Shantaram, with his magnificent mythologicals such as *Shakuntala*, was another favorite.

Whether these films were ironic and questioning "socials," or fantasies of the past, engaged with the growing "westernization" of India or immersed in its rich and ancient heritage of music and story, Indian cinema was unashamedly glamorous and fabulous. Stories, songs, actors transported people into an enchanted, if remote, world.

Never content with watching his dreams from afar, Ismail was determined to realize them in his own life. His first chance came when his family became close to an aristocratic family with whom they stayed on pilgrimages to Ajmer, the tomb of a famous Muslim saint. "I would hear the grown-ups speak about Jaddan Bai (Nargis's mother) and Wahidan Bai, another celebrated singer who was married to the Nawab's aunt."

Years later Ismail met Wahidan's daughter Nimmi when she called on the Nawab in Bombay. Ismail was entranced. "She had exquisite eyes: piercing, hazel, and arched eyebrows like swords; he reminisces, lapsing into the language of Urdu poetry. "She must have been eighteen, maybe nineteen. She took me to the premiere of her film *Barsaat Barsaat*. We went in her green Cadillac and people threw flowers. It was her first film and she was an instant hit."

Hooked by now with the glamour and the stardust, fourteen-year-old Ismail took to haunting Nimmi's house in Marine Drive, the exclusive area where many stars lived. Soon they were firm friends. "We would go to the Eros cinema and watch English and American movies together and Nimmi would tell me I should become a film star so that we could play opposite each other."

But Ismail had other aspirations: he wanted to make films—to run the show. "Cinema creates this magic in one's life," says Ismail. "If used constructively, it permeates religion, politics—every kind of communication. Its power is huge." And it was his conviction that the fantasy and the thrill were accessible to everyone, if only they reached out, that prompted him to court the star, and bring them into the lives of his fellow students. "I was president of the Music Society at university and I regularly invited the top stars to be the guests of honor. We could sell many more tickets if the visiting celebrity was a film star.

"I invited Nargis once. She said she would have to come direct from her shoot to be there for the starting time of 6:30. When she still hadn't come at 7:30, I went to her house, Chateau Marine. She came to the door, relaxed—not at all as if she was going anywhere. Someone had told her the event had been cancelled. I told her no, it was on and I was here to collect her. She got dressed immediately and we got to the show in her black and white Riley just as people were beginning to think she wasn't coming.

"Movie stars," he adds, "are one step down from gods and goddesses. I'd say they're higher in status than politicians. Politicians have to court them to attend their campaigns and rally votes. Look at M. G. Ramachandran in the south—he's hardly less powerful than a god. He began as a film star. It's a reliable route for an idealist who wants to change things for the better. Become a film star first."

Indeed, Nargis, and her husband Sunil Dutt who co-starred with her in *Mother India*, both became prominent politicians as did numerous others including Dilip Kumar, one of the "Big Three" male superstars of the 1940s and 1950s, and Vyjayanthimala, the dancing megastar of the 1950s and 1960s.

"People associate them with their roles and everyone wants to follow someone else's charisma and superior identity. That's why even though the quality of Indian cinema isn't the same anymore, the worship continues."

James Ivory

Geoffrey Macnab/1999

From *Clips*, Winter 1999, 8–11. Reprinted by permission of Geoffrey Macnab and Quantel.

James Ivory limps across the ballroom of the Des Bains Hotel in Venice, looking every inch the old colonial grandee. Seventy-one now, he has been making movies for more than forty years. No, Ivory says, having finally put down his walking stick, maneuvered himself onto a sofa and stretched his leg in front of him, the limp is nothing to do with gout or affectation. "I fell down in St. Mark's Square yesterday and then the person I was with fell on top of me. The full weight of someone falling on your leg is not a good thing—especially if you're falling on stone."

Ivory is in Venice for the festival screening of his latest feature, *A Soldier's Daughter Never Cries*, which was produced by his partner Ismail Merchant. He co-wrote the script himself, together with his regular collaborator, Ruth Prawer Jhabvala. The trio has been making films together since the 1960s, when they first met in India. Even so, *A Soldier's Daughter* seems a departure. An adaptation of an autobiographical novel by Kaylie Jones about growing up in Paris in the 1960s, it might best be described as a family melodrama. It has few of the period trappings we have come to expect in Merchant-Ivory productions. Take a closer look and you realize that the film deals with familiar themes. It's about an American adrift in Europe (a subject Ivory knows well). This may not be a Henry James or E. M. Forster adaptation, but it was inspired by a well-known writer: Kaylie's father was James Jones, author of *The Thin Red Line* and *From Here to Eternity*.

There is also one character in *A Soldier's Daughter* with whom Ivory feels a particular affinity, the cultured, effete young rebel, Francis Fortescue (Anthony Roth Costanzo). "Like Francis, both as a small boy and later as a teenager, I lived a life of constant self-dramatization—a fact most people meeting me now might not imagine," Ivory observes. Although he didn't grow up in Paris himself, he claims he too was a precocious school child. At high school, he had his own stage act, "Solid Ivory," which involved him walking back and forth with an utterly deadpan face until the audience succumbed and started laughing. Later, when he was in the army, he used to pull stunts on the firing range. He would pretend to be a lousy shot and would dangle his glasses over the end of his nose as if he was myopic. Then he would take aim—and hit the bull's eye every time. "I'm surprised I wasn't beaten up," he says now.

Ivory may have avoided the wrath of the NCOs, but he hasn't always been as lucky with the press. Merchant-Ivory films are regularly lambasted as snobbish, pretentious, and full of unnecessary detail. All those big hats, frilly dresses, and ornate furnishings in the E. M. Forster adaptations have even led some British critics to suggest the team takes its inspiration less from Forster himself than from Laura Ashley.

"But we've been accused of so many things," Ivory chuckles when asked if the criticism affects him, "we've even been accused of murder." He goes on to tell an extraordinary story about *The Deceivers* (1988), a film he and Merchant made which included a scene depicting suttee— the rite by which a Hindi widow throws herself on her husband's funeral pyre and is burned to death. The scene in the movie was never shot. The Indian government wouldn't allow it. "Suttee is almost unheard of today. The British stamped that sort of thing out 150 years ago—it's a crime," Ivory points out. By coincidence, though, while the crew was on location, a real-life incident of suttee took place in a nearby village. The Indian newspapers held Merchant-Ivory responsible, suggesting the filmmakers had staged the burning (and the death of the woman) for the sake of their film. "Perhaps it was because our love of authenticity is so well-known."

After the accusations of murder, the charge that Ivory makes literary, hidebound, heritage cinema doesn't seem quite so stinging. "It's said that it's the English who are saying these things," he reflects, "but in the years that we have been making the E. M. Forster films, it has slowly dawned on me that the English don't like Forster very much. They see him as a hectoring old auntie who should shut up."

Ivory holds no truck with the idea that the English are buttoned up and repressed. "In all my years of dealing with English characters in my films, I've never found that they are emotionally restrained. If anything I think they're nakedly emotional . . . often far more than they themselves may realize." On his travels in England, he adds, he is constantly surprised by how ready complete strangers are to unburden themselves to him in a way Americans never would.

Do classic novels make classic movies? The very question annoys Ivory. "Sure they do," he snarls. "They have again and again. For me, it's the scenes and the characters—not so much the story. That has always been the fun of it for filmmakers." Ivory is renowned for his painstaking approach to his craft. It doesn't make any difference whether he is making a period piece like *Jefferson in Paris* (1995), or more contemporary films like *A Soldier's Daughter Never Cries* or *Slaves of New York* (1989). "Just because it's a modern film doesn't mean that I don't need a good designer. Everything has to be prepared and done well. If you're setting up the Court of Louis XV and you see someone coming marching into the Hall of Mirrors, that's obviously one kind of effort, and if you're filming a very fifth-rate small town in 1970s North Carolina where high school students go (as we did in *A Soldier's Daughter*), that also takes a lot of effort. I'll be damned if I'm going to listen to people who criticize me for taking great pains to do things in the proper way. That's what I call production value." At this point Ivory's brow furrows. "It is not, absolutely not, some morbid preoccupation with detail for the sake of detail."

Filmmaking is a labor-intensive craft. All films, Ivory argues, are "collections of details of every kind." The unseen detail, the exhaustive editing process for instance, is like the bottom of an iceberg. "People don't recognize it." He suggests that his detractors are intimidated by the grandeur of the settings found in Merchant-Ivory's work. "I can't help it if their eyes are wandering all over the set and they're not listening. That's their problem."

There is one exquisite moment in *Remains of the Day* (1993), Merchant-Ivory's adaptation of Kazuo Ishiguro's prize-winning novel, which shows how well his meticulous approach sometimes pays off. The elderly butler (Peter Vaughan) is serving the guests at a dinner party. A little bubble of snot dribbles out of his nose into the wine just as he is about to pour for his lordship (James Fox). It's a throwaway incident, but it captures brilliantly both the butler's mortification and the unstated tension between servant and master "That was in the book," Ivory remembers. "I thought, how in the world are we going to show a runny nose so that you can really see it? In order for the audience to be able to see it, you have to have the camera right up under the tip of the nose. We worked and worked and worked and worked to get just that right drop," says Ivory, describing what was, clearly, a labor of love. No, he adds, it is not Vaughan's own snot. "It's like tears—they came out of a little tube." *Remains of the Day* ends on a downbeat note. The retired butler (Anthony Hopkins) watches impassively as the woman he loves (ex-housekeeper Emma Thompson) disappears over a rain-swept horizon on the back of an old bus. Ivory recalls that senior Hollywood executives frowned on such a bleak finale. "The supreme pontiff of Columbia saw the film in a private screening and jumped up and said, my god, there goes $50 million. But the happy ending he wanted wasn't the story that Ishiguro wrote and it certainly wasn't the film that we wanted to make."

In the event, *Remains of the Day* tested well despite the final scene. Even if it hadn't, Ivory would have left it alone. He points out that he has always had final cut on his pictures. "That's part of the deal, as they say, and I couldn't imagine making a film with a studio when I didn't have that."

The septuagenarian hauteur looks quite at home sitting on a sofa in the ballroom of the Des Bains, the grandest hotel on the Venice Lido. This is where Thomas Mann wrote *Death in Venice*. It is one of those places that boasts precisely the kind of fading European grandeur that characterizes the world of E. M. Forster and Henry James. Ivory and Venice go back a long way. It was here that he directed his breakthrough film, the half-hour documentary, *Venice—Theme and Variations* (1957), more than forty years ago when he was still a student. "I came here when I was twenty-two as a tourist on my first trip to Europe. I had twenty dollars in my pocket. I stayed in a hotel where people were getting drunk and throwing up all the time. I'd get out of that by going round Venice and I was intensely struck by the beauty of the place," he remembers. A year or two passed. Ivory, who had originally studied fine arts at the University of Oregon with a view to becoming a designer, went to film school at the University of Southern California instead. The course didn't inspire him. In fact, he says, he was bored out of his mind. He talked his father into paying for him to come back to Venice to shoot his thesis film. "The university didn't mind as long as they didn't have to pay."

Ivory knew precious little about shooting a movie ("I hadn't paid attention in class because it was so dull") but somehow managed to cobble together an impressionistic film about why Venice inspires so many artists. The film was well-reviewed in the US, quickly found a distributor, and his career was launched.

It seems that Ivory's attention to detail rubs off on everybody he works with. He recalls that when he cast Nick Nolte as the lead in *Jefferson in Paris*, the burly American star spent the best part of a year researching the role. "He read every possible thing on Jefferson and made all kind of contact with scholars and historians. He was very, very thoroughly prepared."

Even Ivory was a little surprised when Nolte turned up on set for the first day's work, looking like Jefferson sprung back to life. "But then again, we work with incredibly gifted make-up artists and costume designers. When they turn a person out, it normally is a fantastic sight."

He pays extravagant compliments to these designers, most of whom are English. They're far superior, he says, to their counterparts in the US. "It used to be that the Hollywood studios were masters at that kind of thing. But when the studio system fell apart, the best people left or died, everything was sold and all the rest of it."

Ivory is currently in pre-production on a new film, an adaptation of Henry James's *The Golden Bowl*. He has already tackled James before, both in *The Europeans* (1979) and *The Bostonians* (1984), but acknowledges the novelist's work is fiendishly difficult to bring to life on the big screen.

Of James's adaptations other than his own, Jack Clayton's *The Innocents* (1961) is the one he admires most. "It's a long time since I saw it, but I remember it as having a wonderful atmosphere. Photographically, it was eerie and interesting." He didn't much care for either Jane Campion's *Portrait of a Lady* (1998) or Iain Softley's *The Wings of the Dove* (1997). He suggests they were miscast and misinterpreted. "The directors haven't always done their homework and sometimes they've had a tin ear. There is a tendency to rewrite James's dialogue. You have to trim it, yes, but you shouldn't rewrite it—especially not that badly."

Even as he makes the criticisms, Ivory backtracks. "Obviously I've made films myself based on E. M. Forster novels and Henry James novels. Naturally, when I see other films made from those writers' work, I'm ten times more critical than the ordinary cinemagoer would be—maybe harshly and unfairly so." Suffice it to say, he announces loftily, he would have made the films differently. With this last remark, he is ushered off by the publicist to have lunch. He limps slowly away.

Conversation
with Ruth Prawer Jhabvala

Philip Horne/2000

From *The Guardian*, October 27, 2000. Reprinted by permission of Philip Horne.

Academic and author Philip Horne interviewed one of the world's fore-
most screenwriters, Ruth Prawer Jhabvala, at her London home earlier
this week. Recipient of two Oscars for her previous work with Merchant-
Ivory, Ruth Prawer Jhabvala has most recently adapted Henry James's
most complex and ambiguous novel, *The Golden Bowl*, to great acclaim.

Philip Horne: After escaping from Nazi Germany you came to London
in 1939, and later studied English at London University. Does English literature, or Anglo-American literature, have a special meaning for you?
Ruth Prawer Jhabvala: Well, I was very lucky to come here when I
did. I was also very lucky to have the years of doing nothing but reading, mostly English literature. So my whole background is that. It was
extremely fortunate for me. Also, English became my first language.

PH: Do you think studying literature is a better preparation for writing
screenplays, or at any rate adapting classics for the screen, than going to
film school would be?
RPJ: Well, I started off and still am primarily a novelist, and not a screen
writer. Studying English literature is really not studying—to have all
those years to read is a gift. Particularly as I wasn't really very good at
anything . . . It was wonderful to have all those years to read. But I will
say that while I was preparing for my degree I never wrote. I wrote before
and after, but during those years I just read. I even wrote a thesis on the

135

short story in England from 1700 to 1750. There weren't any, of course, but that was my thesis!

PH: Do you think that studying literature at university is why you were interested in adapting classics?

RPJ: I was never interested in adapting classics at all. I've written four novels. I was never interested in film. Never. I never even thought of it. I wasn't even a film buff, I didn't see many films, ever. I never thought of it until Merchant-Ivory came to India and filmed one of my books— they said "Why don't you write the screenplay?" and I said, "Well, I've never written a screenplay and I haven't seen many films," because I was in India by that time and hadn't really had any opportunity to see new films or art films or classic films or anything. So they said, "Well try. We haven't made a feature film before." So that was really my introduction into film.

PH: Is there a main purpose in adapting classics for film?

RPJ: The main purpose is, well, you have to . . . well the main purpose is that I have such a good time—I mean, think of all that marvelous material. Just think of spending all that time in *The Golden Bowl* and other James and Forster books we have done. But especially Henry James because, not so much in *Golden Bowl*, but the other two [*The Europeans, The Bostonians*]—he has such marvelous characters and he has such strong dramatic scenes. You just put your hand in and pull them out.

PH: There isn't an educational impulse?

RPJ: I'm afraid not! Maybe there should be, but I'm afraid I only think of myself.

PH: I suppose you are trying to communicate your enjoyment?

RPJ: Yes, yes. I suppose, yes. And in a way it's an homage to a great author. You know I never write any critical articles or critical reviews, never write anything except fiction and screenplays, so it is a kind of homage. But I never think I'm doing a public service or anything . . .

PH: Do you have any idea why American literary classics from the turn of the century seem to be so fashionable at the moment?

RPJ: Is Henry James particularly fashionable? Well, let me think. Well, yes, I think so.

PH: Over the last few years . . .
RPJ: Yes. Well, it is such grand material, wonderful scenes, great characters, such wonderful relationships between the characters—the material
is there.

PH: The French director Jacques Rivette said, in 1974, that James is one
of the "unfilmable" authors, who "can be filmed diagonally, taking up
their themes, but never literally." You obviously don't agree . . .
RPJ: No, I do agree! Any adaptation you do it diagonally. You can take
up the theme but you can never, never, never do it literally. You'd come
up with a kind of travesty, if you tried to interpret anything literally.

PH: But fidelity, is that important?
RPJ: Fidelity is not the first [thing]. No, I don't think so. Like I said, the
theme and the feel of the characters, the ambience and their relationships, that is what you try and—but never, never literally.

PH: So it's a separate work, really?
RPJ: In a way. I'll tell you what I usually do. I read the book several times,
usually it's a book I know very well anyway, but I read it several times and
make some notes and make a kind of plan that I think I would want to
follow—usually I don't, it breaks down at some point—and then I put
the book away and really don't look at it again until I've filled out my
own thing. And then I look at it again and see what I have missed. But
there is a period when the book and I are two separate entities.

PH: How much changing do you do when you go back to the book at
that stage? Or what kinds of things do you change?
RPJ: Nothing really—usually I find that I look for some poignancy or
some scene that might contribute more, that might point something
out that should be there in the screenplay. I try and find that. Or even
just half a line of dialogue can be a God-send to me at that point.

PH: How well do you find Henry James's dialogue works?
RPJ: Well, again, it works diagonally. You really have to transcribe it.
He's not the only person—all the others—you can never just take it off
the page. However colloquial the language might sound, this is not how
actors can speak.

PH: Could I ask what you liked or what you didn't like about any of the recent James adaptations?

RPJ: Well, I like *Portrait of a Lady* very much, and that was a book we had wanted to do over twenty years ago, but we never had the money for it. We did two other James's, it was easier, we started with *The Europeans* because that was all in America so it was much easier and a much smaller film so it was much easier to raise the money. And then again with *The Bostonians*, that was all in America, easier for us to shoot. Then other things came in-between and *Portrait of a Lady* went, I'm afraid.

PH: Did you ever get as far as a script?

RPJ: No.

PH: I really should congratulate you on making a film, and on getting a film made, of *The Golden Bowl* at all. Was it hard work getting it made?

RPJ: To get it made? Well, no, we got—people said "This is not a good novel" or "This is not one of Henry James's really good novels." They didn't want to go ahead with it. But we did get money for the screenplay, money for the development, and once we had that we didn't have too much difficulty.

PH: How did you pitch the story?

RPJ: I wrote a sort of outline of the book—how we were going to see it and a background of the characters—and that's what we sent out. Because I didn't really expect anyone to have read the book.

PH: Was there an emphasis that you thought was central to that?

RPJ: Well, yes, I think that we said that this was a passionate encounter between four people, and we thought that might sound good to them. So if this had been our first, second film or our third film we may have had more difficulty, but we did have a good record, so people came forward and said, "Well, it may not look like much, but, you know" [*laughs*]. But certainly if we had started out and it had been an early film, we might have had real difficulties.

PH: How different is *The Golden Bowl* to how you would have done it, say, straight after *The Europeans*?

RPJ: I don't think it would have worked so well for me. No, I think I needed a lot more practice, because this was a very difficult script. This was the hardest. This was the nicest and the hardest. The only other one that has been equally difficult and equally rewarding was *Mr. and Mrs. Bridge*—I don't know if you know that one, by Evan S. Connell. Well, it was two books actually, which we adapted into one. And that was one of my favorite films. But those two were the hardest.

PH: When Jack Pulman adapted *The Golden Bowl* for the BBC in 1972, in the famous version directed by James Cellan Jones, with Cyril Cusack, Daniel Massey, and Gayle Hunnicutt, they had six forty-five-minute episodes—a total of four-and-a-half hours. At 130 minutes, your version is only half that length. Are you at all envious?

RPJ: Oh no, no, no. Not at all. That's the difference between television and film, television rests so much on dialogue, not as visual as a film is. You can develop things much more slowly and carefully. But in a film, I mean you just couldn't do it. I wouldn't want to.

PH: But were there sections you would have liked to have taken longer on?

RPJ: No, not really. We were in a two-hour format. Since we did not have time for four or six hours, I thought, well we might as well adapt ourselves to what we have, and just take the essence of the situation and each incident and turn in the story. We couldn't dwell on it.

PH: You obviously have a wonderful working relationship with James Ivory. But late Henry James is notoriously ambiguous and difficult, and no two readers of *The Golden Bowl* read it quite the same way—in fact, a single reader often sees different things in it at each reading. Did you always see it the same way?

RPJ: Yeah. I think we must have done. I mean the screenplay—he read it, and he had some objections, but there was nothing fundamental. I don't think we ever had a fundamental difference of opinion.

PH: Could you talk about how your process of collaboration with James Ivory works?

RPJ: Well, when I lived in India and he lived in New York, or wherever he was, we did a lot through correspondence. But now we all live in New York . . . I am still so used to working on my own that I do several drafts for myself first and then send them to him to make marks in the margin. And then I rewrite, and this goes on over a few months. And then finally, before he really starts to get it all together, we sit together and see where we still might have disagreements. Then he goes and shoots the film—I have nothing to do with that—I only go along to see some rushes. But I will see the rough cut, which is usually twice the length of the final version, then I see it again, and we sit in the editing room for some time and, you know, fiddle about.

PH: So you are involved in the editing?
RPJ: Yes, I am involved in the editing but not in the actual production, or in the casting.

PH: Whose idea was it to begin the film in Renaissance Italy with the discovery of adultery and the killing of the lovers?
RPJ: Well, I put that in right from the beginning because I thought to myself, well, how am I going to show who this prince is and where he comes from? So I read a lot of books about the Renaissance and I came across a story in which a duke actually does kill a stepmother who was involved with her stepson, so I thought, well that's a good background for this film! You can't do these sort of things in a film, but in television you could, you could say that [just] in dialogue. You know, [a narrator] could sit there and expound and talk about it and everyone could listen, but in a film you just can't do that.

PH: The duke is one of the ancestors?
RPJ: Yes. And then there is the slideshow [later in the film], of the families, and then the story of the duke is told.

PH: Later on, in your story, the role of the duke seems to be closer to Adam Verver.
RPJ: Well, yes, you know, you're supposed to think that!

PH: In the book, the figure of Adam Verver is ambiguous to the end, so that we don't ever really know whether he has any clear idea what's been going on, or whether he's a bit of a simple soul, all of whose subtlety is used solely on his business. In your film it seems to me we know very clearly that he knows [what's going on between his wife and stepson].
RPJ: He's immensely clever. A man doesn't become a billionaire and a patron of the arts if he's dim!

PH: So that ambiguity . . .
RPJ: There is no ambiguity. How could he have become a billionaire? In

the book he manipulates the entire situation—he and Maggie between them. He [is] in silence, but he knew what everyone else was thinking.

PH: I was struck by the sympathy with which you presented the predicament of the Ververs who, in much academic criticism since F. R. Leavis, are taken to be capitalistic vampires, an essentially incestuous father-daughter team, draining the passionate blood from their weaker partners. Do you think there's a sinister side to what the Ververs do in the book that doesn't appear in the film?

RPJ: Not at all. I think Henry James loved Maggie Verver. He loves her and he enters into her more than any other character in any other novel. All of the passion that she has for the prince, this is Henry James's passion that he has given her. I really don't see this reinterpretation. Though I like Gore Vidal's introduction [to the Penguin edition] very much, but I didn't really like his thesis that they are the manipulators, and the prince and Charlotte are the victims. In a way they are the victims because they are social victims, because they have nothing and are dependent on them. But that has nothing to do with the character of the Ververs, who are all goodness, and Henry James painted them as goodness, in a way that an earlier Bostonian knows goodness, I think.

PH: I admired your courage in actually having the golden bowl itself appear and also be discussed as a symbol. Could you say something about what it means for you?

RPJ: Well first of all it's an object, we had to have it there, it's a physical object, which one person buys and another does not. The moment when the golden bowl is delivered in the film is also the moment when she [Maggie] discovers about the relationship between Charlotte and her husband. The golden bowl itself—Fanny says she does not believe it—it has a crack, it's damaged, and Fanny says, "Who would think? It looks so perfect?" And then she [Maggie] says "yes, a perfect fake." And that's how she sees the situation that has been created for her, her marriage, and her father's marriage in fact, is a perfect fake. Like the golden bowl. And shortly afterwards [Amerigo] asks, well, "What do you want?" and she says, "I want a happiness without a hole in it, I want the bowl without a crack." So it's a perfect symbol for us, and in the film we do see it.

PH: You seem to agree with the idea that the man in the shop who sells Maggie the golden bowl, and intervenes decisively in the plot, is Henry James appearing in the action. Am I right?

RPJ: No, that was an accident.

PH: Really? It was an accident? Because many critics think it intentional. [The shop owner] says "my golden bowl" in a rather emphatic way.

RPJ: Yes, he does look like [Henry James] [*laughs*]. But no, I never thought of that. Plus I wasn't there when he was cast.

PH: You also seemed to have rethought Prince Amerigo, making him less languid and passive than he appears in the book. I noticed that he drives his own car and has his chauffeur sit in the back; and he even wins a bicycle race. What is the logic behind that?

RPJ: Well, you can't have a languid central character, otherwise why would these two women be in love with him? You need some kind of driving force.

PH: In the first edition of *The Portrait of a Lady*, Isabel first comes across Mme. Merle playing Beethoven on the piano; in the revised edition it's Schubert, a more beautiful, sadder, less stirringly courageous composer. You have Charlotte play Adam Verver a Debussy Sarabande. Does that characterize her? [In the novel she just plays Adam some of his "favorite things."]

RPJ: No, not at all. Charlotte plays very badly and Henry James says she plays like you would play a game of tennis, you know, correctly but . . . Debussy was at that time a modern composer, so . . . I think in *Room with a View* we had Schumann a lot.

PH: Incidentally, you have Fanny near the end of the film tell the story of *The Portrait of a Lady* as if it's something that's happened to a friend— she's a friend of Isabel Osmond, née Archer.

RPJ: You spotted that? Good! In fact I put it right in, and then she turns round and says, "That dreadful husband, what was his name?" I had in fact put in his real name, but Jim [Ivory] thought that was going too far . . . so he used another name.

PH: Was that a joke?

RPJ: Well, I thought it was as good a story as any!

PH: So that's twenty years after the action of *Portrait of a Lady*?

RPJ: Yes.

PH: Do you think Isabel is happy?

RPJ: No, no. I'm afraid not [*laughs*]. I think this is the one book with a happy ending.

PH: *The Golden Bowl*? You think Charlotte is happy?
RPJ: Well, yes. She is going to be one of these great patronesses of the arts like Isabella in *The Bostonians*, and he will probably die twenty years before her, and it will all be hers.

PH: Adam and Charlotte do seem here to have a marriage in which sex might happen. Is that right, and is she lying when she says to Amerigo that she will never have children?
RPJ: I'm afraid there is something that we had to cut out there. She could not have children. We had that in one scene that we had to drop. In fact two scenes. There was one where she comes back from the doctor's and tells Adam that they all say the same thing, and he says "Well, you know . . ." And then there is another scene where she says, you know, "I have been to Sir Matthew This and Sir William That and they all say the same thing." She is barren. And in the book she says that she can't have a child but it is not her fault. But we didn't want to undermine Adam Verver's manhood! [*laughs*] Since we had Nick Nolte! It is very different from the book because in the book Adam Verver is not such a fine figure of a man.

PH: Is there a literary critic on *The Golden Bowl* whose work you admire or agree with, or have been influenced by?
RPJ: No, I never read about anything, I always read the thing. I read around the social life and where it all came from, but it would disturb me to read other people's opinions I think. I really want to go to the text itself, or to how the text came about—the personal and social circumstances behind it.

PH: The book was published in 1904, but your action runs from 1903 to 1909. Were you inspired by the recent [1997] film of *The Wings of the Dove*, which also pushed its action forward to the end of the Edwardian period in order to get in those modern things—like the ballet you include? What is the ballet?
RPJ: It's an invention by an American choreographer called Carol Armitage with whom Jim has worked with before. Our usual composer, Richard Robbins wrote the music.

PH: So it's a pastiche, like Bernard Herrmann's pastiche in *Citizen Kane*, the opera that Kane's second wife performs and fails to hit the top note?
RPJ: Yes, it's completely a pastiche.

PH: So Charlotte likes modern things and Adam doesn't?
RPJ: Well, he's not very musical anyway, remember when she plays the piano, he's half asleep. Art is his thing, not music. With her everything would tend to be somewhat fashionable, like a woman like that would be today . . .

PH: So you think she doesn't have a deep appreciation of art?
RPJ: I don't think so, no. Although she will, already in the later scenes she has learnt a lot. And certainly when they reach America and start this museum, she is going to make herself a great expert.

PH: When Maggie brings the book out to Charlotte in the garden at the end, you introduce a detail that's not in the novel. Charlotte comments, "I read something else by the same author. I found it rather contrived." Is the book meant to be a book by James?
RPJ: No! No, absolutely not. "But the social scenes are well done," that's the next bit [of their conversation]. But no, absolutely not, never.

PH: I thought it might be James, because Charlotte wouldn't understand James.
RPJ: No, no. I wouldn't do that.

PH: Would Charlotte like James if she had read him?
RPJ: Well, she might like early James—*Daisy Miller*—up to, well, not *The Europeans*, too American, but the early ones that were really popular. She might even have read *Portrait of a Lady*—she's not a fool, although they do say a lot in the book that she's really stupid, and compared with the others perhaps she is, but she does have her wits about her.

PH: When they go to see [art dealer] Mr. Guterman-Seuss, in the book it's supposed to be Brighton but you made it Camberwell. Why?
RPJ: Well, we didn't want to take a trip to Brighton, and some London suburb was easier. In fact we did have a scene where he laid out the tiles and Adam Verver sees how appreciative Charlotte is of it and that brings him closer to proposing—as he did in Brighton—but we had to cut that

scene out in editing. A lot gets lost! But you don't regret it afterwards, you really don't feel regret for the scenes that have gone.

PH: What other scenes were cut at editing stage?
RPJ: Oh, many [*laughs*]! Very, very many. At the beginning there were scenes about inviting Charlotte to stay at Fawns and how poor she is, and the prince listens to all of this, and how she had a great romance with somebody but no one knows who it is, and the poor prince is having to sit there . . . but all that went. We don't cut scenes out because of length, we just want the scenes that really work for us. If you only have two hours the essence is what you come down to.

PH: Do you have any other James adaptations in mind?
RPJ: No, I don't think so. I think that *The Golden Bowl* is the ultimate for him, it's his last novel . . . so I don't think I'd particularly want to. There's none that I could think of now that I would want to do.

James Ivory Interview

Mike Goodridge/2002

From *Screencraft: Directing* (Crans-Près-Céligny, Switzerland: RotoVision SA, 2002), 143–53. Reprinted by permission of Mike Goodridge and Elsevier.

James Ivory and his partners, producer Ismail Merchant and screenwriter Ruth Prawer Jhabvala, have carved out and maintained a unique niche within film—a cottage industry of intelligent, consistently successful productions which they generate and raise the finance for independently from bases in New York, London, and Paris. Although most famous for his impressive canon of literary adaptations, the range of films directed by Ivory is intriguingly wide. His first feature, The Householder *in 1963, a comedy of a schoolteacher coping with his arranged marriage, was the first collaboration between the trio and the first fruit of Merchant-Ivory Productions. Later,* Bombay Talkie *(1970) looked at the affair between a British writer and an Indian movie-star. It wasn't until his sixth film,* The Wild Party *in 1974, that Ivory tackled a period piece, which was in this case an adaptation of Joseph Moncure March's poem about 1920s Hollywood. The first of his adaptations of literary classics was Henry James's* The Europeans *in 1979. Since then, he has mostly stuck to novel adaptations, tackling Jean Rhys (*Quartet, *1981), more James (*The Bostonians, *1984;* The Golden Bowl, *2000), E. M. Forster (*A Room with a View, *1985;* Maurice, *1987;* Howards End, *1992). Other films include* Heat and Dust *(from Jhabvala's own novel, 1982),* Slaves of New York *(1989), Mr. and Mrs. Bridge *(from books by Evan S. Connell, 1990), his masterful* The Remains of the Day *(from Kazuo Ishiguro's novel, 1993),* Jefferson in Paris *(1995), and* Surviving Picasso *(1996).*

I had been commissioned by The Asia Society of New York to make a documentary about Delhi, and travelled to India. There I became friendly with Satyajit Ray, and on a trip to Calcutta he invited me to go to the set of *Two Daughters*, (or *Three Daughters* as it was originally called; one of the stories was cut out by Ray's American distributor because it was too long). I remember getting up at absolutely the crack of dawn to be out there on set in the country. It was the last day of work on one of the stories, "The Postmaster," and I just watched and watched. It was the first time I had ever seen a director at work. Even though I had gone to USC film school [University of Southern California], we had never visited a Hollywood film set in all the years I was there. I don't think I knew what a director did until I went on Ray's set and I saw him communicating all sorts of things to the actors in various kinds of ways, and muttering things to his cameraman. At that point, he had begun to operate his own camera, which is something his cameramen were not thrilled about, but they could hardly stop him. And I understand now why a director would want to operate his own camera if he could, especially for Ray, who couldn't do a lot of takes because Kodak film was so hard to get in India at the time. He would know at once whether he had got what he wanted out of his actors in terms of timing and composition in a way the cameraman could not.

And when I came to do my first feature, *The Householder*, two years later in Delhi with Ismail, we were able to hire his first cameraman, Subrata Mitra, and about fifteen of his crew, including his first assistant. So in a sense, what they knew was what I learned during the nuts-and-bolts part of making a movie. I had never sat down and done a breakdown of a scene or a shot before then. It was like jumping into cold water, but I had to be able to do that.

I think *The Householder* naturally benefited from the fact that I was with Ray's long-time collaborators, and aesthetically there was further benefit, because I was looking at a scene through the eyes of his cameraman. When we came to editing the film, as we weren't happy with it—it was long and draggy and not cleverly edited—Ismail and I asked Ray if we could bring the film to show him, so we put ten reels of sound, ten reels of pictures, and a lot of rushes in some big tin trunks and went on a train from Bombay to Calcutta. He liked the film and agreed to help us shape it, but on the condition that he do it freely with his editor, Dulal Dutta, and we not interfere. "Leave me alone for two or three days," he said. Anyway, he worked out a whole new scheme for the actual story and shortened it considerably, and gave it the flashback form it has today, within bookends. When we did *Shakespeare Wallah* later on, we again showed it to Ray, who suggested how we might tidy it up a bit, and he agreed to do the music.

I feel that I have never really found a better way to set my scenes than the way Ray taught me, or a way I *like* better, to put it another way. Somehow unconsciously and without a tremendous amount of analysis on my part, simply seeing his films over and over has worked on me in a way, so that, although I'm dealing with different kinds of subject matter and in countries thousands of miles away from India, I feel his influence very strongly. Some years after I've finished a movie and I'm looking at it, I realize that I wouldn't have done it that way if it had not been for Ray's lingering influence.

I never talked to Ray about this, but I feel he must have had similar ideas about working—in that I feel that if you hire good actors, then they are artists through and through, and what they give you is the gift of their talent. A director is crazy not to recognize this and accept it. There are times of course when actors get on the wrong track and you have to guide them back. But I've always felt that actors are very deep and not wide—that they go into the depths of their own character to create this new character for you. And on the other hand, directors are wide but not deep, because a director has to deal with hundreds of things going on horizontally and he must deal with all of those things confidently, but he may not be able to deal with them in the depth that he would like. He hasn't got the time; he has to spread himself more thinly than the actors do. But that makes for a good balance, and it carries over into his working relationship with his other collaborators. A director, for example, can't know every tiny nuance of every single take, whereas the editor has an incredible memory for that and knows exactly where any shot goes out of focus or where an actor stumbles on a line. It's impossible for a director to know all that—anyway, I can't. I'm famous for my sets and costumes, but I don't begin to know how the designers come up with these things. I just get very good people to do them, and I let them do what they know best.

So I think I work with actors in the same way that Ray did: I have a tremendous amount of respect for them. It's hard for me to understand how some directors can push actors around and humiliate them—and I hear terrible things from actors about the most famous directors. I couldn't work in that way. I don't tend to shove people around or yell and scream anyway. There was a famous actor we worked with once who had too long fingernails, and I felt that the character he was playing wouldn't have such long nails. It was very hard for me to bring it up without saying, "goddamn it, cut your nails," so I didn't say anything, and there he is in the film with long nails.

Sometimes you can't get your own way because you will offend the actor and disrupt something else that they are doing, which is not worth it. It's better to have long nails and wonderful performances. A director sees a million things. A leading lady might be conscious that one angle is better than another, yet you see that the angle she thinks is bad is really her best angle and you have to work to maneuver her in such a way or into such a position that the camera will take advantage of the better angle which they hate. Often you have to work secretly with the cameraman to do something or other. There's a lot of secrecy that goes on all through the making of a movie to enable the director to get his way.

When I'm casting, I've learned to be more open-minded than I used to be. There have been casting mistakes in some of our movies—more in the earlier ones—and one has to be more receptive to suggestions from agents and one's friends about actors. What I'm always looking for—and this is true even when casting a well-known star—is a kind of individual distinction. I don't like them to be conventional in appearance or personality; I want there to be some additional thing that brings some extra life. When we're casting new, young actors, we rarely choose some pretty girl or good-looking guy. Leelee Sobieski [in *A Soldier's Daughter Never Cries*], for example, was only fourteen when we cast her, but she doesn't look like your average girl. She's about seven feet tall and has a marked aquiline nose, which gives her face a kind of strength and character that an ordinary pretty girl wouldn't have.

We always intended to have long dialogue scenes in our films. Earlier on when we worked with Subrata Mitra, we would very often do a whole scene in one shot, a combination of tracking and zooming and so forth and we'd get all the dialogue in one shot. Later on I did less of that. Such shots were difficult to edit. With conventional scenes from one viewpoint, such as the actors acting Shakespeare in *Shakespeare Wallah*, we have always worked in the classical way, which is to light for the long shots and then, on a particular angle, go in closer and closer to the tighter shots, and then reverse and light the other way and again get closer and closer. That's pretty traditional, and Ray's crew had been trained to do that. We still stick to that way of shooting. In India, it was very hard sometimes to do elaborate tracking shots because they don't have good dollies, and the floors were often uneven so it was difficult to lay rail—or sometimes we didn't have enough rail. Nevertheless in *Bombay Talkie*, we made very good use of long travelling shots in that film, which Mitra and I worked out carefully and which really paid off.

There are all kinds of ways of breaking a scene down. If it's a straight-

forward dialogue scene with people moving around a room and alight-
ing here and there and sitting and standing, it's all rehearsed before we
start and we don't need these tracking shots. The scene is broken down
into shots so we know what we're going to do, and we follow that plan.
But sometimes the scene is covered in one long master-shot, which we
then break into with closer shots for emphasis.

I'm considered to be a perfectionist, but I also don't believe in doing
too many takes because the actors hate it, and chances are they've given
their best already and from then on, they get worse and worse.

Because of the kind of money we have, it's very rare to be able to bring
the actors together before a shoot begins for rehearsal. Emma Thompson literally arrived on *The Remains of the Day* the day before we began
shooting because she had another film going. There are only two films
where we've had proper rehearsals—*Autobiography of a Princess*, which
was very short, but we were able to plan rehearsals with James Mason
and Madhur Jaffrey which really paid off; and *Mr. and Mrs. Bridge*, where
we were able to have a proper two-week rehearsal period because we were
all in New York. Also, Paul Newman and Joanne Woodward wanted very
much to get to know the actors playing their kids. We even blocked some
of the scenes, although I remember that when we got to Kansas City to
shoot, I threw them all out of the window because they didn't apply to
where we were shooting. I'm sure the rehearsals helped the wonderful
performances in that film. Usually we do read-throughs beforehand,
and when we're going to shoot we rehearse thoroughly on the day. For
example, when we shot the scene where Maggie tells the Prince about
her dream in *The Golden Bowl*, it was Kate Beckinsale's second day of
work. But she felt confident and so we went into the room and rehearsed
it several ways. She ended up sitting on that couch at the foot of the bed
with him down on his knees in front of her. I think there's a logic to any
scene which is set in an existing room with furniture in it and doors and
windows. You have to manage something within that—it's not like a set
where you can take a whole wall out or shoot from above. It's therefore
slightly inflexible, but the actors always manage it. You just rehearse it
over and over until they're happy that they've moved about in a way that
seems logical. It's an actor's logic. I have very good cameramen who, if
the actors want to do their lines under a bed, will find a way to shoot it.
Anyway, after we've organized a scene and the actors are satisfied, they
then go into make-up and costume and the lighting is arranged, and we
shoot it when they reappear.

Ruth and I go on working on the script right the way through shooting. She rarely comes on set because she doesn't like to; she always feels she's going to get in the way. But we keep in close touch over the phone and fax or by letters sometimes and she watches the rushes all the time. She often picks up on things which feel repetitive and rewrites scenes we haven't shot accordingly, or if I tell her that someone is not working out as well as we thought, she will simplify speeches—or vice versa; if someone turns out to be brilliant, she will pump up their part. Sometimes she'll think we don't need a scene and will tell me to look at it again carefully because it could be a waste of film. That happened in *The Golden Bowl* with the Prince, Maggie, and the little boy asleep in the bed at the end—that was originally two scenes.

When I'm doing films based on very well-known novels, I am not keen on actors improvising all over the place, nor am I keen on them taking the novel and suggesting we re-insert scenes from it. When we were making *The Europeans*, everybody had a paperback copy of the book and was wandering around reading it all the time. Ruth knows exactly what she's doing; she's thought it out five hundred times, and on the whole there is no need not to speak lines as written. Most actors tend to respect that, although any director's a fool if someone comes along with a better idea for a line and he doesn't accept it. Ruth also gets involved in the editing room. I change the film enormously in the editing. The first full screening is usually a vast, shapeless monster, and we do a lot between then and the final cut. There's stuff in the movie which isn't first class, but sometimes you are forced to keep such scenes in because they help the story. You must find a cut to present them in the best possible way. We don't reshoot. It's never as good as what we did the first time, even when it was done badly. We do add scenes sometimes, like the scene in *The Golden Bowl* where Maggie is reading the letter in the courtyard, which strengthens a particular strand of the story, and which was shot months later.

Critics of course only respond depending on whether we are in a fashionable or unfashionable phase in our career and reputations. We have been in and out of favor numerous times the whole forty years we've been working. It all just washes away finally. We just carry on making films, and what we do is often the only thing like it out there. I do feel that we're a little bit like aliens in a way—from outer space.

Ismail Merchant Transcript

Chris Neumer/2003

From *Stumped Magazine* (Chicago), February 2003, http://stumpedmagazine.com/inter
views/ismail-merchant-transcript.html. © Stumped Magazine. Reprinted by permission.

Chris Neumer: Thanks for taking the time to speak with me.
Ismail Merchant: You're welcome.

CN: It's much appreciated. I was curious, just to get things started, what caused you to choose this particular novel—to address in *The Mystic Masseur?*
IM: Actually, I read it when I just finished my college in Bombay and I enjoyed it so much I laughed. Then, years later, a friend of mine said, "Have you read *The Mystic Masseur?*" I told him, "years ago." He said, "Why don't you reread it," and so I reread it and I liked it so much that I laughed again. The characters were very rich and interesting. And particularly when you talk about Trinidad, most people think it is black people from Africa. Half of the country is populated by Indians who came almost two hundred years ago. It grew, sort of a cultural evolution with the local people and Indians who brought their food, their culture and music, all of that. So that grew and it's become a fascinating country. The people are so interesting and the language that they speak is exactly like any Trinidadian speaks.

CN: You certainly haven't seen that particular setting or that particular culture examined at all.
IM: No, this is the first time. I was absolutely bowled over by it. I wish I could speak like that with that wonderful musical rhythm they have. I was very taken by that. We were blessed with these marvelous actors

who bring the same kind of manners of rhythm in their day-to-day conversations and the characters became richer. So, I was very pleased with that.

CN: Tell me this. Having already adapted several E. M. Forster works in your career, did you have any trouble procuring the rights to the novel that this was based on or did any elements at all of the Naipaul-Forster mini-feud ever come to a head with you?
IM: Naipaul is a difficult man.

CN: How so?
IM: Well, he is very protective. He doesn't have faith in anything. He never took this seriously that this would be made into a film. But he didn't realize that Merchant-Ivory, when they want to do something, they just go ahead and do it! They don't wait for people to come, whether they like it or they don't like it, we are just there making the kind of film we do best. Taking good story and characters and bringing them to life, and that really pleased him very much, that the film was made. It added a lot to his work and people are enjoying it. In whatever country I've shown it, France or Italy . . . I was just in Rome for the festival and it was the opening night film. People enjoyed it so much. It's not just that one has to think about Indians or people who know that world, because it's a human story and it connects with people.

CN: You had said that Naipaul was a difficult man and that he didn't necessarily take it seriously that this would ever ultimately turn up in feature film form.
IM: Other people bought his option, his novels and all. They were never made, including *Good in Love*, a Francis Ford Coppola option. Nothing happened. Jonathan Miller optioned *A House for Mr. Biswas* but nothing happened. So he was a little skeptical about it.

CN: It was sort of a case of, "I'll believe it when I see it." Did he ever come on set with you guys or offer any advice about the script?
IM: No, no. And we bought it outright. We didn't even buy the option. We bought the book outright.

CN: That's even nicer. Now this was shot in India, correct?
IM: No, no. In Trinidad.

CN: Oh, was it? I had seen different reports.

IM: The whole idea was to shoot in the actual authentic location.

CN: Okay, I was gathering that. Did it pose any specific challenges to you or the production, shooting in Trinidad, that you hadn't encountered previously when you were shooting in India or in other locations?

IM: We were using the Trinidadian film industry, so we had to take everybody from here. They didn't have any equipment so we had to take our equipment, but they were most welcoming, most helpful. Then we hired local actors and they were just wonderful. That was a great challenge and an enormous advantage for us. We were all living together and being there together. That also helped produce a kind of family atmosphere.

CN: How long was the shoot?

IM: The shoot was eight weeks long.

CN: Have you returned to Trinidad since?

IM: I've been to Trinidad and showed the film to the, then, Prime Minister and other people who were helpful to us. And they loved it.

CN: So it wasn't the type of experience that would get you to write off a particular island to return to.

IM: No, no. I would feel happy to go back and do another film there.

CN: This was one of your first projects that you had made in a while that wasn't in collaboration with Ivory. Was there any particular reason for that?

IM: No. The film is presented by Merchant-Ivory and he [James Ivory] is always there in the editing room helping me with things. He came on the set. Nothing is done without having him involved in it. The collaboration is a very close collaboration.

CN: Let me ask you this, then. Normally, on your productions he is either credited with directing or producing or executive producing, something along those lines. Was there any reason . . . Granted, it was a Merchant-Ivory production, but was there any reason he was not credited with more involvement on this?

IM: He was never credited on *The Proprietor* or *Cousin Mary* or *In Custody*.

These are the films that I directed. He is most generous with his time and help. It's my film that I wanted to do and he was there to help me.

CN: And this gave you an opportunity to get behind the camera as well.
IM: Correct.

CN: You had been talking about how you had read this book and found it amusing. Was there something inherently visual about this or something that provided you with the drive to direct the material? Or that you wanted to specifically land behind the camera and grab the reins?
IM: No, the story propelled me too and the characters, the old aunt. Have you seen the film?

CN: Oh, absolutely. I wouldn't talk to you if I hadn't.
IM: The old aunt, you know, is such a wonderful character. Zohra [Segal], the actress who played it, is so delightful. I was really drawn to these people. I had such a ball doing this film. If you are not drawn to something, and you are forced to do something that really doesn't appeal to you, it shows in the film. But if you are, yourself, so keen on it, that is, of course, a different thing altogether.

CN: It's funny you mention that because you would assume that would be the way it would be in most cases. If you don't have a drive or a love of the material, you wouldn't hop on board. As you hear with the huge, hundred-million-dollar films, time and again, it's more of a hired job for the director. I guess that's one thing that sets your productions apart from the others.
IM: Right.

CN: It's interesting to me, though, because one of the things that has always fascinated me about the Merchant-Ivory name is that there is this sort of consensus among the American public that any given movie of yours is excellent, well-made, and critically well-received, but no one goes out to see it because they perceive it to be boring or hard to follow. Do you ever find this to be the case—that you run up against audiences of that nature?
IM: No, not really.

CN: Or that if they are paying money to see it, they have to be interested in it?

IM: Absolutely. The whole idea is that you are making a film for, what do you call it, a *civilized* audience. Whenever they see a Merchant-Ivory name, they go with the expectation that this will be something interesting, exciting, entertaining, and they are satisfied with that. We have an exceptional and devoted following, which is very gratifying for us.

CN: Robert Altman is fond of saying that most people make clothes and he sells gloves, that sort of thing. I'm assuming this metaphor rings true with you as well, that you are not necessarily making movies for the same crowd that is going to go out and seeing *Men in Black 2* or something of that nature.
IM: Exactly.

CN: I guess touching on this one more time, it's such an interesting phenomenon because to me it marks the decline of the American civilization—because, in certain cases, your films are being shunned because they are viewed as being smart and literate and passionate. In my eyes it seems like it should draw more of an audience as opposed to pushing people away.
IM: The day before yesterday I went to speak at Fairfield University. My book, *My Passage to India*, has come out. In less than two months, we have sold out eight thousand copies and it is now in the second print.

CN: I believe I have a copy on its way to me in Chicago.
IM: You will enjoy it enormously. It is a very, very entertaining book. It is my personal journey from Bombay to Hollywood and beyond. I was just telling you about Fairfield University. It was the Super Bowl on Sunday. I was told, "You are fighting with the Super Bowl and not many people will show up." They had to remind me, I guess. I said, "It doesn't matter. I'm going there and I'm going to speak about my book and my career and all of that." So I went there. There were about 750 people who came. Every seat was taken. It was an amazing response. With clips of the new film *Le Divorce*, we talked about my work and people interested in our films. It was so gratifying. Here you are talking to an actual audience who supported our films. They may not see all the films, but they supported us over the years, almost forty years. Young people in the audience, all age groups were there, so I felt very elated and happy. I thought, "My God. This is going against the Super Bowl and attracting such audiences." It was a very good thing.

CN: That does sound interesting. You do hear about that, though. This is the movie that opens opposite the big blockbuster and proves to do very well. What types of traits do you identify with your audience that identifies with your particular film?

IM: People who read, people who understand things, people who enjoy a particular world or a particular civilization, a clash of culture, knowing about other people across the continent or from the continent to here, from India, to East, to the West. All of those themes are quite substantial themes. That's why those who come want to be our avid supporters.

CN: Does it ever frustrate you, and I mean it in a very, very light sense, that your audiences are not bigger than they are? I was looking at the box office for *The Mystic Masseur*. It grossed about $400,000 I believe.

IM: Half a million dollars.

CN: Half a million. Is it ever something that you strive for to get a bigger box office, like, "Let's see if we can crack seven figures," or is that just gravy on the side?

IM: I would have been happier if we had grossed about $2.5 million because the film deserved a wider audience. It was such an amusing, witty, entertaining film. The reviews were just spectacular, as you know, from Kenny Terrain to the *New York Times* to Roger Ebert to *The Washington Post* . . .

CN: To watching the film myself, yes. Well, thank you for speaking to me. Thank you for the interview.

IM: Thank you very much.

Interview with Ruth Prawer Jhabvala

Declan McGrath and Felim MacDermott/2003

From *Screenwriting* (Oxford: Focal Press, 2003), 100–112. Reprinted by permission of Elsevier.

Ruth Prawer Jhabvala was born in Cologne in 1927 and has been writing since the day she learned the alphabet. Her parents were Jewish and as a result she was forced by Nazi regulations to attend segregated schools. In 1939 Jhabvala and her family fled Germany and the Holocaust, finding refuge in England. At twenty-four, after receiving her Masters degree from London University, Jhabvala moved to Delhi where she began her prolific career as a novelist. Jhabvala had no interest in cinema until director James Ivory and producer Ismail Merchant bought the rights to her novel The Householder *in 1960, and asked her to write the film script adaptation. That was the beginning of her collaboration with Merchant-Ivory which has lasted over forty years. Early films include* Shakespeare Wallah *(1965) and* Autobiography of a Princess *(1975). Working closely with James Ivory, Jhabvala identified an affinity between his sensibility and that of novelists E. M. Forster and Henry James; from James she adapted* The Europeans *(1979),* The Bostonians *(1984), and* The Golden Bowl *(2000); and from Forster* A Room with a View *(1985) and* Howards End *(1992), both of which gained her an Academy Award. Jhabvala received an Oscar nomination for her adaptation of Kazuo Ishiguro's novel* The Remains of the Day *(1993). She has continued to write novels, and adapted her own work,* Heat and Dust, *in 1982.*

This is the way I set about adapting a book: I read it once, twice, three times and then I put it away. After that I work without the book for a bit. I have to find a form that is *not* that of the novel, the form of the film is *never* that of the novel. This form is a sort of construct in my mind. It is very difficult to describe. It is easier to describe the difference between

writing a novel and writing a screenplay. When I write a novel, I don't really have an idea in which direction or in what manner it is progressing.
It has to be allowed to grow. But with a screenplay (an original as well as
an adaptation) I must know from the start in which direction it has to
go. By that I don't mean the progress of a story from beginning through
middle to end. It is more a concept of what would best express the essence of the film. For instance, the film *Mr. and Mrs. Bridge* was based on
two novels by Evan Connell that are written as a series of short sketches.
I used these sketches but in a different form. This form was the progress
of the seasons: the film starts off in spring and ends in deepest winter,
not of one year but of a succession of years during which the parents
grow old and the children grow up. So the form of the film has become
the course of human life, which is reflected in the course of the seasons.
It is only when I have some conception, however vague, of the form
(which is not the structure) that I can begin to focus on the content. At
this point my method of working can vary. Much of it depends on how
much or little time there is before I turn the screenplay in (or surrender
it, as I tend to think).

Sometimes I have to do what is really a rush job. For example on *Hullabaloo*, Merchant-Ivory had to have a script in a matter of weeks, in
fact they were already on location before I had finished writing it. But
if I have a lot of time then I do like to prepare more elaborately and go
through many different versions. If I love a project, that will make a difference. I must confess that this has not always been the case. There have
been instances when I have not been very keen on the project in hand,
yet knowing that we had to have a script I wrote it cold, almost like an
exercise, like one might solve a problem in chess or math. That is a different kind of enjoyment, the pleasure of using one's technical skill.

But when I love a project I do spend as much time on it as I can. My
two favorite adaptations have been *Mr. and Mrs. Bridge* and *The Golden
Bowl*. I set about doing both of them the same way; through analysis.
Going through the books, I made a separate analysis of each character,
marking their individual characteristics. So I might have a heading for
appearance; for turn of speech; for simplicity; for complexity; for integ-
rity; for deviousness; for selfishness; for altruism, and so on, running the
whole gamut of human personality and passions. Of course this can only
be done with the greatest books where the characters are real, complex
and leap at you off the page. I also had headings for the relationships of
the characters with one another, marking passages where they seem to
love one another, where they can't stand one another, where they put up

with one another. This can go on indefinitely, since it applies not only to each character with one other, but each character with everyone. There are endless cross-references and entanglements. That is really fun.

If there is time, I read a lot around the project although the moment the project is finished I completely forget everything I learned. For a while (while reading about Jefferson in Paris) I became a little expert on Jefferson and American slavery and the French revolution. I can't dignify this reading as research, it is just reading around a subject and as much as possible of what has been written or recorded about it. For something set in the past I like to read contemporary books with the project, in order to feel my way into it. With authors I admire, like [Henry] James and [E. M.] Forster, I would want to read not only all their own novels but also those of their contemporaries, and their biographies in great detail. One thing I don't read is literary criticism—that is, other people's interpretations of their work, which I feel is none of my business while I am struggling with my own.

While I have the greatest reverence for some books, I feel that in turning them into a film it is necessary to be absolutely irreverent. At that stage, it is only the screenplay that matters, and getting that screenplay to work is my sole concern. I have no compunction about radically changing scenes or inventing new ones. Sometimes what works triumphantly in a book does not work at all in a film. *The Golden Bowl* is a prime example. The novel is told entirely obliquely, with nothing stated directly but only by hints, guesses, flashes. Nothing is explicit, but my goodness what a lot is implied. The film had to work the other way around and turn what was so deeply implicit in the novel into scenes where people attempt to explain their extremely complicated feelings.

As for dialogue, it is a tricky business to turn literary dialogue into its cinematic equivalent. When the former appears to be at its most colloquial, it is often at its most literary—in fact the most expressive dialogue in a book *is* literary, reflecting the art of the novelist. But try and put this dialogue directly into the mouth of an actor and it will sound stilted—not art, but artifice. To sound colloquial film dialogue has to be a lot starker than it is in a novel. And one must never forget that added to the words on the page of a script is the entire range of expression brought to the screen by the appearance, manner, and personality of the actor speaking those words.

Calculating the amount of dialogue necessary to write has given me a lot of headache. In my first screenplay, *The Householder*, I had no idea that far fewer words were needed than in the novel, and I wrote reams of dialogue in the same way as I would for a novel. I quickly found that most of it had to be thrown out. Later on, trying to learn, I went in the opposite direction and wrote far too few words. Two of our earlier films, *The Guru* and *Bombay Talkie*, just don't have enough dialogue. The characters don't express enough to each other, it is all very thin. Over the years I have developed a method where I write down what I want my characters to say and then compress that as much as possible into what they need to say. Therein lies the danger that in my eagerness I compress too much. I often do, which means that I am not giving the actors enough stages to get to the emotional point that they have to reach. I then have to go back and expand again, giving back those intermediate steps that I had so recklessly flung out.

I hold onto the script for as long as I can. I keep writing drafts and thinking of new things to try out. At last, when I can't delay any more, I hand it over to the director—who fortunately in my case has always been the same one so he knows what I mean and I trust what he does. I have nothing to do with casting and almost never have any particular actor or actress in mind when I am writing. I don't go on the set, there's nothing for me to do there. Sometimes I see rushes just to see if things are working out the way we thought (they are usually different, but that is alright, they are supposed to be taking on a life of their own), and also to see if there are any scenes we could do without and thereby save money.

But there have been occasions when I see nothing until the rough cut. At that stage I begin to be very interested again. I go into the editing room and, together with the director and editor, fiddle around with what we have there. Here is another advantage of always being with the same director: we both know what the other is aiming for and it is usually the same thing. Mostly the film is much too long—I don't know why we never get this right—and so we have to decide how and where to cut. There are two criteria. One is that the story should move forward in the best (which is usually the clearest) way possible. The other is to throw out scenes that have not come out well and to retain those that have come out very well, even if they are not as strictly necessary to our purpose (the story and theme) as the former. There is some conflict of interest here, but in the end I think that the individual good scenes must win. One would simply not wish to discard something that is beautiful or interesting, or a wonderful bit of performance even if it is at a tangent to the main purpose. On the other hand, the main purpose has to be sacrificed if a scene is a failure. In *Howards End* one of the most crucial scenes is where the two sisters talk about their philosophy of life, which is to connect the different aspects of humanity. "Only connect!" is the entire motto and theme of the book! However, we had to ditch the scene where this is expressed because it was dull, and a dull scene equals disaster.

I always regard my sessions in the editing room as one more chance—the last—to improve the screenplay. It is magical to be able to switch scenes around, to contrast or correlate or counterpoint them with one another—even to change performances by eliminating tricks or devices actors have used unsuccessfully or excessively. It is amazing how one can do without certain steps that one thought at the time were absolutely essential for the story. For example in *The Golden Bowl*, we had a series of scenes where the Ververs decide to invite Charlotte to visit them—only to find in the editing room that we didn't need them; it was far more dramatic just to show the motor car with Charlotte inside it arriving at the door.

Quite frankly I feel that I have come to films from the wrong direction. They were never my prime interest, which was from the beginning literary. People who actually make films have a passion for them from a very young age. Not only did they see and were deeply impressed and influenced by films, they also learned about cameras and lighting and all the visual and technical stuff that to this day remain a mystery to me. I enjoy writing scripts but I know that I am doing no more than giving a blueprint for others to build from. Of course the blueprint is essential and has to be worked out to the last possible detail—but I do not think that it has any value in itself. I don't find scripts interesting to read. It is as though they are waiting for something more, someone else to breathe life into them, as a composer breathes life into a libretto. This is one of the reasons why I do not like visiting a set. It's not only that there is nothing for me to do there—there isn't—but also that I am in the way: physically, insofar as I stumble over wires and have to be jostled aside by irritated crew members, but more seriously I am in the way of others doing their creative job of making the blueprint come alive. And in the process I don't want them to think of me at all—that is, of the script I've written. I want them to feel as free with the script as I was with the original novel. I love it when actors change the dialogue to make it fit them better, or add to it, or subtract, or reinterpret, or do whatever they wish to serve themselves. I want them to take possession of it for themselves, knowing that they will do so, much more than I could on the page, by infusing the words with their own talents and personalities.

And the same goes even more for the director, whose view or vision has to prevail over and transform the script. Often the chosen location offers unprecedented new angles—for instance, in *The Golden Bowl* the father delivers his warning to the errant son-in-law inside a huge and noisy steam engine which then acts as a sort of giant punctuation mark. And in *Mr. and Mrs. Bridge* so much is said of the relationship between husband and wife when in the Louvre the husband slyly glides his eye along the flank of a nude while at the same time aware of his wife innocently watching him. So while everyone is working on the set, what they are doing is transforming the script, transcending it. Yet the script has to be strong enough to bear such treatment—the basic foundations and framework of a building, while the individual scenes must have an abundance of content in order to have every drop of meaning squeezed out of them.

I have very much enjoyed being involved in films and think of it as a great privilege that I owe to Merchant-Ivory. However I do feel that, if I had not at the same time continued to write fiction, I would feel somewhat frustrated—because a film script is an unfinished thing, waiting to be brought into existence by the director and a whole team of artists and crew. If I had wanted the same creative fulfillment that have found in writing fiction, then I would have needed to direct the scripts I had written. But for that I know myself to lack every spark of the necessary talent, or interest—let alone the passion of those who are born and dedicated film-makers the way I regard myself as a born and dedicated novelist.

James Ivory on His *Final Destination* and Working without Ismail Merchant

Eric Larnick/2010

From *Moviefone*, April 15, 2010, http://blog.moviefone.com/2010/04/15/james-ivory-interview-city-of-your-final-destination/. Content by Eric Larnick © 2010 AOL Inc. Used with permission.

James Ivory—the thrice Oscar-nominated director of *A Room with a View*, *Howards End*, and *Remains of the Day*—has created some of the most stylish and elegant films of the last twenty-five years. With co-producer and partner Ismail Merchant, and screenwriter Ruth Prawer Jhabvala, Ivory is the rare filmmaker whose productions—literary tales set in different pockets of the globe and known simply as Merchant-Ivory films—are practically their own subgenre.

When Merchant passed away in 2005, the future of the prestigious production company was called into question. But Ivory returns to art-houses once again this week with *The City of Your Final Destination*, an adaptation of Peter Cameron's 2002 novel of the same name. *The City of Your Final Destination* tells the story of a young grad student (Omar Metwally) hoping to write the biography of a reclusive author who has committed suicide. But first, he must travel to Uruguay and convince the writer's widow (Laura Linney), mistress (Charlotte Gainsbourg), and brother (Anthony Hopkins) to grant him permission, struggling with family secrets and temptations along the way. Ivory sat down with *Moviefone* to discuss shooting his first film after losing his long-time partner and the struggles that came with filming *City*.

Eric Larnick: What drew you to the story of *The City of Your Final Destination*?

James Ivory: All those one-on-one confrontations which were so wittily written. I like things like that. Secondly, the fact that it would need to be made in South America. The attraction of going to South America was really one of the big things.

EL: This is the first Merchant-Ivory film since Ismail's passing. He once referred to you, himself, and Ruth Prawer Jhabvala's relationship as a three-headed monster. Has the creative relationship between you and Ruth changed?

JI: Well we don't have Ismail there to question, to reassure, he's not there to collaborate with. He was our closest collaborator, and he was the person we needed and hoped to please with everything we did. We hadn't done anything since the time he died, except for the reworking of the scenes that we shot in Montreal; you can call them the American scenes. In reworking [them], it was really the first time that Ruth and I had worked together since Ismail died. But it all went quite well. There's no change in the way we worked.

EL: Did you feel like your confidence level was affected in any way?

JI: Absolutely. Some very mysterious things happened; things to do with banks and loans. Financiers just disappeared. He was used to dealing with those kinds of events, and I had never had to before. I felt able to finish off the film, do whatever I had to do as the director, and get the film done and out—I had already done that on *The White Countess*. But *The White Countess* was a studio film, it was financed by Sony, so I didn't have those kinds of fears. This was another matter and I had to deal with a lot of stuff I hadn't dealt with before. Still having to deal with.

EL: Anthony Hopkins sued Merchant-Ivory in October 2007, accusing you of failing to pay him for his part in *City*. What is the latest on that legal situation with Anthony Hopkins?

JI: He's doing press as we speak in Los Angeles. That all was taken care of. We couldn't pay him. Nothing to hide. When we left Argentina, we were beginning to run out of money, and he had come to work and finished, and naturally he wanted to be paid, but we didn't have any money to pay him with.

EL: Even though you've worked with him extensively on multiple projects, has the legal drama changed your relationship with him at all?
JI: No, it hasn't. Oddly [*laughs*].

EL: How were your experiences filming in South America?
JI: We were working out in the country, about ninety miles south of Buenos Aires, in what is really the Pampas. It was along the gigantic river between the two countries of Argentina and Uruguay. It was hot, I can tell you that. Both houses are right on the water. It was quite a relaxed shoot. Occasional car crashes. [Actor] Hiro Sanada was in a car crash, the car turned over twice and he was left hanging upside down; luckily he was all strapped in.

EL: Have you already started planning your next project?
JI: Oh yeah. There's an American project, that's set in Iowa, that's based on two books by [Pulitzer Prize winner] Marilynne Robinson. That's called *Gilead*. And then there's another one, it takes place at the same time with the same people, called *Home*. We're going to put those two books together and come up with a film. I'm also doing another project, which is a long-time project that I've been working on for years—a film of Shakespeare's *Richard II*.

EL: Looking back, are there any projects of yours that you feel were underrated?
JI: *Mr. and Mrs. Bridge.* That's one of my really all-time favorites and it was certainly very well-received but it didn't go down with the public I think; they probably didn't like to see Paul Newman play a part like that. Probably went against their idea of Paul Newman. And he was underrated in that film. I thought what he did was just marvelous.

EL: You pull from a lot of literary and biographical sources. What draws you to that?
JI: Let's say the literary and biographical sources are in themselves autobiographical. I don't always know it at the time, but I wouldn't be choosing some of this material if it didn't already resonate with me in some unseen kind of way. When it's all done, I realize sometimes that I've been, or that we all have been creating our own three-part autobiography out of our films. They're full of our interests and the stuff that was meaningful to us in different kinds of ways, and in some cases deeply psychological. Sometimes it's just for the sheer possibility of enjoy-

ing making something. *Howards End* was something like that. I hadn't thought to make *Howards End* and Ruth said, "Okay, you've made two other E. M. Forster books, sort of minor works, why don't you do a great E. M. Forster book, and climb a mountain?" So we did. But years after I've made a film, for some reason watching it, I think, "Oh, that's what it was all about. That's what I was thinking. That's why I made it."

Additional Resources

Bailur, Jayanti. 1992. *Ruth Prawer Jhabvala: Fiction and Film*. New Delhi: Arnold Publishers.

Chakravarti, Anna. 1998. *Ruth Prawer Jhabvala: A Study in Empathy and Exile*. New Delhi: B. R. Publishing.

Dannenbaum, Jed. 2003. *Creative Filmmaking from the Inside Out: Five Keys to the Art of Making Inspired Movies and Television*. New York: Simon and Schuster.

Higson, Andrew. 2005. *English Heritage, English Cinema*. Oxford: Oxford University Press.

Hill, John. 1999. *British Cinema in the 1980s: Images and Themes*. Oxford: Clarendon Press.

Hipsky, Martin A. 1995. "Anglophil[m]ia: Why Does America Watch Merchant-Ivory Movies?" *Journal of Popular Film and Television* 22, no. 3: 98–107.

Long, Robert Emmet. 2005. *Conversations with Ivory: How Merchant-Ivory Makes Its Movies*. Berkeley and London: University of California Press.

———. 1997. *The Films of Merchant-Ivory*. New York: H. N. Abrams.

Merchant, Ismail. 1999. *Filming and Feasting in Paris*. New York: H. N. Abrams, 1995.

———. 1989. *Hullabaloo in Old Jeypore: The Making of The Deceivers*. New York: Doubleday.

———. 1994. *Ismail Merchant's Florence: Filming and Feasting in Tuscany*. New York: H. N. Abrams.

———. 1986. *Ismail Merchant's Indian Cuisine*. London: Futura.

———. 1994. *Ismail Merchant's Passionate Meals: The New Indian Cuisine for Fearless Cooks and Adventurous Eaters*. New York: Hyperion.

———. 2002. *My Passage from India: A Filmmaker's Journey from Bombay to Hollywood*. New York: Viking Studio.

———. 1996. *Once Upon a Time . . . The Proprietor*. London: Bloomsbury.

Pym, John. 1995. *Merchant-Ivory's English Landscape: Rooms, Views, and*

Anglo-Saxon Attitudes. New York: H. N. Abrams.

———. 1983. *The Wandering Company: Twenty-One Years of Merchant-Ivory.* London: British Film Institute.

Spinelli, Italo (ed.). 2002. *Indian Summer: Films, Filmmakers and Stars between Ray and Hollywood.* Milano: Edizioni Olivares.

Index

Printed in the United States
by Baker & Taylor Publisher Services